D1060907

Floyd Clymer's
Steam Car Scrapbook

CALVIN T. RYAN LIBRARY
KEARNEY STATE COLLEGE
KEARNEY, NEBRASKA

BONANZA BOOKS • NEW YORK

STEAM CONVERTED PACKARD

STEAM CONVERTED NASH

Floyd Clymer's
Steam Car
Scrapbook

© MCMXLV by Floyd Clymer

This edition published by Bonanza Books,
a division of Crown Publishers, Inc.,
by arrangement with the author.
a b c d e f g h

Printed in the U.S.A.

INDEX — STEAM CAR EDITION

DEDICATION

I dedicate this Steam Car Edition of my SCRAPBOOK to the memory of F. E. and F. O. Stanley. These twin brothers were truly pioneers in the development of the automobile in America. During the many historical and eventful years in which the steam car played such an important part in the transportation system of America, these brothers were as outstanding in their efforts to produce good steam cars as in their business ethics. Americans will long remember the Stanley twins and the Stanley Steamer.—*Floyd Clymer.*

UNUSUAL PHOTOGRAPHS OF THE STANLEY TWINS

Shown here are two interesting photographs of the Stanley twin brothers. —the first one taken in their first steam carriage on the road in 1898. The other photo was taken in a 1918 Stanley touring car — just two months before Mr. F. E. Stanley was fatally injured in an automobile accident enroute to Boston from Maine on what was known as the Newburyport Turnpike. Mr. F. E. Stanley died July 31, 1918, and Mr. F. O. Stanley died of a heart ailment on October 3, 1940. Note that although these two photographs were taken twenty years apart, they were taken in the same place, with the same house in the background. — Clymer.

C. F. Stanley Photos

In Appreciation

THE illustrations and data appearing in the following pages of this Steam Car Scrapbook have been taken from my own files and a large collection of photos, newspaper articles, magazines and other material which I have accumulated throughout the years. Many of my good friends have sent additional material, which appears on several pages in this book. It would be impossible for me to list all the persons who have cooperated so generously in assisting me to compile this historical book on steam automobiles, but I desire to thank each and every one of them.

Arguments both for and against steam cars are included, so that the reader may draw his own conclusions as to the future possibilities of steam as motive power for vehicles on the highways of America. While steam-powered automobiles have seemingly been replaced in the minds of millions, there are many steam car advocates who claim that steam vehicles on the highways may be down temporarily, but they are never out!

The interest in steam cars is at a new high pitch in recent months, due to the air pollution and smog situation in many of our large cities. Steam car advocates claim, and with justification, that if our cars were powered by steam engines the gas fumes produced by internal combustion engines would be eliminated.

So much criticism of our car manufacturers has caused a leading car manufacturer to build some experimental steam cars. General Motors Corporation recently announced that they would build some steam-powered cars for testing purposes by the California Highway Patrol. The Williams Brothers of Ambler, Pa. have developed a steam car that attracted the attention of the United States Senate Committee on Commerce and the Air and Water Pollution Sub-Committee of the Senate Committee on Public Works in Washington, D.C. Besler Developments of Oakland, Calif. reportedly received a contract from General Motors Corporation to develop a steam engine for testing in the Chevelle. The Besler firm has had long experience in developing steam engines and were involved in the development and manufacture of the Doble. An airplane powered by a Besler steam engine actually flew in 1933.

This book is not intended to deal with modern steam automobiles but to highlight the interesting history of steam automobiles of the past. There are many new developments, and several comments in this book, that no longer are valid. Many of the pioneers such as Abner Doble, Thomas S. Derr and Fred Marriott are dead. Others have moved, and their addresses are unknown.

I hope you enjoy this book.

Floyd Clymer

Floyd Clymer's
Steam Car Scrapbook

By HARRY W. GAHAGAN

President, Stanley Steam Motors Corporation

Mr. Floyd Clymer is to be congratulated on publishing his Historical Motor Scrap Books. He has made a real contribution to posterity, and these unusual books are published at a very opportune time; opportune because the Automotive Industry is such an important and determining factor in the defeat of the Axis, just as it was vital to the defeat of the Central Powers in World War 1.

The Automotive Industry, directly or indirectly, affects the lives of every human being in the world, in fact civilization depends upon it. Therefore, this great institution must and will continue to grow. The Aviation Industry, born of the Automotive Industry, has extended the American sphere of interest and influence to cover the world.

The publication of The Steam Car Edition is timely. Interest in steam for motor transport is mounting daily—therefore, the history of the steam car will be welcome.

STEAM IS A POWERFUL INFLUENCE IN WAR AND PEACE.

Steam is America's No. 1 source of power, so you can see how important it is to our successful conduct of the war. Years ago someone called steam "that great civilizer." Never before has it been more so—more useful in the service of man. By overwhelming odds, not water power but *steam is still the prime mover of industry*. In the United States more than 60% of the Central Electric Power Stations are actuated by steam, and 90% of the individual power plants.

In our great battles at sea we find all of our capital ships propelled by steam. The reason is they must have *power to move at will, speed, maneuverability and, above all, dependability.*

It is a little known fact that the first automobiles built were powered by steam. The story of the automobile finds its beginning in France, between the years 1760 and 1770, when Nicholas J. Cugnot built three machines, all powered by steam. The last one was intended for use as a tractor for a field gun.

The first American automobile was constructed by Oliver Evans in 1787, and it too was a steam car.

In England, in 1823, the first bus was built and it was powered by steam. This development was stymied by Parliament passing what was known as a Red Flag Law. This law made it compulsory for any vehicles carrying passengers to have a man carrying a red flag walk in front of the vehicle. This law was not repealed until 1885, and at that time the solution to riding on wheels and moving about without the use of rails seemed as far removed as ever. In 1896, Duryea, Ford, Haynes, and the Stanley brothers were beginning to find success in their experiments.

And here is the beginning of the world's greatest business—the Automobile Industry.

The steam cars immediately attracted attention by establishing world records for hill blimbing and speed. These records were publicized the world over, and thereby played an important part in interesting inventors, engineers, capital and industrialists in this new industry.

In addition to these records the steam cars set goals of performance such as *smooth and rapid acceleration, simplicity of power control, and maximum torque at zero speed.*

The Automotive Industry has spent millions in research in an endeavor to produce a vehicle that would approach the *steam engine smoothness, rapid acceleration and controlability or ease of handling.* The development of the transmission and self-starter contributed much to the success of the internal-combustion engine. Perhaps it would be simpler to use a steam engine: with modern engineering, utilizing materials and processes available today, steam may yet become an important factor in the Automotive Industry.

Since steam can compete successfully with water power and since it contains so many more wild horses of potential power, is it strange that it continues to dazzle the imagination of inventors and industrialists?

MY MOTOR SCRAPBOOK

By Floyd Clymer

This is the first volume of my MOTOR SCRAPBOOK series dealing exclusively with steam automobiles. In my MOTOR SCRAPBOOKS numbers 1 and 2, recently published, I told of my experiences, when as a youngster at Berthoud, Colorado, I was the youngest automobile dealer in the world. At eleven years of age, I was the dealer for Reo, Maxwell and Cadillac cars. Frankly, I was never very enthusiastic over steam cars; however, the steamer always did hold a certain fascination for me. I enjoyed riding in steam cars and talking with their owners. The magic of steam power is a subject that never dies; and even today there are those who believe the steamer will come back. This of course is a debatable question, with the proponents of the gas-propelled car having a tremendous advantage.

The first steam car I ever saw was when I was a kid seven years old, in 1902. My father, a small-town doctor, had just purchased a new, curved-dash, single cylinder Oldsmobile, which of course we thought was the finest thing on wheels. On Sunday afternoons, Dad would usually attach the Dos-a-dos seat which clamped onto the rear deck of the Olds. The passengers rode backwards. With father and mother in the front seat, my brother Bill, my sister Ethel and I occupied the rear seats. After we climbed aboard, Dad would place a strap across the side rails for us to hold on to and keep from falling overboard. It was quite a sight to see the small Olds rolling along with father and mother in the front seat and three kids with their short legs dangling, not long enough to reach the foot-board. When the Olds needed water, usually taken from an irrigation ditch, as they were common in Northern Colorado, we had to remove the rear seat to fill the water-tank.

The first steam car I ever saw stopped at Berthoud en route from Denver to Fort Collins. It came through town very slowly—and along with some other kids, we chased it down the street as fast as we could run. The driver stopped at a blacksmith's shop, as he was having burner trouble. Along with the other kids, I watched everything that was done to get the steamer going again.

A STEAMER TRIMS US

On one of our Sunday drives, we went to the nearby town of Longmont. On our way home, when we were about four miles from town, (from our rear view seat, we could see what was coming and what we had passed) we noticed another automobile coming, and in a few minutes it caught up with us. About two miles south of Berthoud there is a hill that in the early days required low gear for the Olds to make it. As we were slowly chugging up this hill, probably doing five miles an hour, the other car gained quite rapidly and passed us before we reached the top of the hill. The driver must have been doing at least eight miles an hour! We knew it was a steamer. The driver waved rather enthusiastically as he went by our Olds—and he must have arrived in town at least a half mile ahead of us.

Being an inquisitive kid, I immediately got the idea that Dad had made a mistake in not buying a steamer. He wasn't exactly pleased at my questioning his judgment and replied with a little sarcasm that "those steamers are apt to blow up or explode" and that he did not want anything to do with them. Then he told me that the car was a new Stanley that Mr. Morgan, the jeweler in Longmont, had purchased. Mr. Morgan was en route to Berthoud to visit his daughter and son-in-law, Billy Lyons. I could hardly wait to get up to Billy Lyons' house and have a close look at this marvelous steam car which had so completely outclassed our Oldsmobile on the way home from Longmont.

The car was standing on the street—and I could detect a slight odor of kerosene. Dad knew a little about steamers, and he explained that the pilot light was on and that the car was quite warm around the boiler. After looking the car over a few minutes, Dad went back to his office—and I camped alongside that steamer for about three hours—until Mr. Morgan came out. He was a good-natured man and showed me a few things about the steam car—and I rather

This early Locomobile is another of the collection of antique cars owned by J. C. Van Sciver of Philadelphia, Pa. This car was built by the Locomobile Company after they purchased the steam car business of the Stanley brothers. This is a duplicate of the first steam car I ever saw, when the owner stopped in my home town for repairs.
— Clymer.

1902 STANLEY STEAMER

This model Stanley was one of the early chain-drive models turned out by the Stanley Brothers when they resumed the manufacture of cars in 1902, after they had again acquired the Stanley tools, equipment and patents they had previously sold to the Locomobile Co. — Clymer.

MR. F. E. STANLEY

Mr. F. E. Stanley, inventor of the Stanley Steamer, is shown here with the car in which he made the famous "climb to the clouds" up Mt. Washington in 1904. The time was just over 27 minutes. The car has a folding front seat — Clymer.
R. W. Stanley Photos

suspect he was a little elated and really quite proud over the demonstration he had given for the steam car.

MY FIRST RIDE IN A STEAMER

Mr. Morgan said he was returning to Longmont soon and he had to go down to the Davis & Brown store to get some gasoline, or kerosene, (he could burn either) on which to return home. Gasoline was then much less expensive than kerosene. A small town merchant thought nothing of going down on Sunday and opening his store if it would help a motorist in need. I waited a few minutes and soon he came out. After turning on what seemed to be several valves and waiting probably 15 minutes to steam up, Mr. Morgan told me to get in. I was thrilled, and at the same time I remembered Dad's remark about "those steamers were apt to blow up or explode." Nevertheless, I was curious enough to want to know how the car operated. The smooth operation fascinated me, and the acceleration was much faster than that of our Oldsmobile. The steamer owner seemed to get a lot of enjoyment out of accelerating rapidly, and he could always be sure of getting favorable remarks on the quick get-away for which the steamer was noted. Mr. Morgan went around a few extra blocks; and by the time we arrived at the store I was almost a steam enthusiast; at least, I was convinced that the thing was safe; and occasionally I would tell Dad about the fine ride I'd had in that Stanley steamer.

In the months to come I saw a few other steamers which came through our town; and occasionally I would go to Denver and always visited the automobile agencies that displayed steam cars. A short time later, another steam car came to our town, and it was also a Stanley, owned by County Judge J. Mack Mills of Fort Collins. It had a folding seat in front and tiller steering. The Judge came to Berthoud quite often to visit his brother, Warnie Mills. When the Judge arrived in Berthoud, almost every kid in town knew it, and of course they would gather around to look over any new or strange car. The Judge once gave me a ride around the block—and it was the second steamer in which I rode. J. Mack Mills is the father of the famed orchestra leader Felix Mills, now of Hollywood. Judge Mills did exactly like Mr. Morgan—that is, he opened the throttle rather quickly to demonstrate how much better the steamer was than the gas car on acceleration.

Every few Sundays Mr. Morgan would return to Berthoud, and after Dad had purchased an underground gasoline tank, Mr. Morgan would sometimes come to our house for gasoline on Sunday afternoon. I always considered it a great honor to unlock the gasoline pump and measure out three or four gallons in a one gallon measure for Mr. Morgan. We always strained the gas through a chamois. Our tank was on the edge of what we then called the "auto-shed." "Garage" was a French word, and we were not quite sure that it was going to stick as the name of a building to house automobiles in America.

In 1904 I heard of an automobile race at Denver, and Dad let me go to see it. It was at Overland Park, and was to be a race between a Stanley Steamer and a foreign car called a Daimler which was gasoline-propelled. I got there early. The little Stanley seemed very small and light compared with the heavier Daimler. However, the Stanley driven by George Herring won the race.

In the early days, few steamers were purchased by any of the automobile buyers near our town. However, in nearby towns it seems there were one or more steamers; and I recall an early White owned by a man named Neiheisel at Boulder. Occasionally I would go to Boulder to visit Tom Hussie, the Reo dealer there, and I was always anxious to see any of the new steamers—and there were a few in Boulder.

ANDY BERGLIN - OUR FIRST MECHANIC

As a dealer in gasoline cars, it seemed I had very little steam car competition—but occasionally a steam car would come through our town for repairs. The local mechanic who knew most about steam cars was a good-natured Swede named Andy Berglin. Andy was a steam engineer at the local flour mill—and Andy could do anything for a steam car owner from cleaning out a defective burner to retubing a boiler. Andy was also a good gas car mechanic in the earlier days. Dad would many times call on him for his expert knowledge of gasoline engines. Others who repaired our early cars in Berthoud were the Preston Brothers and A. G. Bimson, the local blacksmith, who was an expert at

AN EARLY STANLEY RACE WINNER!

The first automobile race I ever saw was at Overland Park in Denver in 1905. The car shown above was driven by George Herring who defeated a high-priced foreign Daimler. The usual seat was removed — and George Herring is seated on the floorboard; he is shown crouched low with the steering lever in his hands. Even in the early days they did what they could to reduce wind resistance. — Clymer.

THE VERY FIRST STEAM CAR THAT I EVER RODE IN WAS IDENTICAL WITH THE 1903 STANLEY SHOWN IN THIS PHOTO. A duplicate of this car was owned by a jeweler named S. C. Morgan, living in Longmont, Colorado, 11 miles from my home. On Sundays he would come to my home town of Berthoud, Colorado, to visit his daughter and her husband, Billy Lyons. I was then a gas-car enthusiast, as we owned a curved-dash Oldsmobile, but I always got a big thrill out of riding with Mr. Morgan a few blocks to the horse-watering trough where he would fill the water tank for his return trip to Longmont. Notice the full elliptic spring and the engine operating directly on the rear axle, with a metal case for protection against dirt. The steam throttle is alongside the seat railing. Parcels could be carried under the front seat when the folding lid was closed. When opened, it formed a foot support. The car shown in this photo is in excellent condition today and is one of the fine collection of early automobiles owned by J. C. Van Sciver of Philadelphia, Pa. — Clymer.

R. W. Stanley Photo

welding our broken springs. Mr. Bimson is still active, and at an advanced age as a skilled machinist has produced hundreds of knives which he has hand forged for use of our boys in jungle warfare in the South Pacific. Townspeople of Berthoud are justly proud of Mr. Bimson, and his contribution to the war effort, and of his son Walter Bimson, who rose from obscurity to the Presidency of the Valley National Bank of Phoenix, Arizona, one of the largest banking institutions in the Southwest, with branch banks throughout the state.

The earliest heater that I can recall was a series of pipes that Andy Berglin installed on our Oldsmobile. These pipes were placed on top of the floorboard and extended across the floor-board, possibly 8" in width. Andy connected this heater to the radiator and a surprising amount of heat was made possible through this ingenious device. I am not so sure but what it might have been one of the first automobile heaters. The only thing—we could not control it. When the engine became warm enough to heat the radiator, the heater was on full blast. With no windshield or top, it was a very satisfactory heater, (when covered with a lap-robe).

A STEAMER COMES TO BERTHOUD

Time went on, and at length a steamer came to our town. A livery stable owner by the name of Lew Hertha purchased a Model "F" Stanley, five-passenger touring car to use in his livery stable business. In the early days, many owners of livery stables decided if they wanted to keep pace with the times and remain in the livery business they should purchase an automobile and use it for hire. Lew was no exception—and about the same time his competitor and the owner of the other livery stable—Sim Jeffries—purchased a 2-cylinder Reo. I had been the Reo dealer at Berthoud; however, the shaft-drive Maxwell seemed more popular and I was selling more Maxwells than Reos then. The Reo distributor in Denver therefore decided to change his dealer in Berthoud. I lost the Reo agency because I was selling more Maxwells probably because the shaft drive was then an improvement over the chain-driven Reo.

A fine young mechanic named Ed Wray, and Sim Jeffries, opened up a garage and secured the Reo agency—and Sim bought a new 5-passenger Reo for use in his livery business.

The automobile rental business really started with a bang. Hertha, with his steam car, and Jeffries, with his gas car, competed for the business. A few months later I sold a two-cylinder, 5 passenger Maxwell to a local man named Charlie Breon—and Charlie quit his position as a clerk in the McCormick General Store to engage in the automobile rental business. We now had three rental cars in our small town. While Berthoud was a small town, it was an overnight stop for traveling men out of Denver, and once a week certain travelers would leave Berthoud with their sample cases to make a trip around a circuit to the nearby towns of Johnstown, Millikan and Mead, a distance of about 34 miles. Each of the men in the automobile rental business had certain traveling men whom they carried on these trips. Competition became very keen, especially between Hertha and Jeffries who had long been rivals in the livery business. On certain days, when the customers were coming in on the morning train, Hertha would start a few minutes earlier to start getting up steam and would drive his Stanley steamer around the block very slowly several times—probably not over 8 miles per hour.

Those who know anything about the early Stanley Steamers will recall the whistling or hissing sound that was so common, which was caused by the burner. It was a sort of a mournful tune; and the louder it became was more indication that the burner was working perfectly. You could hear Hertha's Stanley Steamer with that low moan for a couple of blocks. By the time the train arrived, Hertha always had up a good head of steam. Once loaded, he would really tear out of town, and in some instances would make quite fast time to his nearest stop. Later on, Hertha bought a Stanley Mountain Wagon. The rear seats were removable, and it could carry quite large trunks.

Jeffries continued in the livery business—and became an Overland dealer. He sold many Overlands in Berthoud in the early days, when they had a two-speed planetary transmission located on the rear axle. Both Sim and Lew were fine men, although both were a little gruff at times, and did not get along well with each other at all. They were both my friends, and while at times I must have appeared to them as an impudent kid, they seemed to enjoy talking with me about automobiles. Lew had absolutely no use for a gas car. He never owned one and said he never would—and up to the time of his death several years ago I do not believe he ever owned anything but a steamer.

Occasionally, I would ride with each of them on the trip to the nearby towns when the cars were not loaded. I had to be rather diplomatic in talking with Lew about gas cars as he did not like to be told anything good about a gas car,— and Sim had absolutely no use for a steamer. Occasionally I would get in an argument over something—and once Sim ran me out of his livery stable because I told him that one tire chain on the rear wheel would not keep the other wheel from spinning in the snow. A couple days later he saw me on the street and said, "By gosh, Doc, you were right." The name "Doc" was a nickname that the localites had given me on account of my father being a doctor. Sometimes they called me "little Doc" or "young Doc." That name adhered, and even in recent years when I stop over in the old town, about half the people still call me "Doc." Once when our Maxwell broke down Hertha towed us home with his steamer. He went out of his way to pass Jeffries' livery stable and had a sort of an "I told you so" expression on his face as he passed Sim, who was standing on the sidewalk.

Charlie Breon, who was competitor in the rental business of both Hertha and Jeffries, soon moved to Denver, where he later became foreman of the Fernald Automobile Company, Maxwell distributors for Colorado. Charlie became one of the finest mechanics in the West.

Another employee of the Fernald Auto Company was later to become nationally famous as a hill-climber. I refer to Glen Shultz, who during the period that I sold Maxwells was sort of a handy-boy around the Fernald Agency in Denver. Glen later moved to Colorado Springs and won the famous Pike's Peak hill-climb for automobiles many, many times. For years, he was invincible in Pike's Peak races and competed in practically every Pike's Peak climb until his death a few years ago.

THE WHITE STEAMER RACER

In the early history of automobile racing in Colorado, road races were popular in and around Denver. Quite a famous road race was called the Model Road Race, held on the Brighton Road between Denver and Brighton. It was a triangular shaped course, turning East from the Model Roadhouse, crossing the railroad tracks and going Northeast through Derby and back across to the Brighton Road, and again towards Denver to the Model. Many famous races were run on this course. One of the most interesting races I can recall was one about 1909 when two White Steamers were sent out from the White factory at Cleveland, Ohio. These cars were very fast. One thing I can remember distinctly is that they were very high off the ground. It seemed as though the driver and the mechanic in these White Steamers were seated at least two feet higher than the drivers of the stripped gas car racers. These White steamers had tremendous speed and at times would run away from the gas cars. At other times, it appeared that their steam pressure became low and the gasoline cars would pass them. However, the White steamer won one of the events as I recall and a Denver-made Colburn gasoline car won another.

Quite a few steamers were appearing on the streets in Denver. The Colburn Automobile Company which was owned by Judge E. A. Colburn were dealers for White Steamers. Judge Colburn was a great race-horse man; therefore, intensely interested in all types of competition. With his two sons, he was quite active in all automobile racing in Colorado—and the Colburn car once won the Model Road Race, the outstanding racing event in Colorado from about 1907 to 1911. I will describe the Colburn activities and illustrate the Colburn car in my MOTOR SCRAPBOOK No. 3. Colburn once built in Denver a car with a sloping hood. The radiator was located back of the hood, similar to the famous French Renault.

The Denver Dry Goods Company used a number of small White Steamers for many years for delivery service; and the Flint Oyster Company in Denver used Stanley Steam cars for many years for the delivery of fish and oysters to restaurants and hotels in Denver. I am sure they were the last commercial users of steam cars in the City of Denver.

I later on had many interesting experiences with steam cars at Loveland, Colorado; and when I lived at Berthoud I would go to Loveland quite often—

a distance of six miles—to learn what I could about steamers. Loveland actually became the center of steam automobile activity in the entire West—for reasons I will relate in the following paragraphs.

THE STANLEY STEAMER - KING OF THE ROCKIES

Estes Park, Colorado, which is now known as a summer resort in Rocky Mountain National Park, was a mecca for vacationists and Eastern tourists. There was no railroad into the park—and it was necessary to secure transportation from Loveland to the Park. In the very early days, horse-drawn stages were used. About the year 1908, the Loveland-Estes Park Transportation Company was formed by a man named Osburn. With his three sons,—Will, Otto and Estes —they started what became one of the earliest stage lines or bus transportation systems in the United States.

This firm purchased several Stanley Steamers, and every morning during the summer season, these cars would meet the morning train at Loveland. A person in Boston or Chicago could purchase his ticket by rail to Loveland right on through to Estes Park by Stanley Steamer Stage. The business grew rapidly —and as time went on, I can recall as many as twelve of these Stanley steamers lined up at the Loveland station, ready to start on the 34-mile trip to Estes Park.

For the first two or three years these cars were used they had no tops or windshields. The passengers were furnished with raincoats and in some instances with Gordon storm aprons. These aprons would button tightly around the necks of the passengers and would protect them from the rain that was almost sure to come every afternoon in the summer-time between Loveland and the Park.

I MEET ONE OF THE STANLEY TWINS

Let me state here that undoubtedly the fact that Mr. F. O. Stanley resided in Estes Park and built a very fine exclusive hotel called the "Stanley" was responsible for the growth of this company—and I might say that the experience gained in this early-day transportation system did much to develop and perfect the Stanley Steamer. Mr. Stanley came to Colorado for his health and always in summer resided in Estes Park. He came to Loveland quite often; and as later on my parents moved to Loveland, several times during the summer I would ride to the Park with him. He was a fine man and had much patience in explaining the numerous features of his steam car to me. He knew that I had sold many gasoline cars and seemed to want to impress me with the fact that the steamer was really more dependable.

Many times during the summer I would also ride up with some of the Osburn boys or some of their drivers. I recall a number of them—such as Carl and Ed Gooch, Charlie Hess, Tony Ilg, George Wales, Palmer Richardson, and Bill Baudette.

There were times when all cars were not loaded, and about twice a week during summer vacation I would hop into any car that had a light load and ride up in the morning and come back in the afternoon, or sometimes stay all night in the Park. I usually earned my passage however by polishing the cars after arrival and working the water pump hand lever alongside the driver.

By making these frequent trips I learned a great deal about the operation of steam cars. These cars were usually very heavily loaded and they ran on schedules the same as trains. They were very seldom late, and even through the summer rainstorms that were sure to occur two or three times a week, these Stanley steamers carried their passengers and cargo high into the Rockies on schedule and with a dependability that any transportation company today would consider excellent. They would usually leave Loveland about 11:00 A.M., and wind through the famous and scenic Big Thompson Canyon. In those days the roads were very narrow for considerable distances. The roaring Big Thompson River was but a few feet below the road and very high mountain walls of solid rock were on the other side. The curves were sharp and treacherous. On meeting an oncoming vehicle, it was sometimes necessary to back up 100 or 200 feet to a wide spot in the road where two vehicles could pass. The Forks Resort—about half way—was usually reached about noon. There the passengers would have lunch and the Stanley steamers took on water, sometimes by hose from a hydrant and sometimes by siphoning the water from the river. This was done by inserting a long hose with a strainer on the end of it into the river and starting the water pumps.

LOVELAND CANYON
OF THE
BIG THOMPSON RIVER

This roaring river flowing out of the heart of the Rockies is shown in the first canyon, 10 miles west of Loveland, Colorado.

It was through this canyon, over early-day roads that were narrow and winding, that the first Stanley Steamer Stages passed en route from Loveland to Estes Park. With solid cliffs of rock on both sides, the road wound its way alongside the river.

The cabin of the frontiersman Indian Louis Papa was about two miles from where this photo was taken.

—*Clymer.*

Harold M. Dunning Photo, Loveland

STANLEY STEAMER STAGES

Operated for many years between Loveland and Estes Park, Colo. These Stanley cars, owned by the Osburn Brothers and their father, met the train daily during the summer season and transported the vacationists from Loveland to the Park, a distance of 34 miles.

I have seen as many as 12 of these cars loaded for the trip into the heart of the Colorado Rockies where no railroad facilities existed. They had reserve power and outperformed the gas cars in the early days on this famous trip.

Mr. F. O. Stanley, who with his twin brother, F. E. Stanley, manufactured the Stanley Steamers, built the exclusive Stanley Hotel in Estes Park. During several of the years that these cars operated I lived in and near Loveland and would ride to the Park two or three times a week with the drivers when they were not loaded. This photo, taken about 1909, shows three Osburn brothers and their father and a driver named Carl Gooch ready to start the trip. I am the 14-year-old kid on the right side in the front seat of the first car, driven by Will Osburn. Most of my knowledge of steam cars was gained in and around Loveland riding in, observing and driving them.—*Clymer.*

DUST, RAIN AND INDIAN LOUIE PAPA

To those of us who had lived in the West, some of the wealthy Easterners appeared rather uppish or not quite sure that they had made a wise selection for a vacation in making such a dangerous trip. Many of course had heard about the Indians, who had long since left the country. However, many Indian relics were still in evidence, such as flint stone, and flint stones could still be picked up in the foothills. To add atmosphere, there was an old Indian named Louie Papa who lived as a recluse in a lonely cabin a few feet from the road on the trip to the Park. The drivers of course would always call attention to Louie Papa's cabin as they passed by. Louie actually was as civilized as the rest of the local population. On occasion when he could be seen, the Easterners would be thrilled at seeing an honest-to-goodness real, live Indian!

They used to tell a story about Louie that caused a lot of amusement among the localites and a lot of discomfort to some of the newly-arrived Easterners. For $1.00 Louie would come down and stand alongside the road, with his Indian headdress, (a lot of colorful feathers), a beaded vest, an old tomahawk in his hand, and three or four cocoanuts dangling from his belt. The cocoanuts were carved, so that from a distance they looked a little like human heads—and Louie had some old hair pasted on what appeared to be the tops of the heads. You can well imagine the reaction from the Easterners as they passed by Louie standing thus alongside the road! The drivers had of course in most instances prepared the passengers for what might be expected, except they never explained that it was a put-up affair.

The cars would usually go in a caravan—and occasionally some of the drivers would have a little fun with the Easterners who had never been West before by telling them that it was unsafe to make the trip alone and that was why it was necessary for the cars to go in a caravan—so that one could protect the other in case of an Indian raid! Strange as it may seem, a really surprising number of the visitors swallowed this story as a fact! I suspect that some of the visitors who had seen Louie en route actually magnified the situation in their own minds until they took part in a full-fledged Indian raid by the time they returned home.

Soon after the loaded steamers left the Forks, they came to a long and very steep hill known as The Rapids. Probably this very steep grade was responsible more than any other one thing for the use of the steam car instead of gasoline cars between Loveland and Estes Park. Many gasoline cars could not climb The Rapids even in low gear without the passengers having to get out and assist by pushing. The Stanleys were always able to climb this long, steep grade with very little effort—much to the surprise and amazement of the owners of gas cars. It was not until about 1917 when greatly improved roads and much better gasoline cars were made that the gasoline cars climbed this famous hill called The Rapids at a speed comparable to that of the Stanleys.

Many times when the passengers arrived at the Park, they were covered with dust, if there had been no rain, or if they ran into showers on the way up they were usually quite damp and sometimes wringing wet, if they did not have enough time to change to their slickers or get into the long capes which fastened tightly around their necks. Now and then some Easterner came prepared, with a fine set of goggles, a leather cap, and a pair of gauntlet gloves, with the usual linen duster. Others were sights to behold—some coming with Derby hats and high-wing collars, spats, and wearing neatly pressed suits. You can well imagine their appearance when they arrived at their destination over dusty roads or through rainstorms! One could never be sure when the rain or afternoon showers would appear either. Many times the sun would be shining brightly—and ten minutes later it would be raining hard.

As time went on, the later Stanley Steamers of course had protection with top, windshield and side-curtains.

I am going to have to end my story on Steam Cars at Loveland, Colorado where I had practically all of my early experience with Steamers.

As years went on, the Osburn Brothers, who were the real pioneers in motor stages, passed out of the picture; and with improved equipment and better roads, later types and more modern gasoline cars replaced the famous Stanley Steamers of the Rocky Mountains. Thus a never-forgotten era in automotive bus trans-

THE BELOVED INDIAN
OF THE ROCKIES
LOUIS PAPA

An unusual character among the early settlers of the Big Thompson Valley of Colorado has a place in early history of automobile transportation. During the declining years of this unusual and loved pioneer of the West, the Stanley Steamer Stages began operation . . . and passed his cabin on their daily trips from Loveland to Estes Park. Louie had as much fun with the tourists from the East as they had with him. While Louie usually rode his horse to Loveland, he was always welcome to ride the Stanley Steamer to and from town and he sometimes did!

Louis Papa once bought a Model "T" Ford and according to Harold M. Dunning, Loveland historian and former mountain guide, Louie sold it on the spot . . . after trying to drive it . . . and said, "Ugh—him no go straight!"

It was my pleasure to have known Louis Papa . . . almost the last of his kind . . . and to know the affection and esteem in which he was held by his friends and neighbors at the foot-hills of the Rockies.

The history of Louis Papa is vividly told in the book, "NAMAQUA," by Pierce Egan. Louis Papa was born at Snake Creek, Utah, about 1844. His father, Joe Papa, a Frenchman, traded his family, Louis' mother, Marie, a Flathead Indian (also called John), Louis and his sister "Namaqua" to a Spaniard named Mariano Modena for four ponies. Louis father remarked to Modena, "You got damn-fine bargain."

The Old Stage Post, home of Mariano Modena, still stands three miles southwest of Loveland. It is named "NAMAQUA" in honor of the beautiful sister of Louis Papa.

—Clymer.

The burial grounds of Mariano Modena, his wife Marie (John) and daughter Namaqua. In an orchard three miles southwest of Loveland, surrounded by a wall of stones, rest the remains of these early settlers.

The life of Louis Papa ended at Loveland, Colo., Sept. 18, 1935, at the age of 81. Held in high esteem and respect by those who knew Louis, a tribute is carved on the headstone at his grave in the Loveland Cemetery.

portation passed out of existence. Mr. Stanley continued to spend his summers in Estes Park at his hotel and nearby home which had become famous to the thousands of tourists who visited this scenic playground of the Rockies.

Thus ends my actual experience with steam cars. While of course I have always been interested in all types of steam-propelled vehicles, something about the steam car seemed to me to pass out of existence when the Stanleys of the Rockies were no more.

FLOYD CLYMER.

MY FRIEND, THE LATE F. O. STANLEY

In this photo Mr. Stanley stands alongside an early Stanley Steamer with the round hood raised. He is pointing to the boiler. This photo was taken at Estes Park which is now Rocky Mountain National Park (Colorado). Mr. Stanley built the famous Stanley Hotel in Estes Park and lived there for many years. When I was a kid, I made many trips with Mr. Stanley from my home in Loveland, Colorado, to the Park — a distance of 34 miles. Stanley Steamers were used to transport passengers from Loveland into the Park, for many years. Mr. Stanley was a kindly man, and he and I became good friends. Although I was a gas car enthusiast, he would occasionally let me drive his Steamer and would point out the many advantages that the steam car did have over the gasoline car, especially in the mountains of Colorado. — Clymer.

R. W. Stanley Photo

THE STANLEY STEAMER

By R. W. STANLEY*

Today almost everyone who grew up with the automobile industry, and even many a youngster who never wore a linen duster, has a kind word to say for the Stanley Steamer. The chances are they'll tell you their father or grandfather had one and that it was the first car their family owned. Furthermore, they'll insist that the Stanley Company would give a car free to anyone who would drive it and hold the throttle wide open for one minute, which, of course, was not true. Next, they'll want to know if any steam cars are still being made, and if not, why not? Many still insist that the Stanley Steamer gave you a ride that has never been equaled by any gas car. Personally, we are inclined to agree with that.

From the safe distance of some forty years away, people who used to think the Stanley was a pretty crude means of transportation now look back to it with real affection. The Stanley is the subject of good-natured jokes on the radio and screen. Jack Benny traded in his lowly Stanley Steamer for an archaic Maxwell. Edgar Bergen and James Melton actually have Stanleys in use on the road today, and their steamers have been the objects of some entertaining banter on nation-wide broadcasts. Yes, the Stanley has come to typify all the inelegance of that era when horseless carriages were sneered at, when their owners were looked upon as being more than a little queer, but when more people had a secret hankering to own one than would admit it.

The story of how the Stanley Steamer first came to be built has been printed in books and magazines many times, but, as is usually the case with the telling of beginnings by people who were not there, as well as those who were, the true facts of its birth and infancy rarely appear. After the passage of so many years it is enough to say that in September, 1897, a little car with a body like a two-seated buggy, leather dashboard, whipsocket and all, set on oversized bicycle wheels, made its appearance on the streets of Newton, Massachusetts. First to see it was a horse hitched to a produce wagon. He took one look, snorted and jumped so quickly that he broke the whipple-tree and ran four miles before he was stopped. As the little car continued along people stopped and gazed open-mouthed at the man with whiskers and derby hat, his exact counterpart seated beside him, guided his little "teakettle on wheels" up the main street and back. The second trip, made the next day, also produced a runaway. It was quite clear from the first that the life of an automobile driver was not altogether enviable.

My earliest recollection of this first Stanley was the day my father tried to teach my mother to drive it. When she steamed up our driveway, after a short spin, she tried to drive right up the front steps. She didn't quite make it, but she did make up her mind she would never drive a car again. She never did.

The first time this little Stanley had a real chance to show what it could do was about a year later at Charles River Park in Cambridge. This was an oval track, one-third of a mile long, used mostly for bicycle racing, with a grandstand seating over 5,000. Here, on November 9, 1898, was held one of New England's first "Open-Air Horseless Carriage Meets." The outstanding feature of the day, so the newspapers said, was when my father, with his twin brother again beside him, drove his car around the track three times in two minutes and eleven seconds, a rate of over 27 miles per hour. The enthusiasm of the crowds was boundless. My father was kept busy the rest of the afternoon answering questions and explaining the construction of his little steamer, how it worked, and what could be done about getting one like it. The news spread fast, and within two weeks more than 100 people had said they would buy one if they could. Convinced that this little steamer of my father's was more than a toy, my father's twin brother, who was his partner in the business of manufacturing photographic plates, joined with him in forming the Stanley Motor Carriage Company. They purchased an old bicycle factory and immediately began the manufacture of 100 cars with standardized interchangeable parts. The sources of supply in those days were extremely limited. Practically everything that went into those first cars had to be made by the Stanleys themselves, or in neighboring machine shops under their direction. The bodies were supplied by a maker of fine carriages, and it is laughable to recall now that when they were received at the factory each one was actually equipped with a leather dashboard and a whip-

Here is a Special Stanley Steamer that was the only one of its kind. It was built in 1908 and was the first car owned by R. W. Stanley, son of one of the Stanley twins. Mr. Stanley's article on his early experiences with Stanley cars appear in this SCRAP-BOOK. — Clymer.

R. W. STANLEY AT THE WHEEL OF A SPECIAL STANLEY RUNABOUT
In this car young Stanley defeated a National Vanderbilt Cup-racer in an informal three-mile race. The race was held on Commonwealth Avenue near Boston, in the days when races on that famous highway were reported in the sports columns of the newspapers — Clymer.

A special Stanley steam runabout that would go close to 90 m.p.h. back in 1912. This car ended up in the junk pile in 1913 after crashing through a stone wall and dropping 12 feet below. A broken steering gear caused the accident. Quite a nice job of streamlining for 1913. — Clymer.
R. W. Stanley Photos

socket; but even whipsockets were not entirely useless, for some of those early drivers actually carried fancy whips in their cars, both for looks and in case they met with horse trouble along the way.

In the spring of 1899 the Stanleys sold their business and the purchasers, soon after, split their interests and organized two steam car companies, The Mobile Company and The Locomobile Company. Subsequently, the Stanleys bought back the Newton plant and all the patents, and in 1902 again began to turn out cars embodying many important new refinements. The rest of the story is comparatively modern history. In June, 1917, the Stanley brothers retired, sold The Stanley Motor Carriage Company to a Chicago investment firm which controlled the affairs of the company until 1924, when it was resold to a newly formed concern called The Steam Vehicle Corporation of America. The Newton plant was disposed of by the new owners and headquarters transferred from Newton to Allentown, Pennsylvania, but no cars were ever produced there. In the year 1925 the word *finis* was written at the end of the last page of the annals of the Stanley Steamer.

The Stanley Steamer was anything but finished in the memories of those who drove them and rode in them, for the "Whistling Billies," as they were often called, in a little over a quarter of a century, made a most notable mark for themselves, not only on the road but on the race track as well.

My father and uncle were both firm non-believers in paid advertising. They belonged to that hardy Yankee school that felt if a product was good enough it could speak for itself much more convincingly through performance than any number of boastful words and phrases concocted by advertising men.

So in order to bring the unusual qualities of the Stanley to public notice, like Winton, Duryea, and Ford, the results on the race track were permitted to tell the story of what the car could do, and a good story it was, too. But fate stepped in and dealt the team of Stanley twins a serious blow. In 1902 my father's twin brother became seriously ill and was forced to go to Colorado. First, staying in Denver under his doctor's care, he later moved to Estes Park, where he built a home and eventually the Stanley Hotel. Because of this, the designing, building, and testing of the Stanley racers were carried on by my father, who even drove some of the cars himself.

In April, 1903, a hill-climbing contest was held on Commonwealth Avenue. The Stanley entry was a little folding-front-seat model, tiller steered and powered with 5½ horsepower. Entered against it were such comparative leviathans as a 16-horsepower Peerless, 16-horsepower Darracq, 20-horsepower Winton, and a coterie of Packards, Stevens-Duryeas, a Cadillac, Knox, Toledo, and many others, even including electrics. Just before starting time it was discovered that each car must carry two passengers, so my father, who wished to keep his car's load to a minimum, put me on the seat beside its driver, Frank Durbin. I was just nine years old and not very large for my age. Well, the cars had been taking all the way from 43 seconds to over 2 minutes to make the run, and the crowd which lined the entire length of the course had been getting into the middle of the road and stepping slowly aside to make way for each car as it came up. There was plenty of time. When we made our first run we actually had to put on the brakes to keep from running over people who scrambled madly to get out of the way. So we were given a second run and this time made it in 16⅗ seconds. This was 10 seconds under the fastest time made by a gas car, a Stevens-Duryea. It was a great day for steam and this performance layed a solid foundation to the Stanley's reputation as a hill climber. When my mother, who was watching the race from a car parked some distance from the course, found out I was the passenger in the Stanley she told my father what she thought of his "risking" my life in no uncertain manner.

The first of the Stanley racing "Wogglebugs" made its appearance at Readville Track, near Boston, on May 30, 1903. It was shaped like a cigar, painted red, and its lines were such that wind resistance was reduced to a minimum. From its unusual appearance it was dubbed a "freak" by gas car owners and dealers, as were all subsequent Stanley streamlined racers. This was an attempt to belittle the records that they set up. Some called these cars "Bug," "Teakettle," "Wogglebug," "Torpedo," "Whistling Billy," and many other picturesque names. On this particular Memorial Day at Readville the only car that seemed to have any real chance of giving the streamlined Stanley a run for its money was a steamer designed, built, and driven by a Harvard student and member of the Class of '04, George C. Cannon. The Cannon car was steered by one man in the front and controlled and operated by another in the rear. It was low and rakish and very formidable looking with a successful record of track racing back of it. Present also was a Grout steamer that was advertised as being able to make the mile in several seconds less than a minute. A battle royal seemed in the making. What became of the Grout and other contenders I do not recall, but young Cannon pushed the Stanley very hard. They both went faster than any car had ever before gone on a track in the United States. The Stanley, driven by my father, made the mile in 1 minute 2⅘ seconds, with Cannon's best less than 2 seconds behind. But this record only stood for a few hours, for later that same day at the Empire City Track near Yonkers, New Jersey, Barney Oldfield drove an 80-horsepower racer for a man named Ford a mile in 1 minute 1⅗ seconds. Of the Stanley racer the papers said, "A trail of steam followed the red-painted machine as it skimmed around the Readville Race Track and overhauled and passed other larger and seemingly more powerful automobiles. The machine resembled somewhat an inverted boat. The top was rounded and from the center could be seen the head of its operator, F. E. Stanley."

The car that established the name of Stanley in the Hall of Fame of world-wide motordom was the streamlined racing car my father designed that went a mile in 28⅕ seconds at Daytona Beach, Florida, on January 27, 1906. The following year the same car was sent back to the beach and, but for a long string of misfortunes, might well have lowered its own world's record by several seconds. As it was, the car was wrecked when traveling over a rough spot on the beach, but its driver, Fred Marriott, lived to tell about it first hand. The 1906 record stood for four years when Barney Oldfield drove his 200-horsepower "Lightning Benz" a mile in 27.33 seconds on the same beach.

About this same time two special Stanleys were built to compete in the Vanderbilt Cup Race. Though they never competed in that event, they both established great records as racers. It was in one of these cars that I rode with my father at Daytona Beach in 1906 when we struck up a race with Walter Christie, who was driving one of his famous front-wheeled racers. We were traveling along faster than I had ever ridden before and rapidly overtaking Christie, who was quite a bit ahead. There was no windshield on the car and I had no goggles on. Each grain of sand thrown up by the tires of the Christie car seemed to hit me right in the face. I covered my face with both hands, but even so it looked like a raw beet when we finished. We beat the Christie soundly, but I never saw much of the race. I was quite cool to offers to ride in a racing car after that. At this race meet, as at most others, the war between gas and steam flared out in full force. Even the officials were partial to the gas cars. They once changed the starting time of a 30-mile race, pushing it ahead from 9:00 a. m. to 7:00 a. m. This change was not posted on the bulletin board until after 11:00 o'clock the night before the race. My father had retired, but the gas car boys didn't know that he was such an early riser. It was 6:35 a. m. on the day of the race when he first saw the new time of the start. He started getting up steam on his racer, literally pulled Fred Marriott out of bed and got to the starting line several minutes after the gas cars had started; but the Stanley won the race with three minutes to spare, much to its opponents' displeasure.

The Stanley was the first car to climb Mount Washington. It was one of the original models driven by my father's twin brother, F. O. Stanley. He made the trip in 2 hours and 10 minutes on September 16, 1899. In 1904 my father drove a folding-front-seat Stanley to the summit, over the same treacherous road, in a few seconds over 27 minutes. In spite of its fine reputation as a racing car, a hill climber, and for easy riding, the Stanley began to give ground to the gas car by way of numbers in use. Though the production of these cars was never large, the average turned out for each year was close to 1,000 cars. I can remember well one evening when my father returned home and announced that he had just learned something that made him feel very badly. It seems he had seen a report covering the number of automobiles registered in Massachusetts, and for the first time there were more gas cars registered than steam. The ascendency of gas over steam as a motive power moved along slowly at first, but with startling rapidity as time went on. In 1902 registrations for the State of New York totaled 909 and of this number 485 were steamers, such as the Stanley, or its offspring, Locomobiles, Mobiles, and the White. On December 30, 1916, there were 779 Stanleys registered in Massachusetts. At that time Ford headed the list with 30,871, and there were 25 other makes of gasoline cars that exceeded the number of Stanleys.

With the battle for supremacy well on its way to complete victory for the internal combustion engine, when the self-starter came in, many a driver of the die-hard Stanley Steamer began to wonder secretly if he wasn't perhaps just a little bit queer. Why should he bother with fusible plugs, dripping pilot lights, and steam gauges when all you had to do with a gas car was to step on a button and drive away? Then, too, there was the bother of "firing-up" which took from 10 to 25 minutes, depending on how smart you were, and it was pretty important to remember where the watering troughs were located if you were going very far from home. It was always embarrassing to have your gas-car-owning neighbor ask you how far you could go without stopping for water and how long it took you to get up steam. Furthermore, your wife was always annoyed at the whistling of the burner which was music to your ears because it meant everything was working well. There was also considerable criticism as to the body lines of the Stanley. With the majority of cars having flat-fronted radiators, why should the Stanleys stick to that ridiculous looking round hood? "They look more like grasshoppers than automobiles," I once heard someone say at the Boston Automobile Show. Yes, I don't think there is any doubt but what the people who rode in Stanley Steamers suffered more or less from an inferiority complex. I know I did until 1914, when I had a special Stanley that looked for all the world like a Mercedes, with a V-shaped radiator and low slung body. It was painted white with black wire wheels. Wherever it went it caused more than a mild sensation. If I parked it by a curb in Boston a crowd would instantly gather about and ply me with questions. In reply to their query as to what kind of a car it was, I often would reply, "It's an Italian Ford," and drive away. I sold this car when I joined the Navy in 1917, and the last I ever heard of it was in 1919 when someone phoned me and said he was just back from Los Angeles and that he had ridden in a special Stanley out there that was now a taxi. It was in great demand and he had heard it belonged to me once and thought I would be interested. I was. I'd certainly like to have it today.

The first Stanley I ever had was a little car that had about the same proportions as a baby carriage, only it was a little higher. Its wheelbase was 75 inches, but it could go 60 miles an hour. In 1908 I made a trip to Maine in it, leaving home some two hours before my father, who was to follow me along, and, as he said, "pick up the pieces." I had a list of all the watering troughs on our line of travel and had promised to leave a message in chalk on each one where I had stopped for water. Watering troughs were as welcome to the drivers of Stanley cars as they were to horses in those days, and the messages we wrote were: "Reached here at 5:40 a. m., everything working well . . ." "Two punctures to here . . ." "Blew a fusible plug, but filled boiler with borrowed hose and went on." The last message was one of triumph. I had filled my tank at the last trough and knew I could make our destination, Bath, Maine, so in triumph I wrote: "All's well! Catch us if you can." There was a real thrill to touring in those days. When I drove back I took an old sea captain from Boothbay Harbor back with me. We made it, but when he was asked how he liked the ride he said with his salty, down-east drawl: "Ride? That wasn't no ride, I was in the air most o' the way!"

I was in the eighth grade at grammar school when I had this first car. I drove it to school for awhile but some of the boys couldn't resist taking it. They wouldn't know which handle turned on the main burner, so when the steam was used up they'd leave the car wherever it happened to stop and then after school I'd have to hunt it up. Today taking a car without the consent of its owner is a pretty serious affair, but in those days it was just good fun. Once someone took a Stanley I had parked at Harvard Square, in Cambridge, and four hours later when it hadn't returned I went to the police. They only laughed at me, for reporting a stolen car was something new to them. The car turned up eventually, several miles away, with a burned boiler. I found out who took it, but let the matter drop. He was bigger than I was. Thereafter I used to padlock the throttle and had less trouble.

Speaking of the police reminds me that being arrested for speeding in the early days of automobiling was taken pretty much as a matter of course. Even 19 miles an hour made a lawbreaker of you. But it wasn't until you had been arrested two or three times that you felt like a real veteran and somehow you were really proud of your transgressions. Once when my father was testing the speed of a racing car on a long, straight road back of a town near Boston, he went right by a policeman at a mighty fast clip. When my father came back he stopped his car by the officer, for he knew him well. Apologetically he told my father that he would have to swear out a warrant for his arrest. This he did and the case came up in court several days later. The officer told his story and stated that my father was going nearly 60 miles an hour. My father entered a plea of "not guilty" to this charge, much to the judge's astonishment. When he asked him how he could plead not guilty when the evidence was so clear against him, my father replied, "I plead not guilty to going 60 miles an hour. When I passed the officer my speedometer showed I was going 87 miles an hour!" He paid a fine of $5.00 and all the Boston papers carried the story.

What are the chances of the steamer coming back to some of its former glory? Personally I think they are pretty poor. There are bound to be attempts made, as there always have been, but there are a lot of tough hurdles to get over, as anyone who has tried it will tell you. Just the other day I had a letter from a man who said he was a representative of the Chinese Government. He wanted to know if the Stanley burner could be converted so that it could use wood for fuel. It seems that the gasoline problem is very acute in China and some people over there figured that the Stanley Steamer might be the solution to their problem. My correspondent wanted to know how quickly a certain number of Stanleys could be made ready for shipment. The letter I had to write in reply made me wonder if American manufacturers weren't missing a bet. With the automobile industry centered in the Middle West it was impossible for a small company located in New England to survive. The maker of 1,000 cars a year could hardly compete with a maker of several hundred thousand. In its later years the Stanley was forced up into the high-priced car market, and it certainly never belonged there. But there are plenty of people, even today, "queer" enough or wise enough, whichever you wish to call them, who would still pay good American dollars for a steamer that would give a ride like the Stanleys of the past, but glorified with the modern improvements in design and construction that would be possible with all the new metals and processes that have been developed.

Steam is still carrying lots of people places, even in this age of high-octane gas and synthetic rubber, with all-plastic bodies just over the horizon. But here's a warning to the gas-buggy boys: "You'd better watch out or jet propulsion will get you if you don't!" And if it ever does, perhaps some little folding-front-seat, tiller-steer Stanley, in some long forgotten auto graveyard, will stir just a little bit and have the last laugh, after all.

*The writer of this article is Mr. R. W. Stanley of Boston, Mass., son of Mr. F. E. Stanley. His early recollections on Stanley cars are of interest to almost everyone interested in automotive history.—Clymer.

STANLEY VANDERBILT CUP RACER

This is one of the two Stanley Steam race cars built to compete in the famous Vanderbilt cup races. It was in one of these cars that F. E. Stanley drove in the race against Walter Christie in his front drive special at Daytona Beach, Florida, in 1906. The driver of the car is F. L. N. Baldwin. The Stanley special racing cars were known as the Vanderbilt Cup Models, although they did not actually compete in any of the Vanderbilt Cup Races. — R. W. Stanley Photo.

EARLY HISTORY OF THE STANLEY COMPANY

By CARLTON F. STANLEY*

The Stanley brothers' interest in building self-propelled vehicles began in the fall of 1896, when they attended the Brockton, Mass., Fall Fair. It had been advertised that a "horseless carriage" would be shown. The vehicle however was not able to make a complete lap of the track without stopping.

On the way home, the conversation turned to this not-too-good exhibition and Mr. F. E. Stanley said, "Well, boys, before another fall I will show you a self-propelled carriage that will go around that track not only once but several times without stopping."

From here the development of the first Stanleys is well told by Mr. F. O. Stanley in the book, "The Modern Steam Car and Its Background", by Thomas S. Derr. We may add that the cylinders of the first Stanley were a bronze casting and are now in the Smithsonian Institute in Washington, D. C. These first cars had boilers 14" in diameter and 13" high. The engines were mounted vertically under the driver's seat, so the crank shafts, chains and sprockets were exposed to the dust of the road, of which there was plenty in those days.

The first automobile to climb Mt. Washington in New Hampshire was one of these first Stanleys, Mr. and Mrs. F. O. Stanley making the ascent on August 31st, 1899.

The Stanley brothers marketed only one carriage of this early type before the business was sold to The Locomobile Co., hence any of them found in museums or elsewhere are marked Locomobile rather than Stanley. The Locomobile Co. was organized for the purpose of buying the Stanley business, factory, patents, parts and all.

One of the terms of this sale was that the Stanley brothers would not make motor carriages for a period of two years. At the expiration of this term they began planning again for building cars and late in 1901 or early in 1902 were putting out a much better car. It carried four people, two on a front folding seat.

In 1903 a great improvement was made by placing the engines horizontally and geared to the differential, making it possible to put a sheet metal casing around the engine and gears to protect them from the dust. These cars were known as Model B (with spindle seat) and Model C (with solid seat). Later 16-inch boilers were put into some of them and they were known as BX and CX respectively.

The Newton, Mass., fire department purchased one of the CX cars and used it extensively. It was equipped with fire extinguishers, small tools, etc. So far as is known, this is the first motor carriage ever owned by a city or town that was used for fighting fires.

Next came the Models E and EX cars having 18-inch boilers. These were the first Stanleys having the boilers in front. In 1905 a 5-passenger touring car was added to the list. At first it had a 20-inch boiler and later 23-inch, with a 3⅝ x 5 engine. Late that year the Florida Racer was built, having a 30-inch boiler and 4½ x 6½ engine geared so the driving wheels made two turns while the engine made one turn. Thus at a mile a minute the engine was not turning at its best efficiency. This was the racer in which Fred Marriott made a mile in 28-1/5 seconds and two miles in 59-4/5 seconds, records which have never been equalled by cars weighing not more than 2200 pounds. This was in January 1906. That fall the racer was improved and sent again to Florida. In trying to lower his former record, Marriott was going close to 3 miles a minute. The boiler in this racer was back of the driver's seat, so with the torque of the engine when driving hard there was not a great amount of weight on the front wheels. A little depression in the sand caused the front wheels to leave the ground. As the underneath of the racer was boarded flat, it sailed right off in the air like a kite, neither front or rear wheels touching the sand for 100 feet or more. When it came down it turned over and broke in two. Mr. Marriott was seriously hurt but recovered. This accident effectively dampened the Stanleys' enthusiasm for racing.

By 1907 there were turned out of the Stanley factory between 600 and 700 cars, including at least eight different models. There were the EX Roadsters, F Touring Cars, H Gentlemen's Speedy Roadsters having 23-inch boilers and $3\frac{5}{8}$ x 5 engines, K a faster roadster with 26-inch boiler and $4\frac{1}{2}$ x $6\frac{1}{2}$ engine, and the HX, a cross between the two. There were also two Vanderbilt Racers, the Florida Racer, and a Model J Limousine. The production manager sometimes got a headache. Five of these models were new that year.

The so-called Vanderbilt Racers were long, rangy, two-passenger cars with the same power plants as the Florida Racers. It was originally planned to enter these cars in the Vanderbilt Races which were held on Long Island, N. Y., each fall, but this was never done. Nevertheless the cars retained that name to those familiar with Stanley products.

The Model J Limousine was built for Mrs. F. E. Stanley's use. This was the first closed car made by the Stanley Co. It was also the first closed body made by the Currier Cameron Co. of Amesbury, Mass., and so it was made like a horse-drawn hack. The following year this car was dismantled and a fairly presentable closed model was added to the output.

An incident which caused some amusement in later years but which wasn't much to laugh over at the time, was this. A friend recommended a little change in the design of the boilers; it was not favored at first, as it took away a factor for safety in the construction. Yet as time went on, it seemed likely that the change would become regular practice. It worried the writer, so he decided to make a test without saying anything to any one. With the assistance of the plant engineer a pit was dug out back of the factory building. A small boiler with burner attached and pilot going and water in the boiler was placed in the pit, timbers were placed over the pit and fuel tank, control valve and pressure gauge were all inside the factory building. At the noon hour a sentinel was placed to prevent any one passing near the pit and the fuel was turned on. Soon the steam pressure began to mount. Somewhere between 1800 and 2000, bang went the boiler. Simultaneously bang went between 200 and 300 lights of glass from the factory windows. The glass being out so lightened the window sash that the counter-weights pulled the sash up, creating an optical illusion that the building was settling. A young man returning from lunch saw this and rushed into the office and called out, "There has been an explosion and the factory is settling into the ground!" The Stanley brothers rushed out to the back yard and took a look at the boiler which had been raised out of the pit. "What in thunder, Carlton, were you trying to do?" Mr. F. E. Stanley asked the writer. It seemed the boiler was stark evidence of what had been tried, and all the glass around was sufficient evidence that the experiment was a success. However, something had been learned and within an hour steps were taken to strengthen the part of the boiler which was shown to be less strong than the rest.

One of the early motor passenger busses was the Stanley Mountain Wagon, so called because it was designed by Mr. F. O. Stanley for carrying passengers from Loveland, Colo., into Estes Park. These cars had the same power plants as the Florida Racers, namely 26-inch boilers and $4\frac{1}{2}$ x $6\frac{1}{2}$ engines, only they were geared much lower. The first models carried 9 passengers including the driver. Later they were built to carry twelve and became much used by the summer hotels. Several had rather classy equipment, with built-on tops, side curtains, etc. Among the users were the Hotel Wentworth at Portsmouth, N. H., and the Samosett at Rockland, Me. These cars with the low gear ratio would climb any hill where the traction was good enough. There was no vibration, no odor, and they were very comfortable—altogether important items in the development of bus transportation.

Those who were interested in motor vehicles at the turn of the century will recall that gasoline sold at very low prices. At that time gasoline was merely a by-product of the manufacture of kerosene, which was almost the universal lighting medium, except in the cities. There were but few stationary internal combustion engines. Most motor boats were driven by steam power, so there was a relatively small demand for gasoline and it sold for only a few cents per gallon. As motor cars began to get more numerous, the price of gasoline steadily advanced. By 1911 or 1912, the price of gasoline was much higher than for kerosene, which could be gotten for 7 or 8 cents a gallon in barrel lots. There were no restrictions against keeping a barrel of kerosene in a garage or shed.

It was thought a simple matter to burn kerosene in steam cars by lengthening the vaporizing tube in the burner. This brought about unbearable whistling. While the burners would whistle a little when starting up cold with gasoline, this would stop as soon as the burners got warm. Not so with kerosene. The burner castings were made like a saw tooth affair, and slots were milled in the points to let the gas and air into the combustion chamber. As the flame in this type of burner is simply a rapid succession of explosions, it was thought that having the slots all alike was what set up the whistling, so a burner was made with the casting flat and slots milled all the way across. This burner would whistle at all times, hot or cold. However, this showed the way. In the next burner we used holes about the size of a common sewing needle. This burner would not whistle under any conditions, but did not make quite enough steam. Later No. 56 drills were used and the resulting burners, while they would whistle a little when forced hard, would make very much more steam than anything made up to that time. This type of burner was used as long as the Stanley cars were being made.

More recently a type of burner very like what is known as a gun type of house heating burner has been adapted to steam cars. Two outstanding examples are, one developed by Mr. Thomas S. Derr, of Newton, Mass., on cars which in peacetime he builds under the name of "American Steam Car", and another developed by Mr. Doble. It is the writer's recollection that a house heating unit which had quite a large sale some twenty-five years ago, known as the NO-KOL, came out coincidentally with the Doble type of steam car burner and may have been a joint development.

Two outgrowths from the Stanley business were interesting; one was the building of a Unit Railway Car. One day a Mr. Gentzel came to the factory to get some information about the power plants. The conversation became so eager that a company was formed consisting of the same stockholders as the Stanley Motor Carriage Co., with the addition of Mr. Gentzel as Chief Engineer. One Unit Car was made, the body being built at Laconia, N. H., and the power plant at the Stanley factory. The engine was 6 x 8 and at first had an upright fire tube boiler. Mr. Gentzel designed a burner similar to those used on oil-fired steamships, in which the fuel is driven into the combustion chamber by a steam jet. This burner was powerful; it made steam so fast there was not space enough for it to separate from the water, with the result that the water was raised right up off the crownsheet of the boiler. A water tube boiler was then constructed along lines similar to those of the well known Babcock-Wilcox product. This proved very satisfactory and the Boston and Maine railway used the unit car extensively on a branch line in Vermont.

The unit railway car industry developed slowly, partly on account of the labor unions being opposed to it because it reduced the number of employees necessary. However, quite a number of unit power plants were made. A large proportion of these went to South America.

Another development was the Bell Locomotive Works. Mr. Harvey W. Bell, a grandson of the Mr. Bell who helped the Baltimore and Ohio Railroad, when a school boy had a friend contractor at work on the dam of the great Croydon Reservoir in New York state. Mr. Bell got a second-hand Stanley engine and a boiler and built a small locomotive for the contractor to use in pulling around their materials. This was so successful that another was built and in a short time a going business was built up. This resulted in a company being formed consisting of Mr. Bell and three of the stockholders of the Stanley Company. The plant was at Bound Brook, N. J. and doing a good business when World War I broke out. Mr. Bell, being single, had to go to war, and as he was the whole thing in the business, it was sold to a Mr. Stokes, also a contractor in New York. Many of these locomotives were used on sugar plantations in Cuba and elsewhere.

Another development came with World War I. Some army engineers had built what was intended as a fighting unit at Massachusetts Institute of Technology in Cambridge, Mass. They wanted equipment to supply steam, so some units were made at the factory. In the spring of 1918 they were taken to France, demonstrated to Marshal Foch, General Pershing and others and pronounced the most wonderful thing of the kind ever seen. "But," they said, "it won't do us any good. They cannot be gotten into production soon enough. The war will all be over before Christmas." This was in June 1918. An accurate estimate, one might say.

There chanced to be a high British Medical Officer there and he said, "That is just what we need in order to give the soldiers shower baths." So one Lieutenant Traver was given the job of constructing a platform in sections, and mounting 24 shower sprays on it. The men were taken into a barracks where they stripped. Each was given a cake of soap and ONE MINUTE in which to take a shower bath, after which they went into another barracks where they were given fresh clothing. So this little unit which had been mounted on a small framework with carrying rods so two men could bring it to any desired spot, furnished hot water to bathe 24 men a minute.

Soon afterwards they sent an order for 160 units which were to be mounted on Mack trucks with 800-gallon water tanks, but after only a few were built the armistice was signed and all work was discontinued.

*The writer of this article, Mr. Carlton F. Stanley is a nephew of the Stanley Brothers. He was with the Stanley Company for many years.—Clymer.

Carleton F. Stanley, whose article is above, is shown alongside Mr. F. O. Stanley. The car is a 1903 model; and the photo was taken in the doorway of Fred Marriott's garage at Newton, Mass. Mr. Marriott, who is shown standing, was the driver of the Stanley Steamer Racer that established a world's speed record at Ormond Beach, Florida, of 127.66 miles per hour, in 1906. Mr. Marriott was the first human being to travel at a speed of more than two miles per minute. Photo taken in 1940 —Clymer   C. F. Stanley Photo

FIRST CAR TO CLIMB MT. WASHINGTON

This Stanley Steamer made the ascent on August 31, 1899. Shown in the car are Mr. and Mrs. F. O. Stanley, who made the historical trip.

AUTO·BIOGRAPHIES

BY W. EVERETT MILLER

MAN POWER
1500
THIS IS ONE OF 7 DESIGNS MADE FOR EMPEROR MAXIMILLIAN OF GERMANY (1459-1519) BY ALBRECHT DURER. NOTE WORM GEARING.

WIND POWER
1600
MADE BY SIMON STEVIN AT SCHEVENINGEN, HOLLAND. SPEED 20 M.P.H.

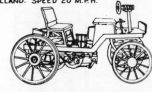

STEAM POWER
1769
THE SECOND CAR BUILT FOR THE FRENCH ARMY BY NICOLAS JOSEPH CUGNOT, FOR HAULING CANNONS. IT IS STILL PRESERVED IN PARIS.

GASOLINE POWER
1868
THE INVENTION OF AN AUSTRIAN, SIEGFRIED MARKUS AND DRIVEN ON THE STREETS OF MALCHIN UNTIL STOPPED BY POLICE.

ADVANCE WITH ADVANCE

3-10-38

TANK DESTROYER

AMPHIBIAN

FIRST FRENCH STEAM DRIVEN CAR (1770)

FIRST AMERICAN STEAM DRIVEN CAR (1805)

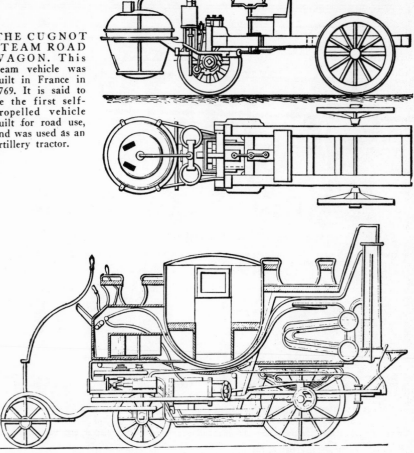

THE CUGNOT STEAM ROAD WAGON. This steam vehicle was built in France in 1769. It is said to be the first self-propelled vehicle built for road use, and was used as an artillery tractor.

The Gurney Steam Carriage — built in 1824.

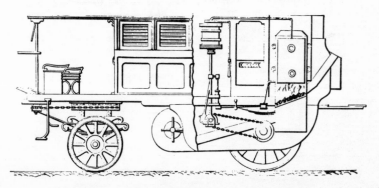

The Hancock Steam Omnibus — built in 1839.

The Ransome Traction Steamer,
England 1870.

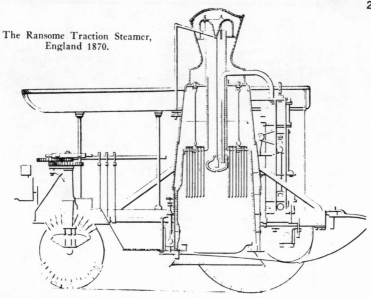

This steam fire engine was built by the Gould
Manufacturing Company in 1900 at Seneca Falls,
New York.

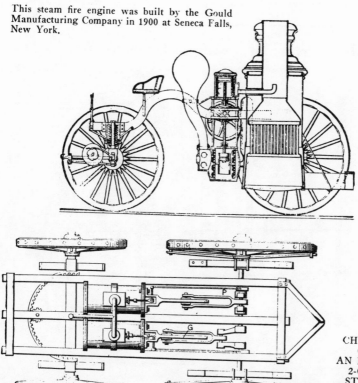

CHASSIS
OF
AN EARLY
2-CYL.
STEAM
CARRIAGE

Carriages without horses shall go,
And accidents fill the world with woe.

Old Mother Shipton has been vindicated insofar as this part of her prophecy is concerned. Of course, it is now generally believed that the verse, of which the foregoing is only a part, was a hoax to the extent that the predictions were circulated after most of the predicted things had come to pass.

But it must be admitted that the author of the introductory lines anticipated present-day traffic problems. The comic sketch here shown appeared in 1828 shortly after the advent of steam carriages which was nearly four centuries after Mother Shipton is supposed to have lived. The artist was himself something of a seer because he attempted to show how the streets would some day be clogged by horseless carriages.

Headline Picture of 1833; an Omnibus Run by Steam

Almost seventy years before the gasoline-driven automobile came upon the scene, passengers were carried between Birmingham and London in Dr. Church's steam omnibus, which ran on flat tires and advertised "22 inside & 22 outside seats." This primitive motorbus could make fourteen miles an hour, but English law intervened. Parliament set a speed limit of three miles an hour and decreed that every steam-driven vehicle must be preceded by a man with a red flag.

1863 AUSTIN STEAMER

THE present generation of (former) motorists have the impression that the first automobiles were developed around the turn of the century when, in fact, self-propelled road vehicles were built and run as early as 170 years ago. The clumsy Cugnot steam tractor made a trial run in France in 1770, steam coaches did a brisk business in England in the nineteenth century, and an inventive American, Oliver Evans, built several tons of lumber and hardware into an amphibian in 1805 which ran, after a fashion, on the streets and waterways of Philadelphia.

Hence, the Austin steam car described in this article is by no means the first, although it was built in 1863 in England. Quaint as it seems, great credit is due to its designer since he had few precedents to start from, with the exception of a horse-drawn carriage body and wheels and heavy steam engines of the locomotive type. In fact, the mechanical principle is much on the order of the English locomotive in which the cylinders and cranks are between the wheels.

A real pioneer, the Austin steam car was built in England in 1863. Connecting rods drive direct on rear axle, like a British locomotive. Water tank is seen behind seat.

Another early steam car was the Mobile, here photographed on Hollywood Boulevard in 1900. Several thousand of these jittery puff-wagons were sold.

This unusual steam vehicle was built about 1880. The driver—or should I say engineer?—was Ike Lehmer. — Walter T. Kelley, Photo.

Reproduced from the first issue of HORSELESS AGE 1895

STEAM CARRIAGE. FRANK VANELL, VINCENNES, IND.

The Vanell Steam Carriage.
——o——

Frank Vanell, 1031 Gurney St., Vincennes, Ind., furnishes a rough sketch of a steam carriage, which he enters in the Chicago Race. The motor which is on the rotary order, is attached to the driving shaft without gearing of any kind. The frame is of wrought iron tubing, so constructed as to be utilized for a water tank. The driving wheels are five feet and the steering wheels two feet in diameter, and all four wheels are fitted with pneumatic tires. The vehicle is steered by a sprocket wheel and chain. The axles are of steel and the bearings anti-friction.

The weight of the vehicle is about 1200 pounds and its cost, so the inventor states, is $275.

MAXIM'S
STEAM ENGINE
1895

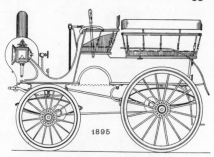

The Sweany Steam Carriage.

Reproduced from the first issue of HORSELESS AGE. This steam carriage was designed by Dr. F. L. Sweany, of Philadelphia and built by the Chas. S. Caffrey Co., of Camden, N. J. Power consisted of four 3-HP motors, one attached to each wheel.

THE OLDS STEAMER

This Steam car was built in 1886-1887 by Ransom E. Olds in his father's machine shop at Lansing, Mich. It was an experimental model and not offered for sale. It had three wheels with a bicycle type front fork and a tiller steering lever. Mr. Olds was the designer of the Oldsmobile curved dash car and later, after disposing of his interest in the Oldsmobile Company, took his initials R.E.O. and built the famous Reo car.

GROUT
4-Passenger Trap
1900

Built by Grout Brothers, early steam car manufacturers of Orange, Mass.
Tires 34x3, wheelbase 63 in., tread 56 in. Speed, 18 miles an hour.

This photo, taken in Pittsburgh, Pa., in August, 1901. shows Mr. H. C. Frick's Gardner-Serpolet Steam Carriage. It was sent to New York as it had insufficient power for the hills of Pittsburgh. Photo, courtesy of Thomas M. Galey.

Birdsall Steam Tractor, about 1900.

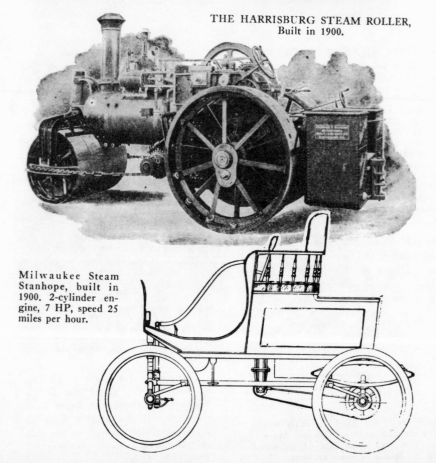

THE HARRISBURG STEAM ROLLER,
Built in 1900.

Milwaukee Steam
Stanhope, built in
1900. 2-cylinder en-
gine, 7 HP, speed 25
miles per hour.

The Only Perfect Automobile!

THE PORTER STANHOPE

Weight only 550lbs.

Order Now to Ensure Early Delivery

THE PORTER STANHOPE

Price $750.00

Has no Rival in Simplicity, Design, Construction Economy.

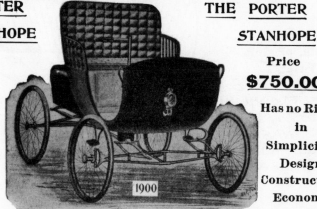

The "**Motor Age**" of Chicago thus describes the Perfect Automobile:

"A handsome, stylish vehicle which can be started instantly and without previous laborious or lengthy preparation, can be stopped promptly, can be run at any speed up to twenty-five miles an hour, can be perfectly controlled by any person without special training, can travel over rough streets and roads, can climb stiff grades, can, in short, do anything and everything that a horse or span of horses attached to a vehicle can do, and do it more satisfactory, do it at a fraction of the expense and at the same time have none of the inherent faults of the horse, and no new ones of its own at the present time." There are vehicles that combine some of these advantages, but none that combine them all except **THE PORTER STANHOPE, price $750.00.** We make only one grade, and that the best, and the best only will be found satisfactory in the long run.

THE PORTER STANHOPE is the Perfect Automobile.

It is handsome and elegant in its lines and conforms in design to the modern horse carriages.

Safe, simple and durable.

Boiler is absolutely non-explosive and water-feed automatic.

It is free from all complications in its mechanism, so that an engineer is not necessary in its use.

Fuel is cheap and obtainable everywhere.

It is noiseless and free from all odor and vibration.

The Burner (or engine fire) is of low draft and so protected from the air as to be unquenchable in all weathers.

It is controlled by one lever only, as in times of danger several levers are confusing. The methods of lighting the burner at first are so simple that anyone can do it quickly and in a manner that is not complicated.

Before you buy an Automobile mention this magazine and write to the **Write Now!**

PORTER MOTOR CO.,

950 Tremont Building, Boston, Mass.

36

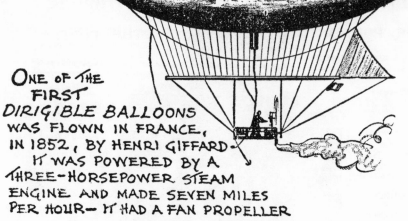

ONE OF THE
FIRST
DIRIGIBLE BALLOONS
WAS FLOWN IN FRANCE,
IN 1852, BY HENRI GIFFARD.
IT WAS POWERED BY A
THREE-HORSEPOWER STEAM
ENGINE AND MADE SEVEN MILES
PER HOUR — IT HAD A FAN PROPELLER

STEAM MOTORCYCLE

SPEED LIMIT UNKNOWN - MILEAGE 17,000 - BUILT BY N.F. GILLENWATERS,

Sacramento, Calif.

Ofeldt's Steam Auto. Specialties.

BLUE FLAME KEROSENE BURNER

Note Its Simplicity.

It is now two months since I installed your water regulator on my car and I am so well pleased with same that I would not take $100 for it. With this regulator I consider you have removed one of the main objections to the steam automobile.

Yours truly,
A. J. PEET, M. D.,
1101 Cortelyou Road,
Brooklyn, N. Y.

Water Level
Water Tube
Boiler

WRITE FOR CATALOGUE.

Built by Boiler Makers of 20 Years' Experience.

AUTOMATIC WATER REGULATOR

Operates the By-Pass Automatically.

F. W. OFELDT & SONS, Foot of 25th Street, Brooklyn, N. Y.

THE TRACTOBILE

1900

SIMPLE   **E**FFICIENT

TRUSTY   **N**OISELESS

ECONOMICAL   **G**EARLESS

AMPLE POWER   **I**NTER-CHANGEABLE

MECHANICAL   **N**O COMPLICATIONS

     ENDURING

Our Tracto-Surrey Price $625; or with Rubber Tires on Rear Wheels, $650.

ANY Vehicle at present drawn by a Horse can be converted into an up-to-date Automobile—one possessing numerous patented improvements not found in any other make. The above illustration shows a "CONVERTED" Surrey, formerly used as a Horse-drawn Vehicle. We have removed the neat shield or guard which is used to cover the Mechanism and the Battery of Patent "Unit" Boilers, in order that the simplicity of design, strength of construction and accessibility of working parts may be appreciated.

The Tractobile is the only motor built on correct mechanical lines. It DRAWS its load; it does not PUSH. No buckling strains are set up necessitating heavy, clumsy frame-work to counter-balance them. The front wheels both draw and steer, and no "differential"—that fruitful source of "skidding"—is needed. The drive is direct from steam cylinders to road wheels—like a Railroad Locomotive. No loss of power from gears and other complications. Legally protected everywhere. Full particulars furnished by the makers.

THE PENNSYLVANIA STEAM VEHICLE COMPANY, Inc.
CARLISLE, PA.

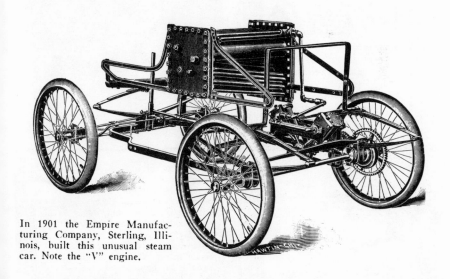

In 1901 the Empire Manufacturing Company, Sterling, Illinois, built this unusual steam car. Note the "V" engine.

NOTE: All ads appearing in this Scrapbook are of course void, having appeared years ago. They are reproduced not for the purpose of selling any merchandise. The ads do, however, show the great progress made by both the automotive industry and the advertising firms of this country.

38

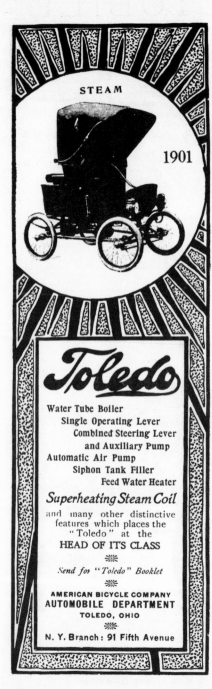

STEAM

1901

Toledo

Water Tube Boiler
Single Operating Lever
Combined Steering Lever
and Auxiliary Pump
Automatic Air Pump
Siphon Tank Filler
Feed Water Heater

Superheating Steam Coil

and many other distinctive
features which places the
"Toledo" at the
HEAD OF ITS CLASS

⁂

Send for "Toledo" Booklet

⁂

AMERICAN BICYCLE COMPANY
AUTOMOBILE DEPARTMENT
TOLEDO, OHIO

⁂

N. Y. Branch: 91 Fifth Avenue

Mr. and Mrs. Malcolm W. Edgar in Toledo Steamer.... Taken in Detroit in 1901.... Notice that this car is identical to the one owned by Mr. and Mrs. Clouse and shown on this page. ... Also note that the right hand of both Mr. Edgar and Mr. Clouse is on the throttle of their respective cars.—*Clymer.*

THEN
AND
NOW

Mr. and Mrs. F. R. Clouse of Auburn, Indiana, are shown here in their 1900 Toledo Steam Carriage.... This photo was taken in 1944 and this car, still in excellent condition, was demonstrated by Mr. and Mrs. Clouse on Sunday, June 25, 1944.... On that date they held "open house" to a large group of friends who came to see the car operate. On the same date the Clouses also demonstrated their 1913 Imp Cyclecar which they also own. This Toledo Steamer is identical to the one shown in the upper photo of Mr. and Mrs. Edgar of Detroit.—*Clymer.*

1901

BUY A SKENE,

A successful steam automobile built by reliable makers, and enjoy the fascination of a horseless carriage. We will be pleased to demonstrate the many points of superiority which our machine possesses to any one who is interested. There is a small amount of **TREASURY STOCK** in this Company still unsubscribed. Those who are looking for a "good thing" will do well to correspond with me immediately.

ARTHUR C. EDDY, Treasurer

Skene American Automobile Company

Carr Bldg., Harrison Ave., Springfield, Mass.

WHITE STEAM CARRIAGES.

1902

The White Sewing Machine Co., Cleveland, Ohio, took such great pains in perfecting their vehicle before offering it to the trade that they find very few changes advisable in their 1902 model. The wheel

Semi-front View 1902 White Steam Carriage.

base is lengthened six inches, making it six feet. The additional length is put on the front, making more room for the occupants.

As the White Steam Carriage has been very fully described in recent issues of the "Journal," it is unnecessary to describe it at this time. The principal feature of this carriage, as is well known, is the flash steam generator.

Side View 1902 White Steam Carriage.

The excellent showing made by these carriages in the New York-Buffalo endurance test was the subject of flattering comment from people prominent in the trade, and the "Whites" have lost none of their popularity in everyday use.

AN ASBESTOS COVERED MUFFLER.

To obviate the noise of the exhaust striking the metal sides of a muffler, the H. W. Johns-Manville Co., 100 William street, New York city, have perfected a muffler covering made of their asbestos fire felt which is a soft, flexible fabric composed entirely of pure asbestos fibres felted together in such a way that the large amount of air entrapped successfully insulates against noise and heat.

James Goold Co., Albany, N. Y., are the manufacturers of the combination brake and fender illustrated herewith.

One cut shows the device in detail and the other shows a mobile with the brake and fenders attached, the operator in the

Goold's Combination Brake and Fender.

act of applying the brake. The standard "A" is clipped to the rear spring and axle, being held tightly in place by the same clips that hold the springs to the axle seat. The small rod "B" is operated by a bell crank on the under side of the rear axle and this in turn by the rod running forward to the lower end of the foot lever. When the foot lever is pressed down, the brake is drawn down onto the top of the tire and it is im-

Mobile Equipped With Goold's Combination Brake and Fender.

possible to move a vehicle when this brake is set.

Parties who have used them state that they would not be without the brake even if it cost double what they paid for it. It is an absolute safeguard against accidents of all sorts and will hold the vehicle on any hill in case the other brake is insufficient or gives out for any cause.

The Kokomo Rubber Co., Kokomo, Ind., has signed the new license agreement with the Single Tube Auto & Bicycle Tire Co., and will manufacture under Tillinghast patents.

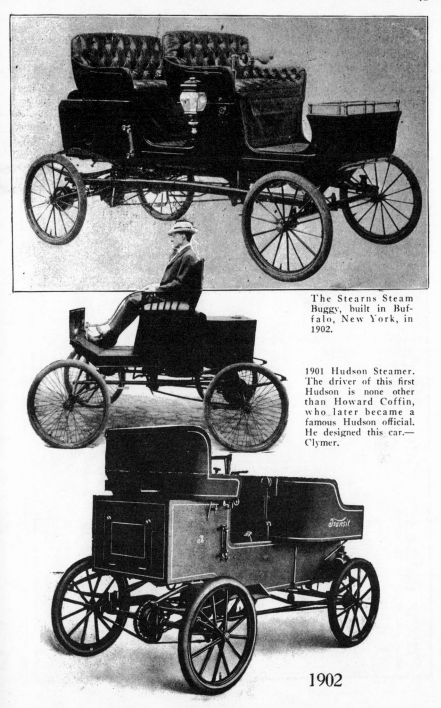

The Stearns Steam Buggy, built in Buffalo, New York, in 1902.

1901 Hudson Steamer. The driver of this first Hudson is none other than Howard Coffin, who later became a famous Hudson official. He designed this car.— Clymer.

1902

THE "TRANSIT" STEAM WAGON, REAR VIEW.

Prescotts Receive First Class Certificates

In the Automobile Club of America's 100-mile Endurance Contest on Decoration Day between New York and Southport, Ct., and return, the Prescott Steam Cars were awarded First Class Certificates.

In the Speed Trials on Staten Island Boulevard, May 31, one of the Prescotts that made the Endurance Run — a regular stock car — nothing special on it, made the mile in 1.37 1-5, thus proving conclusively that the Prescotts are *safe, speedy* and *reliable*.

1902

4 Passenger Open Front.

2 Passenger Closed Front

WHEEL BASE, 68 INS.

WEIGHT, 1250 POUNDS

Boiler Will Not Burn Out
Heavy Running Gear
Two Double Acting Brakes
New Indestructible Burner
Large Fuel Supply
Large Water Capacity
Engine Encased
Superheated Steam

Pilot Light that Holds Steam at any Desired Pressure
Folding Dash
Automatic Lubrication
American Roller Bearings
Steam Air Pump
Steam Water Pump

WHY NOT PURCHASE AN AUTOMOBILE THAT HAS PROVEN RELIABILITY UNDER ALL CONDITIONS? WRITE FOR CATALOG

PRESCOTT AUTOMOBILE MFG. CO.

83 Chambers St., New York

WHEN ANSWERING ADVERTISEMENTS, PLEASE MENTION THE AUTOMOBILE AND MOTOR REVIEW.

The Elite Steam Carriage, built in Utica, New York, in 1901.

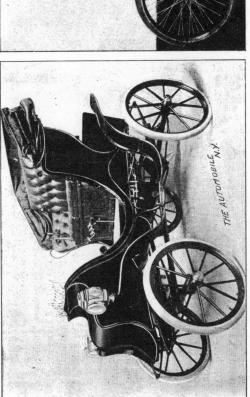

1901 Waltham Steam Carriage, built in Waltham, Mass.

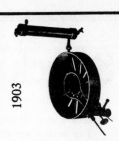
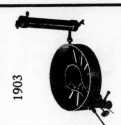

1903

MANUFACTURERS' ENDORSEMENT.
Barber Kerosene Burner for Automobiles
A MANUFACTURERS' ENDORSEMENT.

ORANGE, Mass., May 12th, 1803.

BARBER MFG. CO., *Boston, Mass.*
Gentlemen:—We have now been trying one of your Kerosene Burners for about 30 days on our light Truck, which is fired every day, rain or shine, and is working most of the day. We have found this burner very satisfactory in every way, and will urge you to rush along the two 24 in. burners. You also remember that we tried one of your 16 in. burners on one of our Drop Front's and this also gave us very good satisfaction.
Yours respectfully,
(Signed) GROUT BROS.—By C. B. GROUT.

Points of Superiority.—Economy. No odor. ⅓ more heat than gasoline. No smoke. No lighting back. Absolute safety. No clogging of spray nozzle. Carbon deposit easily removed. Fits any steamer. Each Burner guaranteed. Write for prices.

BARBER MFG. CO., 1005 Tremont Bldg. Boston, Mass.

THE AIR IS ALWAYS PURE AND CLEAN AROUND THE

Storck Steam Carriage

AS THE OPERATOR NEVER HAS TO "CUSS" IT, BECAUSE :—

The boilers don't burn out—they're not built that way
The burner crown sheets don't burn out—they have none
Makes 140 lbs. of steam in one minute—that's enough
Has many a fool-proof, annoyance-saving device—that's nice

And BEST OF ALL for_____

Mr. Dealer or Jobber

if you are in business for the money, and want to sell the best steam carriage made at $725 to $800, and make a handsomer profit than any other gives you, it is high time to write me. My goods, retail prices, and discounts can not be beaten in 1902, and I have features after features, new, up-to-date improvements, and yet use about one-half the piping, etc., used by others. When your customer looks at this wagon he does not say, "Too much for Charley"—he can't ; it's too simple. Ladies run it in one-half hour.

FRANK C. STORCK

Corner Broad and White Sts., RED BANK, N. J.

THE Sturdy **Century** Steam CAR

1903

ONE HAND CONTROL

DIRECT SHAFT DRIVE

NO. 1 STEAM ROADSTER, $750.00
FIRST PRIZE WINNER LONG ISLAND ENDURANCE TEST.
No torch is used.   No Levers in the way.   No wind affects the fire.
New Catalogue Ready.   IMMEDIATE DELIVERY.   Write for terms.
CENTURY MOTOR VEHICLE CO., Syracuse, N. Y., U. S. A.

VICTORIOUS AT HOME AND ABROAD

THE WHITE STEAM CARRIAGE

WINS OUT IN ENGLAND'S RELIABILITY CONTEST

TRUE to its former showing made in this country a WHITE STEAM CARRIAGE completed the 650 mile test with

AN ABSOLUTELY CLEAN RECORD

being one of two out of seventy entries to achieve this distinction.

The conditions of this run were unusually severe, the competing vehicles being required to make five separate journeys over different routes, and submit to brake contests and hill climbing trials.

The WHITE STEAM CARRIAGE used was a six horse=power vehicle taken from stock, and not only scored

1,800 POINTS OUT OF A POSSIBLE 1,800

but demonstrated its fuel economy by using only 13 quarts per day.

Both its track records for speed and its road records for reliability prove that

The White Is A Thoroughbred

Write for full particulars, including Prof. Thurston's report on our steam generator, and the official reports of important endurance contests.

WHITE SEWING MACHINE CO., CLEVELAND, OHIO

(AUTOMOBILE DEPARTMENT)

22 Union Square, New York, N. Y.	300 Post Street, San Francisco, Cal.	12 Woodward Avenue, Detroit, Mich.
509 Tremont Street, Boston, Mass.	609 Main Street, Buffalo, N. Y.	300 Rose Building, Cleveland, Ohio.

BARBER KEROSENE BURNER

FOR AUTOMOBILES

POINTS OF SUPERIORITY Economy. No odor. ⅓ more heat than gasoline. No smoke. No lighting back. Absolute safety. No clogging of spray nozzle. Carbon deposit easily removed. Fits any steamer. Each Burner guaranteed. Write for prices.

BARBER MFG. CO., 1005 Tremont Bldg., Boston, Mass.

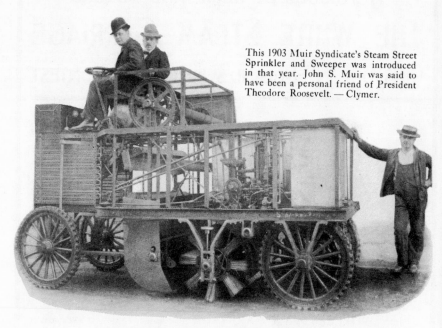

This 1903 Muir Syndicate's Steam Street Sprinkler and Sweeper was introduced in that year. John S. Muir was said to have been a personal friend of President Theodore Roosevelt. — Clymer.

MUIR SYNDICATE'S STEAM STREET SPRINKLER AND SWEEPER.

Toledo Steam Dos-a-dos as it appeared at the international exhibition in Osaki, Japan, May 6th, 1903. The only automobile allowed to run in the grounds.

"Toledo"
STEAM
1903
CARRIAGES

We can make prompt delivery of our superb Model A Steamers, price $800.00. Absolutely the best automobile in the world at the price. These carriages have power enough to go where the ordinary runabout dare not venture. We also offer our very successful Steam Surrey at the attractive price of $1,000.00, and the popular dos-a-dos rigs, like illustration.

If you are looking for a moderate priced motor car with ample power, that is easily understood, easily controlled; that costs little to maintain and operate, and that, at the same time, has style, by all means get a "Toledo" Steamer.

Complete catalogue on request, with address of our depot in your market.

POPE MOTOR CAR CO. 3057 CENTRAL AVENUE, TOLEDO, OHIO
Members Association Licensed Automobile Manufacturers

In answering any advertisement on this page it is desirable that you mention MUNSEY'S MAGAZINE.

The Incomparable WHITE

The Car renowned the world over, for reliability and for flexibility of control. *Steam* the motive-power, but not a steamer in the ordinary sense.

An entirely unique system of steam generation with automatic water feed and automatic fuel regulation. High economy compound engine, *with condenser*; there is therefore no exhaust and the water is used over and over again.

100 miles on one filling of water and gasolene

WHITE SEWING MACHINE COMPANY

CLEVELAND, O., 300 ROSE BLDG.

NEW YORK, 215 W. 48 St.   SAN FRANCISCO, 300 Post St.
BOSTON, 509 Tremont St.   DETROIT, 212 Woodward Ave.
LONDON, ENGLAND, 35-36-37 King St., Regent St.

48

Geneva Steam Cars

mandrine semi-flash boiler; 13-gallon gasoline tank in front; mileage on fuel, 175 with condenser, 125 without; combination 2 or 4-passenger vehicle; metallic fenders; wire wheels; single-tube tires; lamp and tools; price with fire tube boiler and without condenser, $1000; with semi-flash boiler, condenser, wood wheels, mud guards, clincher tires, double-acting hub brake, side lamps and tools, $1200. Made by Foster Automobile & Mfg. Co., 297 State street, Rochester, N. Y. (See also gasoline cars.)

THE GENEVA STEAM TONNEAU.

Geneva Automobile and Manufacturing Co., Geneva, Ohio; 2¾ by 3½ aluminum cased oil-splashed steam engine, placed horizontally under tonneau and direct connected to compensating gear, with spur gears; semi-flash tubular boiler; Geneva patent tubular burner; special condenser; steering by wheel which tilts; 2-inch angle iron frame; 30-inch wheels, with solid bronze hubs; expansion brake, 3½-inch Dunlop or Fisk tires; carries 5; weight, 1600 pounds; price, $1750, including full set of tools, and side lamps.

GENEVA STEAM RUNABOUT.

Long wheel base; hickory reaches; heavy spur differential; double-acting band brake; side throttle; side steering; side or foot reverse; steam air pump; 4 to 6 H. P. double-cylinder steam engine; marine type; 28-inch wire wheels, 3-inch tires; American roller bearings on rear axles, ball bearings on front; carries 40 gallons water, 8½ gallons gasoline.

The Foster Steam Car

THE FOSTER STEAM CAR.

2½x3½-inch steam engine under body,; 6 H. P., 16-inch boiler; pilot light; tubular running gear; wheel base, 66 inches; chain drive; spur differential; side steering; now equipped with condenser making mileage 100 miles on 18 gallons water; without condenser, 35 gallons carries it 40 miles; fire tube boiler or Sala-

Prescott Steam Cars

THE PRESCOTT STEAM CAR, FRONT SEAT CLOSED.

Combination runabout, with folding front seat; tubular running gear; chain drive; side steering; 2 or 4 passengers; weight, 1400 pounds; 2½ or 3-inch Fisk

Avoid Steam Car **Danger**

Substitute safe, cheap, easily obtained KEROSENE for dangerous, costly and scarce GASOLINE, GET MORE HEAT, STEAM and POWER by means of our perfected

KEROSENE BURNER

ENDORSED BY STANLEY BROS. OF NEWTON

the celebrated builders of steam carriages, who say "it developed as much heat as our gasoline burner, and will .in a steam carriage as fast as any burner in the world."

One of our customers on a recent trip used 7½ gallons of kerosene; last year on same run, same carriage, used 14 gallons of gasoline. He saved money and felt much safer with his kerosene burner.

If you will ride with us on our Stanley exhibition carriage, you will leave your order.

We fit any steam carriage made.

Don't put it off. Get out of danger TO-DAY

National Oil Heating Co.
MELROSE, MASS.

tion with reverse lever; centre steering; 28-inch wire wheel; 3-inch single tube tires; tubular running gear; hand buffed leather upholstery; price, with lamps, bell, cyclometer, lock for throttle and tools, $900; with top, $1000.

with adjustable roller bearings; 3-inch solid rubber tires; wheel base, 8 feet, 8 inches; carrying capacity, 2000 pounds; body, 7 feet long, 4 feet wide and 6 feet high inside; price, $2500.

TOLEDO DOS-A-DOS STEAM CAR.

Similar in general construction to Model A with dos-a-dos seat; price, $1000.

CONRAD STEAM MODEL 65 SPECIAL.

Two-passenger; panel back seat; weight, with tanks filled, 1004 pounds; 2½-inch tires; 28-inch wheels; capacity of gasoline tanks, 8 gallons; capacity of water tanks, 35 gallons. Price, $850.

THE TOLEDO JUNIOR.

Practically same mechanism as Toledo Model A, but smaller in size. Price, $600.
Toledo Steam Cars, made by International Motor Carriage Co., Toledo, Ohio. (See also gasoline and electric cars.)

CONRAD STEAM MODEL 70.

Dos-a-Dos; stick back seat; seating capacity 4 passengers; weight, tanks filled, 1000 pounds; 2½-inch tires; 28-inch wheels; capacity of gasoline tanks, 8 gallons; capacity of water tank, 38 gallons. Price, $800.

STEAM AUTOMOBILE
OWNERS OR MANUFACTURERS
EXAMINE THE
Woodward Burner
Gives All the Steam You Want
All the Time under All Conditions
Never Back Fires—Never Clogs
AMERICAN BURNER CO.
State St. and Hubbard Court
Chicago, Ill.

THE SIMPLEX FLASH BOILER
BUILT ON ABSOLUTELY NEW LINES,
and the lower coils will not burn out.
We guarantee to deliver enough
steam, overload or not.
THE BARTON BOILER CO.
Office and Factory, 4112-4230 State St., CHICAGO

CONRAD STEAM MODEL 77½.

Panel seat; seating capacity, 4 passengers; 3-inch tires; 28-inch wheels; gasoline tank capacity, 8 gallons; water tank capacity, 38 gallons. Price, $1200.

Steam Vehicles

Locomobile Steam Cars

Locomobiles are made by Locomobile Company of America, Bridgeport, Conn. (See also gasoline cars.)

THE LOCOMOBILE DOS-A-DOS WITH DISAPPEARING SEAT.

Sixteen-inch boiler and burner, mounted on steel frame; Klinger gauge; generator and Pilot light; new 3x4 Locomobile engine, encased and using superheated steam; Octopus lubricator; steam water and air pumps; 33 gallons of water, 10 gallons of gasoline; artillery wheels with 3x28-inch double tube tires; 2 band brakes on differential; 2 band brakes on rear hubs with ratchet; roller-bearing rear axles; wheel steer; automatic cylinder oil pump; mud guards. Seats four. Price $1600.

single tube tires; steel wheels; band brake on differential; band brakes on rear hubs with ratchet; roller-bearing rear axles; mud guards. Seats four. Price $1200; also made heavier for touring.

LOCOMOBILE RUNABOUT.

Box front; 16-inch boiler and burner; Klinger gauge; generator and Pilot light; 2½x3½ Locomobile engine, encased and using superheated steam; Octopus lubricator; steam water and air pumps; 14 gallons of gasoline, 30 gallons of water; 2½x28-inch tires; heavy steel wheels; roller-bearing rear axles; mud guards; automatic cylinder oil pump. Seats two. Price $950.

The 1903 Whitney Steamer, built at Brunswick, Maine, by the Whitney Machine Company, price $800.00.

Westfield Automobile Parts

COMPLETE AUTOMOBILES READY FOR POWER
Finished or Unfinished

Full line of running gears for runabouts and touring cars.with either chain or shaft drive, lever side steering or center wheel steering, Artillery hub wood wheels or our Standard pattern wire wheels.

Model G Touring Car

Bodies of all styles for runabouts or touring cars.   All panel work of highest grade. Can make immediate delivery of all models.   Send for catalog.

The C. J. Moore Mfg. Co.,   Westfield, Mass.

BRANDENBURG BROS. & ALLIGER
SOLE SELLING AGENTS

103 READE ST., NEW YORK   85 LAKE ST., CHICAGO

GROUT 1903 TOURING MODEL

We make Tonneaus and Light, Frenchy Steam Cars also

GROUT BROS.   ORANGE, MASS

Cut shows Steam Generator.
Made in all sizes.

"BARTON" FLASH BOILERS

Water Regulators, Throttle Valves, Fuel Regulator with floating needle, no Stuffing Box, Engine Pump and Hand Pump. All appliances suitable for flash boiler system. Condenser and Steam Siphons for filling water tanks.

Change your method of generating steam. Any type of steam automobile remodeled and made into an up-to-date car. Special steam tonneau cars built to order. The New "Burnell" Generator, for kerosene, has been perfected, and we guarantee it to give satisfaction.

1903

THE BARTON BOILER CO., 4212-4230 State St., CHICAGO

WE HAVE THE ORIGINAL OF THIS LETTER ON FILE

Boulder, Colo., Sept. 22, 1903.

Barton Boiler Co., Chicago, Ill.

Gentlemen:—We wish to say a few words to express the great satisfaction the 14-in. Barton improved flash boiler is giving us.

With a 7 1-2 H.P. engine geared 2 1-2 to 1, it pulled a 1,400 lb. car up a 12 per cent. grade 1-6 of a mile long with the band brake set tight. We did not know that the brake was set till we reached the top. We started up the hill with 200 lbs. of steam. When we reached the top we had 250 lbs. Since then we have run the car 300 miles without a hitch.

We use the hand pump (only) when we first fire up. In running on level roads the steam stays between 200 and 225 lbs. When climbing hills it runs from 225 to 250 lbs. We have never stopped on account of not having steam enough. Dirty water and oil have no effect on it. It doesn't use half as much fuel as the old fire tube boiler did (it was a 14-in.). It takes one-half minute to get up steam to 200 lbs. after the main fire is started. In running we have nothing to watch but the road. The boiler takes care of itself. It certainly is the greatest steamer on earth. No noise. No smoke. No burnt flues. No broken water glasses. No worry. But lots of good dry steam.

Wishing you every success and again assuring you of our entire satisfaction with your boiler,

Yours truly,		(Signed) NEIHEISEL BROS.

P. S.:—We are using the new model C Mason engine, which they rate at 7½-H.P. at 200 lbs. pressure.

Cut shows "Burnell" Burner. (Pat. May 5, '03)
Uses kerosene or gasolene.

Our Steam Cars

for 1903 are the result of over four years' manufacture, in which time we have made and sold five thousand vehicles. The Locomobile steam car is comfortable and convenient and has won many prizes for speed, reliability, and hill climbing, in all parts of the world. A customer writes, "*I am the owner of one of your earliest steam machines, No. 7 (built in 1890), which still gives good satisfaction.*"

Merrick Road Race, April, 1900. — Auspices Automobile Club of America. — The Locomobile establishes 25-mile Road Record for America.

The 1,000-Mile Trial, May, 1900. — Auspices Automobile Club of Great Britain. — The Locomobile wins two prizes.

Paris Exposition, 1900. — The Locomobile awarded two medals.

Exelberg Hill Climbing Contest, June, 1901. — Auspices Austrian Automobile Club. — The Locomobile wins first place and first prize.

Pike's Peak. — Summit reached by Locomobile, August, 1901. — The most remarkable feat ever accomplished by an automobile.

500 Mile Endurance Run, New York to Buffalo. — Auspices Automobile Club of America, Sept., 1901. — Locomobile wins First-class Certificate.

Glasgow Reliability Trials, 535 Miles. — Auspices Automobile Club of Great Britain, October, 1901. — Locomobile awarded gold medal — highest award.

Pan-American Exposition, October, 1901. — Gold Medal awarded The Locomobile Company. **Speed Trials, Coney Island Boulevard, November, 1901.** — The Locomobile wins the Gold Medal in its class.

Eagle Rock Hill Climbing Contest, November, 1901. — Auspices N. J. Automobile Club. — Open Competition. Locomobile makes best time, wins first prize.

Roslyn Hill Contest, April, 1902. — The Locomobile wins Class "A" Cup.

The Locomobile is the best automobile

Prices from $650 upwards

The Dos-a-Dos herein illustrated is only one of the many sensible and handsome styles.

Write for catalogue or visit any branch office for demonstration on the road.

The *Locomobile* Company of America

General Offices and Factory - Bridgeport, Conn.

BRANCHES
NEW YORK — Broadway, corner 76th Street.
BOSTON — 15 Berkeley Street
PHILADELPHIA — 249 North Broad Street.
CHICAGO — 1354 Michigan Avenue.
LONDON — 39 Sussex Place, South Kensington.
PARIS — 32 Avenue de la Grande-Armée.

Conveniences, Special Features

Indestructible water gauge; Victor steam air pump, obviating all hand pumping and very useful for inflating tires; Victor steam water pump, a reliable auxiliary boiler feed; ejector for convenience in touring; thorough lubrication of engine from one central oil reservoir; positive automatic oil pump for cylinders; forced draught for use in windy weather; superheated steam; solid and substantial construction; fine workmanship and handsome finish throughout.

Liverpool Exhibition, May, 1902. — The Locomobile awarded medal.

Paris-Nice 600 Miles Caravan, May, 1902. — Locomobile finished third, being preceded only by two cars of greatly superior power.

Rex Hill Speed Trials. — Locomobile wins medal.

100 Miles Run, New York to Bridgeport. — Auspices Automobile Club of America. — Locomobile wins three Non-stop Certificates, 100% Records.

Staten Island Speed Trials, May, 1902. — Auspices Automobile Club of America. — Locomobile breaks World's Record, 1 mile, for steam cars. Gold medal.

Chicago Auto. Club, 100-Mile Test, August, 1902. — Locomobile wins Non-stop Certificate, 100% Record.

650-Mile Reliability Trials. — Auspices Automobile Club of Great Britain, Sept., 1902. — Two Locomobiles won Gold Medals, highest award. Only American car to receive this honor.

New York-Boston Reliability Run. — Auspices Automobile Club of America. — Four Locomobiles receive First-class Certificates.

Anniversary Run, October, 1902. — Auspices Automobile Club of Great Britain. — The Locomobile only American steam car to win Non-stop Certificate.

Eagle Rock Hill, 1902 Contest. — Open to all. — Again Locomobile makes fastest time and wins first prize.

WHITE STEAM TONNEAU

1903

"Next to Flying"

STEAM IS THE WORLD'S STANDARD POWER

The only objectionable features of steam as a motive power for automobiles has been overcome, in the case of the WHITE, by a novel self-regulating generator and proper condensers to economize water supply. The swift, gliding movement of the WHITE makes touring a delight.

There are no grinding cogs or terror-breeding explosions, no unreliable sparking-plugs. It starts, stops, and moves in either direction with certainty and smoothness, while absolute reliability on long runs has been proved beyond question in contests at home and abroad.

Write for full particulars, experts' reports, and official results of important endurance contests.

WHITE SEWING MACHINE CO.

(Automobile Department) CLEVELAND, OHIO

22 Union Square, New York, N. Y. 300 Rose Bldg., Cleveland, O.
509 Tremont St., Boston, Mass. 212 Woodward Ave.,
300 Post St., San Francisco, Cal. Detroit, Mich.
35-36-37 King St. Regent St., London, England.

White Steam Touring Car
=== for 1903 ===

Is a Steam Car of Chassis Construction with the Distance of a Gasoline and the Ease of Operation of an Electric.

To the principle of producing great power and wasting practically none of it is due much of the success of the "White," which of all automobiles has to its credit **four first awards** in the **New York - Rochester** endurance test of 1901; **four first awards** in the New York-Boston-New York reliability run of 1902, and its **perfect scores** for reliability in the **great English 650-mile reliability trials** of 1902. But one other car achieved this distinction in the English Trials. These marvelous triumphs may be taken as an accurate criterion of the "**White's**" supremacy.

SPECIFICATIONS:
Price, $2,000.

Seating Capacity,	Four	Tread,	4 ft. 8 in.	Extreme length,	10 ft.
Rated Horse Power,	Ten	Wheels,	30 in	Extreme width,	5 ft.
Engine,	Compound	Tires (Goodrich Clincher),	4 in.	Extreme height	5 ft. 2 in.
Wheel Base,	6 ft. 8 in.	Weight (tanks filled),	1,600 lbs.	Capacity Gasoline Tank,	10 gals.

Capacity Water Tank, ... 15 gals.
Condenser, Two Independent Sets of Brakes, Automatic Cylinder and Engine Lubricator.
Equipment—Condenser, Side Lamps, Set of Tools, Horn, Tool Case.

SUCCESS in everyday use, in reliability contests, in races, and in record trials has proved the "White" system of motive power to be the most noteworthy achievement of automobile developments. The 1903 "White" is equipped with every improvement which our experience has shown would be of advantage to the car. Greater power and economy, and greater ease of operation, combined with noiselessness, have always characterized it.

These advantages are secured by means of a **compound engine**, the "White" **special condenser, a chainless drive, automatic cylinder and engine lubrication, two independent sets of brakes,** and a variety of minor improvements, which assure the "White" purchaser that his vehicle possesses a system of producing and conserving energy unexcelled in the automobile realm.

Safety is the "White" keynote. The "White," as is now well understood, has no boiler, and a boiler explosion is therefore impossible. The power of the "White" car is produced in a generator, in which the possibility of accident is non-existent.

The working parts being entirely encased, the "White" is impervious to mud and dust; while its operating parts are so arranged that a lady need have no fear of soiling even a glove in running the car.

WHITE SEWING MACHINE COMPANY
(*Automobile Department*) CLEVELAND, OHIO.

22 Union Square, New York, N. Y.   212 Woodward Avenue, Detroit, Mich.   4259 Olive Street, St. Louis, Mo.
509 Tremont Street, Boston, Mass.   609 Main Street, Buffalo, N. Y.   1761 Stout Street, Denver, Col.
300 Post Street, San Francisco, Cal.   300 Rose Building, Cleveland, O.   5979 Centre Avenue, East End, Pittsburg, Pa.
Banker Brothers Company, Cor. Vine and Broad Streets, Philadelphia, Pa.
Walter C. White, European Representative, 19 Princes Street, Westminster, London, England.

THE CENTURY NO. 1 STEAM CAR.

28-inch wire wheels; 2½-inch Diamond single-tube tires; single-lever control; fuel capacity, 90 miles; speed up to 20 miles per hour; long wheel base; standard track; carries 2; weight, 1000 pounds; price, including tools and horn, $750. Made by Century Motor Vehicle Co., Syracuse, N. Y.

(See also Gasoline Cars.)

Grout Steam Cars

On Grout steam cars 6½ and 10 H. P. engines are used, capable of developing as high as 10 to 20 H. P.; they have double cylinders, slide D valves, Stephenson link motion, either horizontal or vertical; eccentric consists of only one piece, combining 13 pieces generally used; all parts interchangeable; burner started with a match in 3 to 5 minutes; everything controlled from the seat; either kerosene or gasoline burner is furnished; wood or wire wheels. Made by Grout Brothers, Orange, Mass.

THE GROUT MODEL H.

Runabout for two passengers; length, 7 feet 6 inches; width, 5 feet 2 inches; height, 5 feet 6 inches; seat, 3 feet 4½ inches; track, 4 feet 8 inches; 2½-inch tires; fuel capacity, 70 miles; water capacity, 35 miles; weight, tanks filled, 1200 pounds; concealed panel in back for tools; price, including tools, lamps, etc., $775. The Grout Model E is same as Model H, with Victoria top.

THE GROUT MODEL J.

For 2 or 4 passengers; drop front seat; front seat 12 inches below main seat; height, 5 feet 4 inches;

width, 5 feet 2 inches; length, 11 feet 2 inches; wheel base, 72 inches; 30-inch wood or wire wheel; 3-inch detachable tires; 7 H. P. boiler; fuel tank 50 miles capacity; water tank, 35 miles capacity; condenser if desired; steam air pump; forced draft; price, $1200.

THE GROUT STEAM TONNEAU.

Speed up to 60 miles per hour; wheel base 84 inches; boiler under hood; engine hung horizontally under footboard, accessible from driver's seat; 15-gallon gasoline tank under front seat; water tank under rear seat; height, 5 feet 7 inches; width, 5 feet 8 inches; length, 11 feet 9 inches; 32-inch wood wheels; 4-inch detachable tires; 12 H. P. boiler; 10 H. P. engine; fuel and water capacity 100 miles; steam pumps; forced draft; condenser; price, $2500 with lamps and tools.

THE STORCK STEAM CARRIAGES.

The Storck Steam Carriages are made at Red Bank, N. J., by Frank C. Storck, well known in bicycle circles, who has spent the past three years in perfecting a steam vehicle which would be simple as well as efficient.

NEUSTADT-PERRY COMBINATION CAR.

Complete outfit furnished by Neustadt-Perry Co., St. Louis, Mo., for either steam or gasoline power; 10 H. P. engine; front seat folding; 2 or 4 passengers; manufacturers make a specialty of supplying all parts for complete vehicles.

er gauge; water tank holds 36 gallons; fuel tank,
allons; feed water heater; separate air tank in front
; double-acting brake on differential; price, includ-
lamp, $850.

LANE NO 1 WITH WOOD WHEELS

THE READING MODEL H TOURING CAR.

os-a-dos seat; box front for parcels; tubular run-
g gear, flexible; 30-inch wood artillery wheels; 3-inch
mond detachable tires; same engine, etc., as on
el R. M.; 28 gallons water capacity; 16 gallons
oline; fenders are included; price, $1150.

upholstery; full set tools; price, $1000; solid panel
seat. extra $15; solid seat and buggy top, extra $75;
wood wheels and double-tube tires, $40 extra; wood or
leather fenders, $25. No. 11 is similar to No. 1,
carries 12 gallons fuel, 38 gallons water and has 80-
inch wheel base; weight, 1500 pounds; price, $1100.

HE BURNER is the SOUL of a Steam Carriage

THE
NATIONAL
KEROSENE
OILBURNER

HAS NO PEER.

fills the exact requirements of Steam Carriage owners.
afe, reliable, economical, the best in the world. Hundreds
well-pleased users testify to its merits. Send to us for
escriptive matter and published names of users. We
pply catalog giving new and important improvements.
PRICES REDUCED. Write to
dson L. Thomson Mfg. Co., Owners & Makers, Waltham, Mass.

LANE NO. 2 STEAM CAR.

Similar to No. 1, but water tank is back of boiler,
thus extending the body back of the seat and shortening the forward part of the car; carries 26 gallons
water; ether specifications same as for No. 1.

THE FORD
GASOLINE BURNER
Best and Most Effective
Burner Manufactured
PETER FORD, Somerville, Mass.
CHAS. E. MILLER, Agent, New York
A. L. DYKE, Agent, St. Louis, Mo.

LANE NO. 4 TOURING CAR.

Fuel tank under forward bonnet; engine under rear
footboard and boiler under rear seat; weight 1500
pounds; fuel capacity, 12 gallons; water, 26 gallons;
20-inch boiler; wheel base, 87 inches; tread, 56½
inches; front lever steering; 32-inch wood wheels; 3½-
inch double-tube tires; leather upholstery; full set
tools; price, $1500; wood or leather fenders, extra $28.

LANE NO. 1 STEAM CAR.

me general lines as No. 0, but 2 inches wider
12 inches longer; weight, 1250 pounds; 8 gallons
: 31 gallons water; 20-inch boiler; wheel base, 77
es; tread, 56½ inches; side steering; 30-inch wire
els; 3-inch single-tube tires; leather or whipcord

Century Steam Cars

2½x3¾-inch, double-cylinder, 4½ H. P. "Century"
enclosed steam engine in body on frame; 15-inch "Century" vertical fire-tube boiler; "Century" burner, with
seat adjustment and pilot light; bevel gear drive; lever
and throttle steering; tubular frame, 3 elliptic springs,

holds 22 gallons; fuel tank, 8 gallons; 28-inch tubular wheels; 3-inch pneumatic tires; double-acting band brake; weight, 1600 pounds; price, $1200.

MODEL E, STEARNS VICTORIA TOP RUNABOUT.
Same as Model D, with Victoria top instead of buggy top; weight, 1050 pounds; price, $750.

The Cincinnati Steam Car

Made by the Cincinnati Automobile Co., 807-9 Race street, Cincinnati, Ohio; reachless running gear.

The White Steam Cars
Made by the White Sewing Machine Co., Cleveland, O.

THE WHITE STEAM STANHOPE.

Seats 2; 30-inch wire wheels; 3-inch Goodrich clincher tires; 8 gallons gasoline; 20 gallons water; length, 8 feet; tread, 4 feet 8½ inches; width, 5 feet; height, 7½ feet, top up; weight, 1200 pounds; hickory reaches; tubular arch trusses; live rear axle; enclosed differential; gasoline capacity enough for 100 to 125 miles; White power equipment; price with top, side curtains, rubber boot, tools and bell, $1200; also fur-

nished with condenser, which makes water supply good for about 100 miles running.

THE WHITE STEAM TONNEAU.

10 H. P. compound steam engine under hood in front; "White steam generator; semi-flash; "White" burner; "White" surface-cooled condenser; chainless drive; wheel steering; 30-inch wood road wheels; 4-inch Goodrich tires; automatic cylinder lubrication; two independent sets of brakes; seats 4; wheel base, 6 feet 8 inches; tread, 4 feet 8 inches; length, 10 feet; width, 5 feet; height, 5 feet 2 inches; 10 gallons gasoline; 15 gallons water; aluminum body, removable; weight, 1600 pounds; price, including side lamps, tools, tail lamp and horn, $2000.

THE WHITE DELIVERY WAGON.

Length, 9 feet 8 inches; width, 5 feet; tread, 4 feet 8½ inches; height, 7 feet 8 inches; 30-inch wire wheels; 3½-inch Goodrich clincher tires; 12 gallons gasoline; 30 gallons water; seats 2; weight, 1600 pounds; price, $2000.

Reading Steam Cars
Made by the Meteor Engineering Co., 753 Cherry St., Reading, Pa.

THE READING "R. M." MODEL.

Runabout of 900 pounds weight; box front for parcels; tubular running gear, ball and socket joints; semi-elliptic cross springs; bevel gear differential; 28-inch wood artillery wheels; 3-inch Diamond detachable tires; ball bearings; Mason 4½ H. P., 2½x3½, slide-valve steam engine, Stephenson link motion; steel shell boiler, 346 copper 3-16-inch tubes; Victor steam pump; forced draught; siphon; side lever steering; Klinger

Stearns Steam Cars

Made by Stearns Steam Carriage Co., Syracuse, N. Y.; Stearns steam engines; steam superheater; seamless steel boiler shell, copper tubes; fire controlled by automatic regulator; feed water heated by exhaust; compartment water tanks; air and water pumps driven from crosshead; low water alarm; throttle and reverse lever at right of operator; compensating gear on rear axle; tubular running gears with hickory side bars; all models equipped with fenders; tools, side lamp, water glass mirror, hand air pump, Veeder odometer, rubber foot mat and 6-inch double-stroke bell.

tread, 4 feet 8 inches; 12 H. P. simple 3¼x4-inch engine; 19-inch boiler; boiler capacity, 7.2 gallons; water tank holds 38 gallons; fuel tank holds 16 gallons; 28-inch tubular wheels; 3-inch pneumatic tires; double-acting hub brake; weight, 1600 pounds; price, $1200; locker on front for luggage and supplies.

MODEL B, STEARNS DOS-A-DOS.

Seats 4; length, 8 feet 3 inches; width, 5 feet 3 inches; height, 5 feet 9 inches; wheel base, 5 feet 8 inches; tread, 4 feet 8 inches; 8 H. P. simple engine, 2⅛x3¼ inches; 16-inch boiler, holding 6 gallons, 8 gal-

MODEL D STEARNS STEAM CAR.

Buggy top runabout; seats 2; length, 7 feet 3 inches; width 5 feet 3 inches; height, 7 feet 8 inches; wheel base, 4 feet 8 inches; tread, 4 feet 8 inches; compound, 2x3½, 3x3½ steam engine; 14-inch boiler, capacity 5½ gallons; gasoline capacity, 8 gallons; water, 29 gallons; wheels, 28x2½ inches wire; pneumatic tires; double acting band brake; price, $700. Model A is the same without top; price, $600; weight, 900 pounds.

ONE HUNDRED

FOX VALVELESS STEAM ENGINES

Will be sold at 20% from regular prices

THREE SIZES

5 H. P. Regular Price, $125
7 H. P. " " 150
10 H.P. " " 175

We do this to introduce the engine, and we guarantee it in every respect

ONE LEVER starts, stops and reverses

Very Few Parts   Extremely Simple

Durability

These features should commend it to Steam Carriage users

Orders filled in the order received

It is also built for Marine use, and we will accept orders under the same conditions.

Write for price   Booklet on request

Rochester Steam Motor Works, Rochester, N.Y., U.S.A.

MODEL AA, STEARNS SEMI-TOURING CAR.

Seats 2; length, 7 feet 3 inches; width, 5 feet 3 inches; height, 5 feet 9 inches; wheel base and tread, each 4 feet 8 inches; 2x3½-inch, 3x3½-inch compound steam engine; 16-inch boiler, capacity 6 gallons; water tank holds 29 gallons; fuel tank, 8; 28-inch wire wheels; 2½-inch pneumatic tires; double-acting brake; weight, 1000 pounds; price, $650.

MODEL H, STEARNS STATION WAGON.

Seats 4; length, 9 feet 6 inches; width, 5 feet 2½ inches; height, 7 feet 4 inches; wheel base, 6 feet 9¼ inches; tread, 4 feet 8 inches; 8 H. P., 2½x3½ simple engine; 16-inch boiler; capacity, 6 gallons; water tank

MODEL F, STEARNS SURREY.

Seats 5; length, 10 feet; width, 5 feet 4 inches; height, 5 feet 6 inches; wheel base, 7 feet 4 inches;

READ OUR AD ON PACE 248
Read this List Carefully. These are Plums

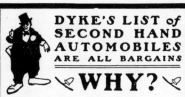

DYKE'S LIST of SECOND HAND AUTOMOBILES ARE ALL BARGAINS

WHY?

Because we pick from a large assortment.

Because all machines we sell are tested by a competent mechanic.

Because we could not risk losing the reputation which we have gained by years of hard work in sending you a misrepresentation.

If you are looking for a good machine, and do not mind getting one that has been used, which is oftentimes better than new, then send for our list.

If you do not want a machine and know or anyone who does, kindly refer them to us.

To parties having machines to sell, will say that we will sell your machine if you will send it to us on consignment and make a reasonable price. If your machine is not up-to-date and will not stand a thorough test, it will not pay you to ask us to sell it.

WE WERE the first concern in America to advertise second-hand Automobiles. We have been selling them for a long time and have never displeased a customer. We have testimonials from them all.

A. L. DYKE
1402 Pine St.   St. Louis, Mo.

STEAM MOTIVE POWER

No. 2 Locomobile. Fine condition. Nothing broke or out of order. Run about 1000 miles. A fine bargain. Guaranteed **$295.00**

White Steam Machine. Purchased last July. Run about 1500 miles. Won last October races at St. Louis fair cup for 5 mile race of steam machines; time, 1.34. Yellow running gear, black body, rear tires almost new, front tires in good shape. Top with side curtains and storm apron; 30x3 Goodrich tires. A fine machine and a fine bargain. Good running order as new. Not worn a particle. Price, **$795.00**

GASOLINE MOTIVE POWER

Packard Model "C," 14 H. P. Engine. Dos-a-Dos Seat, strictly first-class, leather top, (instantly detachable,) (5) good Hartford Herringbone tires; 4-inch batteries arranged for instantaneous removal. Double set of five cells each will last (3) months. Detachable grating in footboard over radiator for use in cold weather. All moving parts fitted with taper pins to take up wear. Two Dietz Brass Lamps. All necessary tools. Engine and running gear are perfectly silent in action. Vaporizer adjusted to furnish correct mixture with thermometer below zero. Entire Auto in as good shape as new. Guaranteed in every respect. Price, **$795.00**

3-Ton Steam Truck—20 H. P., $1800.00. 16 feet long by 6 feet wide, 12½ feet by 6 feet platform area; 9½ feet wheel base; 5½ feet tread; heavy wood wheels, 36-inch and 40-inch front and rear; 3½ inch solid rubber tires, endless; 20 H. P. Robert's water tube boiler (marine model); 20 H. P. double compound expansion engine; 42-gallon — fuel tanks — kerosene. Water tank refilled with steam syphon, usual fittings, oilers, etc.— all best make. No visible exhaust steam. No smoke, no noise. Fuel consumption about ½-gallon per ton mile. Speed loaded about 6 miles per hour. Speed empty, 10 miles.

GUARANTEED IN EVERY RESPECT Will pay expenses of customer to come and see machine if purchased. Machine is not in St. Louis, so write before coming.

Remember we carry a full line of Auto Supplies. Spark Plugs, 85c. up. Jump Spark Coils, $6.00 up. Bike Vaporizers, $3.00 up. Leather Coats, $5.50 up. Send 2-2c. stamps for Catalogue No. 1 and Supplement.

The NEW GROUT

1903 Drop Front

Send for specifications and full description of this model

Notice 12 in. drop of front seat, which allows the operator to see over the heads of passengers. This is our patent.

GROUT BROTHERS, Orange, Mass.

These are the reasons why owners of steam automobiles discard their boilers for the

SALAMANDRINE

NEVER-BURN-OUT

Water Tube Boilers

CANNOT BURN OUT
BURNER DOES NOT BACK FIRE
NO TORCH USED
ECONOMICAL AS TO FUEL

SALAMANDRINE BOILER CO. 220 Broadway, New York

Works: NEWARK, N. J.

Boiler, showing water jacket, fuel and water connections.

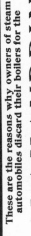

Advertisement

1903 WHITE STEAMERS 1904

BROUGHT UP TO DATE BY ATTACHING

The "CONSTANT" Positive Clutch

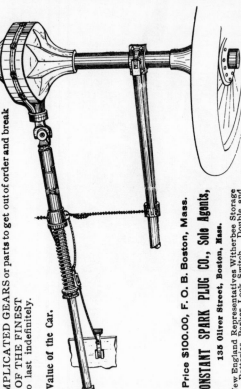

The "CONSTANT" POSITIVE CLUTCH, operated by a foot lever and spring, allows the engine to run free, warm up the generator, and thus avoid HAND PUMPING of water and air.

ADVANTAGES OBTAINED.

Simplicity. NO COMPLICATED GEARS or parts to get out of order and break

Strength. BUILT OF THE FINEST TOOL STEEL to last indefinitely.

Self-oiling.

Adds $500 to the Value of the Car.

IN ORDERING, state whether your car is 1903 or 1904, enclose check for $100, and if shaft is unsatisfactory after ten days' trial after receipt, return shaft, and draw on us for price.

DIRECTIONS. Simply place the shaft in its usual position, which can be done in five minutes, and connect side chains and foot lever.

WE GUARANTEE the "CONSTANT" Positive Clutch against all defects in workmanship and material for one year

Price $100.00, F. O. B. Boston, Mass.

CONSTANT SPARK PLUG CO., Sole Agents,

135 Oliver Street, Boston, Mass.

New England Representatives Witherbee Storage Batteries, Parker Lock Switch. Double and Single Plugs.

Double, $3.00. Single, $1.50.

THE AUTOMOBILE.

1904

GROUT 1905 STEAM TOURING CAR.

GROUT

$1500 SIDE DOOR TONNEAU $1500

Entirely new construction throughout. New and improved 18-inch Boiler and Fuel System. 12-H.P., 2-cylinder Horizontal Engine in dust-proof aluminum case. Positive lubrication to all working parts. Compensating gear in center shaft. Two expanding rear-hub brakes. Grout patented one piece slot burner, noiseless torch, the air being automatically regulated, insuring perfect combustion. Back firing impossible. Irreversible wheel steer: wheel base 86 inches. Weight 1,750 lbs. Wheel diameter, 30 inches, size of tires, 30 x 3½ inches. Water capacity 45 gallons, gasoline 15 gallons. Car sold complete with 4 lamps, horn and full set of tools. NO DANGER OF FREEZING IN ZERO WEATHER.

Agents Now Being Appointed in Unoccupied Territory

We Exhibit at the New York Show—Space J, Main Floor

GROUT BROS. AUTOMOBILE CO., 265 East Main St., ORANGE, MASS.

BOSTON BRANCH
151-153 Columbus Avenue

NEW YORK CITY
Eastman Auto Co.
308-310 West 59th Street

WASHINGTON, D. C.
Clarence Pittman
1310 Staunton Court

THE AUTOMOBILE.

$650 Model with Detachable Surrey Seat.

THE EXCELLENT GROUT STEAM MOTOR CAR

SEE Our Exhibit at St. Louis Exposition. Demonstrations given on the grounds. New Illustrated Catalog, showing all styles, mailed on request. GROUT BROS. AUTOMOBILE CO., Orange, Mass., U.S.A.

BOSTON GARAGE and SALESROOM: 151-153 Columbus Ave., Boston, Mass.

Letter Box

Steam Car with Double Power Plant.

Editor THE AUTOMOBILE:

[244].—No one, so far as I know, has ever built an automobile on any other principle than that of "putting all the eggs in one basket," so I determined to build a steam car myself with a double power plant, so arranged that if half the plant got out of order I could run with the other half. I carried out my intention, and the photograph which I send shows the appearance of the finished car.

The machine has never been towed home, nor anywhere else, for that matter; but on a few occasions, when the car was new and everything not yet working perfectly, I have run as much as ten miles on one engine, stopping only long enough to get out and close a valve; the other occupants of the car knew nothing of the omission of half the propelling power. I have, however, towed others who have got into trouble, and one man was good enough to tell me, after I had pulled him nine miles, that he really had gotten home quicker than he would have done if he had not broken down.

The power plant consists of two Tonkin boilers fired by "Lightning" kerosene burners, and two engines. One engine drives to each rear wheel, no differential gearing being used. The main steam pipes are connected by a 3-8-inch cross pipe, which has the effect of equalizing the steam pressure in the two boilers. The two throttles are connected to one lever, and the links to one reverse lever, so that the control is the same as with a car having a single power plant.

One of the objects I had in view in building this car was to get a machine in which all the machinery should be accessible from above, and all thoroughly protected from dirt. Absolutely the only parts of the driving mechanism of this car that are exposed to dust and dirt are the two side chains and their sprockets. Boilers, burners, engines, pumps (both water and air), and everything else connected with the power plant, are protected by a long galvanized sheet-iron pan, nearly eight feet long, which not only protects the machinery, but, being very stiffly braced, stiffens the whole vehicle and also makes a fine support to which pipes can be attached. It is a decided addition to the appearance of the car. Nearly everything used in its construction was purchased from parts manufacturers. The car is a

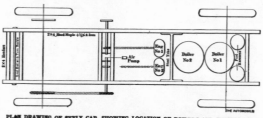

PLAN DRAWING OF SEELY CAR, SHOWING LOCATION OF BOILERS AND ENGINES AND DOUBLE DRIVE ARRANGEMENT.

practical machine, and of very high grade throughout.

The frame is of hard, white Michigan maple, 2 inches thick and 4 inches deep, flitched on the outside with iron plates the same depth as the frames and 1-8 inch thick, fastened every 8 inches with 5-16 inch bolts. The side frames are tied together with 3-4 inch steel bolts with turnbuckles, each bolt pulling against two maple cross frames, the ends of which are let into the main frames 1-8 inch to avoid twisting. In addition to the bolts and cross frames

there is a cross piece of iron 1-2 inch thick and 1 1-2 inches wide, with plates at the ends which are bolted to the insides of the side frames. This iron cross member supports the engines, top and bottom, as well as the rear of the rear boiler, and to it is also fastened the rear end of the galvanized iron pan. It also adds greatly to the stiffness of the frame. The vehicle has a wheelbase of 108 inches; the wheels are 34 inches in diameter, and are fitted with 4 1-2 inch Continental tires all around.

As the plan sketch shows, each engine drives to a separate countershaft by chain, and two more chains drive from sprockets on the countershafts to sprockets on the rear wheels. The chains from the engines to the countershafts are 1-inch Whitneys, while the main driving chains are heavier, being 1 1-4 inch, of the same make. The difference in sizes is due to the fact that the engine chains are entirely protected from dust, and are easily kept well lubricated, while the others are outside where they are exposed to the dust, and consequently require a greater wearing surface.

The boilers are 16 inches in diameter, and have 400 tubes 18 inches long—5 inches longer than is usual in boilers of this diameter. This extra 5 inches gives a great deal more room for steam, allows a higher water level, and, of course, permits more heat to be absorbed from the fire than would be the case with shorter tubes. The products of combustion are discharged downward under the car. There are caps or lids in the tops of the smoke boxes, and these caps can be reached through doors in the top of the hood. When starting the fire the caps are removed to allow the smoke to escape until there is sufficient steam pressure to start the blowers, which are simply small needle valves supplied with steam from 1-8 inch pipes, outside diameter. The exhaust is not used or needed for this purpose when running.

I do not use a condenser. The cardinal points of my car are simplicity, reliability and comfort, and I care more about getting forty or fifty miles out of my car in comfort than two or three times that distance wrapped up in dust coats or smothered with dust.

F. L. SEELY'S HOME-MADE STEAM CAR WITH DOUBLE POWER PLANT.

White Steam Cars

Made by White Sewing Machine Co., Cleveland, Ohio.

WHITE STANDARD TOURING CAR. PRICE $2500.
15 H. P. steam engine; flash generator; automatic lubrication; engine shaft runs in oil; wheel base 7 feet 9 inches;

WHITE CAR, WITH LIMOUSINE TOP.
tires 34x4 inches; water tank capacity 17 gallons, gasoline 15 gallons; weight 2200 lbs.; price $2500, with oil lamps, horn and tool kit. This car is also furnished with cape

WHITE CAR, WITH CANOPY TOP. PRICE $2700.
top at $2600; weight 2262 lbs. With canopy top, price $2700; weight 2309 lbs. Furnished also with limousine body, with

WHITE LIGHT TOURING CAR.
touring runabout body and with extension top. White cars have armored wood frame; compound engine.

Save Your Nerves

BY APPLYING A

Reliance Low Water Alarm

TO YOUR STEAM VEHICLE
SEND FOR ILLUSTRATED CIRCULAR

Reliance Gauge Column Co.
CLEVELAND, OHIO

Boss Steam Cars

Made by Boss Knitting Machine Works, corner Elm and Reed Sts., Reading, Pa.

1905

BOSS, MODEL B, WITH DOS-A-DOS SEAT
PRICE $1000.
Runabout; 2 cylinder, 8 H. P., steam engine under the seat; 17 inch boiler; force feed lubrication; chain drive; tubular frame; weight 1400 lbs.; wheel base 75 inches; 30x3

BOSS, MODEL D, WITH TOP. PRICE $1000.
inch tires; price, with top, $1000, with dos-a-dos seat $1000. Special features: Fuel not under pressure; friction throttle and reverse lever; forced draft.

Clark Steam Car

Made by Edward S. Clark, 272-278 Freeport St., Boston, Mass.

CLARK TONNEAU. PRICE $5000.
Side entrance tonneau; 4 cylinder, 20 H. P. steam engine under footboard; force feed lubrication; bevel gear drive; pressed steel frame; weight 2600 lbs.; wheel base 108 inches; 36x4½ inch tires; price $5000

Summaries of Events in Worcester Hill Climbing Contest.

Steam Cars, Stock. All Prices.

	Driver	Car	H.P.	Time
1	B. Holland ...Stanley	....	10	1:38
2	F. B. Durbin,. Stanley	....	10	1:41
3	G. O. Draper.. Stanley	....	10	3:29 2-5
4	F. H. Marriott Stanley	....	10	5:12

Gasoline Stock Cars, Listed at $850 or less.
(Two persons carried, but removal of tonneau permitted.)

1	G. H. Kimball. Ford	....	10	3:26 1-5
2	F. H. Peabody. Ford	......	12	3:31
3	S. G. Skinner.. Oldsmobile .	7		4:26
4	F. E. Wing.. Queen	......	10	4:32 3-5

Gasoline Stock Cars, Listed at More Than $850 to $1,250.
(Carrying two persons, removal of tonneau permitted.)

1	H. L. Newton. Elmore	.....	16	2:32 4-5
2	W. E. Eldredge Buick	......	22	2:43 4-5
3	W. J. Lee..... Jackson	.....	18	2:58 3-5
4	Fred H. Pratt Reo	....	16	3:22 2-5
5	G. H. Kimball Ford	....	10	3:30 1-5
6	F. H. Peabody Ford	......	12	3:43 4-5
7	F. E. Wing... Queen	......	10	4:04 4-5

Gasoline Stock Cars, Listed at More Than $1,250 to $2,000.
(Carrying four persons; tonneau attached.)

1	H. P. Maxim.. Columbia .	.	16	2:45 4-5
2	Jos. Downey.. Stod.-Dytn.	.	15	3:05 1-5
3	John F. Daley.. Pope-Htfd.	.	16	3:30 1-5
4	A. Dennison .. Knox	....	14	3:44
5	—— Corbin... Corbin	.....	16	4:16 2-5
6	G. H. Kimball.. Ford	....	20	5:09 2-5

Gasoline Stock Cars, Listed at More Than $2,000 to $3,000.
(Carrying four passengers; tonneau attached.)

1	J. F. Duryea.. Stvs.-Duryea	20	2:14 4-5
2	C. S. Henshaw Thomas	...	40	2:22 3-5
3	J.S.Harrington Thomas	...	40	2:50 4-5
4	A. R. Bangs.. Franklin	...	20	2:52 2-5

Gasoline Stock Cars, Listed at More Than $3,000 to $5,000.
(Carrying four passengers; tonneau attached.)

1	John L. Snow. Peerless	....	35	1:43 2-5
2	George Soules Pope-Toledo	30	1:46 3-5
3	John L. Snow. Peerless.	...	24	1:47
4	George Soules Pope-Toledo	24	1:47 2-5
5	Geo. G. Reed.. Stearns	....	40	2:00 2-5
6	E. C. Bald... Columbia	..	35	2:07 1-5
7	Alfred Thomas, Pierce	.....	28	2:10
8	A. S. Lee...... Pope-Toledo	30	2:16
9	A. Mosher..... Columbia	..	35	2:59

Gasoline Stock Cars, Listed at More Than $5,000.
(Carrying four persons; tonneau attached.)

| 1 | George Soules.. Pope-Toledo | 30 | 1:46 2-5 |

Cars Weighing from 1,432 to 2,204 pounds, All Classes.

1	S. B. Stevens.. Mercedes	..	90	1:09
2	W. L. Hilliard. Napier	...	60	1:16
3	Geo. C. Cannon. Grout	.....	50	1:23 2-5
4	A. S. Adams.. Pope-Toledo	30	1:46 2-5
5	John Caswell.. Columbia	..	35	1:58 1-5

Cars Weighing from 851 to 1,432 Pounds, All Classes.

1	F. H. Marriott. Stanley	....	10	1:34 2-5
2	J. F. Duryea... Stvs.-Duryea	20	1:42 2-5
3	F. F. Cameron. Cameron	..	16	1:42 2-5
4	H. Raymond.. Knox	....	14	2:01 3-5

Cars Weighing from 551 to 851 Pounds, All Classes.

1	B. Holland.... Stanley	....	10	1:24 2-5
2	F. B. Durbin.. Stanley	....	10	1:25 1-5
3	E. F. Cameron. Cameron	..	16	1:47 2-5
4	F. H. Peabody. Ford	......	10	3:07 2-5

Cars Weighing More than 2,204 Pounds.

1	E. C. Bald.... Columbia	..	35	1:49
2	Geo. G. Reed.. Stearns	...	40	1:49 1-5
3	C. S. Henshaw Thomas	...	40	1:50
4	John Caswell.. Columbia	..	35	1:54 2-5

Free for All.

1	W. L. Hilliard. Napier	...	60	1:12 3-5
2	Geo. C. Cannon. Grout	......	50	1:21 1-5
3	B. Holland.... Stanley	...	10	1:23
4	F. P. Durbin.. Stanley	...	10	1:25 1-5
5	F. H. Marriott. Stanley	...	10	1:26
6	J. F. Duryea.. Stvs.-Duryea	20	1:36
7	E. F. Cameron.Cameron	16	1:41
8	Fred A. Nagle. Fiat	50	1:43
9	E. C. Bald..... Columbia	..	35	2:01
10	G. O. Draper.. Stanley	....	10	4:15 2-5

Gasoline Stock Cars, All Prices, for Amateur Championship of Worcester County, Owners to Drive.

| 1 | M. P. Whittall Pierce | ..... | 24 | 3:15 2-5 |
| 2 | A. Mosher.... Columbia | .. | 35 | 3:46 2-5 |

CANNON AND GROUT IN THE SPECIAL GROUT STEAMER-CANNON AT THE WHEEL.

THE LANE

STEAM TOURING CAR.

Steel chassis, full aluminum body, compound engine and condenser. No heat under seats. Our new type of boiler combines advantages of the flash system, with constant pressure and reserve of power. All power generating functions automatic. The smoothest and quietest running car built. Price **$2,250.**

LANE MOTOR VEHICLE CO.

POUGHKEEPSIE, N. Y., U. S. A.

1904 and 1905 models White Steamers on the Beach at Daytona, Florida, in 1905.

AUTOMATIC BY-PASS

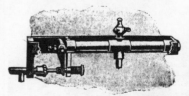

PATENT PENDING.

THERMOSTATIC

Operates positively on half inch variation of water level. More reliable than hand regulation. Applicable to any boiler carrying a water level. Price $15. Discount to the trade.

LANE MOTOR VEHICLE CO.
Poughkeepsie, N. Y.

LANE, STYLE 6, TONNEAU. PRICE $2250. Side entrance, aluminum, King of Belgium body; 2 cylinder, 3¼ and 5¼x3½, 15 H. P. Cross compound engine,

LANE STYLE 6, RUNABOUT. PRICE $2100.

"WHISTLING BILLY" WHITE STEAMER RACER

This photo is of Webb Jay, and was taken at Belmont Track in May, 1906. Webb Jay was one of the outstanding race drivers of America in the early days of automobile racing. He won hundreds of dirt-track racing events in this special White Racer, nicknamed "Whistling Billy" on account of the unusual sound caused by the exhaust of the steam at high speed. Note that the frame is underslung, the axles were above the frame. Notice also the clincher tires are lugged onto the wheels. —Clymer.

MONSTER STEAM CAR RACER

This unusual and powerful steam racing automobile appeared at Morris Park, New York, on July 4, 1905. I am frank in saying that I do not know the make of the car. In early racing cars, the mechanic was called a "mechanician." It appears that the driver of this car is seated on the left-hand side of the car and the "mechanician" operates the emergency brake located on the right side. Perhaps some of my readers can tell me the make of this car and the name of the owner and driver. — Clymer.

=IN THE WHITE MOUNTAINS=

This year the struggle instead of being among the crags and peaks will be in the canyons and ravines, where the best machine will have to win its emblem of victory in the wildest and roughest pass of the mountains, The "Crawford Notch." **On Mount Washington**

in the White Mountains. Stanley climbing, July 18, 1905. Mts. Jefferson and Adams in the background over the Great Gulf.

The mountain is in full view from the **Hotel Mount Washington** and **The Mount Pleasant** at Bretton Woods.

—**Anderson & Price, Managers**—

Send for Route Map from New York and Boston to the White Mountains and Bretton Woods, **also** for Map of "Ten Tours from Bretton Woods."

TWO MILES A MINUTE—IN 1906
A World's Record

THE FASTEST CAR IN THE WORLD
(Rate of 127.66 Miles an Hour)

This car, at Ormond Beach, Florida ,January 21 to 28, 1906, established the following world's records: 1 kilometre, .18-2/5; 1 mile, 28-1/5; 1 mile in competition, 31-1/5; 5 miles, 2.47-1/5; 2 miles, 59-3/5.

Mr. Fred Marriott's description of this car follows (Mr. Marriott, as driver of the above Stanley Steamer, established the above world's records. He is now a garage operator at West Newton, Mass.): Wheel base, 100 inches; wheel tread, 54 inches; width of body at center, 36 inches; gear ratio, 82 teeth on the driving gear; 48 teeth on the driven (ring) gear; wheels revolved 1¾ times to each revolution of the engine; engine is 4½ x 6½ and makes 350 revolutions to the mile; wheels, 34 inches in diameter, equipped with 3 inch G & J tires; wheels make 600 revolutions to the mile; tiller steering; manufacturer's rated horsepower, 30; approximate developed horsepower, 250; plug type pistons, no rings; weight of engine, 205 lbs.; boiler was 30 inches in diameter and 18 inch deep; it contained 1475 tubes, 33/64 inch O.D.; 20-ga. wall thickness, of seamless steel; total heating surface, 285 sq. ft.; steam pressure, about 1000 pounds per sq. in.; when car was demolished on January 27, 1907, while traveling at over 190 miles per hour, the steam pressure was 1300 pounds; the burner was Stanley's vaporizing, slot grate type; gasoline fuel was vaporized and burned as gas; mixing tubes consisted of four of the Venturi type; fuel feed was from two pressure tanks, 180-lb. air pressure on fuel; brakes were 2-band, external, one on each driving axle next to differential gear. In addition, two internal expanding brakes were mounted on the rear wheel hubs. Engine had Stephenson link motion for variable cutoff and reverse. The largest cross-section presented by the body, including the wheels, was only 9 square feet.

WORLD'S RECORD BREAKING
STEAM ENGINE

Shown here is the Stanley Steam Engine used by Fred H. Marriott when he broke the world's speed record in his Stanley racer. This historical engine is now in the Smithsonian Institution at Washington, D. C.

OFELDT'S Steam Generating Outfits

CONSIST OF

Blue Flame Kerosene Burner — **Automatic Water Regulator**
Safety Water Tube Boiler — **Automatic Fuel Regulator**

Diam.	H. P.	Price	Diam.	H. P.	Price
15½ or 16 inches	4-6	$112.50	22 inches	10-12	$225.00
18 inches	6-8	135.00	24 inches	12-15	270.00
20 inches	8-10	180.00		Larger sizes Built to Order.	

WE ALSO BUILD

Compound Double Acting Steam Engines, Horizontal Type, Run in Oil, 12 and 45 H. P.

Feed Water Heaters.

WE HAVE INSTALLED OUR

Kerosene Burner on the White Steam Car and it works O. K. No changes in Fuel System are necessary. Price of 21-inch size, $50.00.

DO IT NOW.

Order parts required for repairing or building a steam car and include our specialties. Readily installed in any steamer including Stanley & White.

Write for "Specialty" Catalogue.

1907

F. W. OFELDT & SONS, Nyack-on-the-Hudson (only) N. Y.

A Steam Equipment

for Automobile or Launch

DIETER ENGINE
OFELDT BOILER

FROM 10 H. P. UP.

Write for full information to

The Dieter Steam Engine Co.
OR **August Ofeldt & Sons**

123 Liberty St., New York

Three Cylinder Dieter Engine.

Ofeldt Semi-flash Boiler.

WHY IS IT

That more Lightning Kerosene Burners are in successful operation than all other makes combined? Investigate. Write us for Catalog B.

E. C. WALKER CO.

1913 Logan St., Louisville, Ky.

Stickney Safety Steam Generators

Can be run dry without injury, and increased mileage on water and gasoline guaranteed. We place them in your auto on trial.

PORTLAND GARAGE
Portland, Maine

21735NJ

The Best License Pad

is made at 896 Eighth Avenue, New York. I make Automobile License Pads and Motor Cycle License Pads, with rings or straps, made entirely of leather. Motor Cycle Pads also made to order. A postal brings the Catalog.

GEO. DENTZEAU, 896 Eighth Avenue NEW YORK

TO ALL USERS OF STEAM AUTOMOBILES

Write for Circulars and Prices about the
NEW OFELDT "NEVER BURN OUT"

Coil, Water Tube & Flash Boilers

We have solved the problem of making a serviceable kerosene burner to fit all size boilers, and to order in any size required. In successful operation for several years. Absolutely guaranteed

AUGUST OFELDT & SONS

Office and Warerooms: 341 West 44th St., New York, N. Y.
Main Factory: Lynbrook, L. I.

1907 WHITE STEAMER

Notice the Prest-o-Lite Tank and running board, the detachable rims, and the large gas headlights. The small wheel above the steering wheel is the steam throttle. Notice the hand-hold on the side of the front seat; and the round spring bumper in front. The front seat is divided—a common design at that time. The top-irons to hold the top, when down, are shown. Apparently the top had been removed when the picture was taken. — Clymer.

1907

THE ROSS STEAM TOURING CAR.

This early photo shows President Theodore Roosevelt in his personally owned White Steamer. Taken about 1907. White Steam Cars were used as White House official cars for several years.

—*Photo, courtesy The White Co.*

Commercial
Applications.

Electric and Steam Road Trains in Europe.

BY FRANK C. PERKINS.

Electric trackless trolley lines are being established in considerable number in Germany and Italy. In the latter country such a system is exploited by the Societa per la Trazione Elettrica of Milan. It is absolutely necessary that the electric current collector be simple and flexible, and it is claimed that by this Italian system the automobile is free to travel 2.5 metres from both sides of the feeder trolley line, which is said to be sufficient for all ordinary requirements.

The current collecting device consists of a rigid tube carrying at the top a special four wheeled trolley truck, the pipe being fastened on the automobile body in a similar manner to the ordinary trolley car pole. There is a ball and socket joint provided, allowing the collector to readily adapt itself to the irregularities of the trolley line, and it is maintained that even if the two wires were not spaced quite accurately little difficulty has been found. In order to insure a good contact there is a pressure of from 5 to 6 kilograms per wheel against the conductor wire.

This car carries from fifteen to twenty passengers and has from nine to fourteen seats. The chassis is designed with a view of obtaining a very easy and smooth motion, the electric motors being fitted with back gears driving a countershaft, from which motion is transmitted to the rear axle by means of chains.

In order to reduce vibration the motor is suspended from the frame at four points. Each motor acts upon the gears through a special elastic coupling, which transmits the movement smoothly, allows the motor shaft to make a small angle with the countershaft, and protects the motor against vibrations due to gears and chains.

Two mechanical brakes are provided, one an internal expanding brake on the rear wheels and the other a band brake on the countershaft. Owing to the provision of these mechanical brakes and the electric brake the automobile may be run safely on very steep grades. A special type of hydraulic brake is also provided for these trolley vehicles for mountain roads where the grades are unusually long.

It is maintained that these trolley automobiles can run with perfect safety at a speed of 35 miles per hour, with comfort to the passengers, and at that speed can be moved to the sides of the road without difficulty, sufficiently to allow of the passage of other vehicles. The Italian engineers claim that the absence of a boiler and supplies of fuel and water makes this type of vehicle simpler and more reliable than the gasoline or steam automobile, while the flexibility of control of the electric motor, doing away with the necessity of a mechanical change gear, insures other advantages.

There is no doubt but that a trackless trolley line requires a greater first cost than a gasoline or steam car line, but the economy in maintenance and energy consumption is said to be to its advantage, even where the traffic is not large. It is claimed that a comparison of several operating plants in Italy has led to the conclusion that where a public service requires more than three complete trips daily the trackless trolley system is more economical than a gasoline or steam automobile service. This rule is not for general application, as the cost of electric energy and the cost of gasoline enter into the question vitally.

It is also claimed that not only the weight but also the energy consumed is in favor of the trackless trolley, a gasoline omnibus requiring greater space and weighing fully one-third more than the trolley automobile, consuming more energy in proportion.

For a fourteen passenger trolley automobile the weight is 2,000 kilograms, and for a twenty-four passenger car 2,300 kilograms. During tests made at Milan with an eighteen passenger automobile operating at a speed of 35 kilometres per hour the consumption of power was found to be 150 watt hours per car kilometre with the roads in good condition, while with muddy roads the power consumption did not exceed 250 watt hours per car kilometre.

It is interesting to note that on the Spezia-Portoevnere line the energy consumption was 160 watt hours per automobile kilometre. This trackless trolley line is 15 kilometres long and has a maximum grade of 7 per cent. The above energy consumption was noted after the automobile had made 50,000 kilometres. On this 15 kilometre line there are two cars for passengers and one for freight. Alternating current is used, and the cost of the plant was about $6,000. The 3 ton freight car cost $2,000 and the three trolley automobiles for passengers somewhat less than $9,000, one of these being held in reserve. The total cost of the line was $24,000 and the transforming station about $2,000, about 15 horse power being required at this station for each vehicle.

The operating expenses are divided into two classes, one being proportional to the number of car kilometres and the other independent of the traffic, including the general expenses, interest on capital, maintenance and depreciation of stationary machines. The operating expense, including the repairs and maintenance of automobiles and depreciation of the same, as well as maintenance of the line, is said to be .16 lire, while the energy cost, counting 300 watts per car kilometre at 15 centimes per kilowatt hour, is .05 lire, making a total of .21 lire, or about 4 cents per car kilometre.

GERMAN TRACKLESS STEAM CAR.

THE INCOMPARABLE
WHITE
THE CAR FOR SERVICE

Clean Sweep for the White in California Hill-Climb

The White Steamer won all three events in which it was entered in the hill-climbing carnival held at San Francisco in connection with the recent automobile show. A 30 H.P. White touring car won the class for cars costing up to $3,500, and a 20 H.P. White touring car won in the $2,500 class. In the free-for-all, the same 30 H.P. car, with body removed, again triumphed. It made the climb in 1:38 4-5, which is 16 seconds faster than that made by its nearest competitor.

The superiority of the White in hill-climbing has been demonstrated in every public contest in which it has competed or, more properly speaking, been allowed to compete. Hill-climbing ability is the true test of real power, of available power, of power at the rear wheels, and it is evident that hill-climbing contests furnish the real demonstration of what the various systems of motive power can do, and that the tables of "rated horse-power" are of purely theoretical interest.

Write for Literature

THE WHITE COMPANY
CLEVELAND, OHIO

The 1909 White Steam Cars

As in 1907 and 1908, the White Steam Cars built by the White Co., Cleveland, Ohio, for 1909 will be built in two distinct models which, while differing from each other widely in power, in size and in price, resemble each other in their general lines of construction. The horse-power ratings of the two models are based on the actual power delivered at the rear wheels, not merely on formulas nor on the power delivered at the engine.

The larger of the new White cars will be known as the Model "M" and will be the successor of the Model "K" of the present season. The Model "M" is rated at 40 horse power and sells for $4,000, f. o. b. Cleveland, equipped with acetylene headlights and tank, oil lamps, horn and tool kit. The wheel base is 122 inches; the front tires 36 x 4 inches and the rear tires

The wheel base is 104 inches and the tires, both front and rear, are 32 x 3½ inches. The car is regularly fitted with a straight-line five-passenger body. The engine, except as regards size, is identical with that in the Model "M." The high pressure cylinder is 2½ inch bore, and the low pressure cylinder is 4¼ inch bore; the stroke is three inches. The frame is heat-treated pressed steel. The front axle is a one-piece forging of I section. The front springs are 37 inches long and 1¾ inches wide; the rear springs are 45 inches long and 1¾ inches wide. Both the foot brake and the hand brake act on drums on the rear wheels, the former being of the expanding type and the latter of the contracting type. As in the Model "M," the water tank is placed under the foot boards and the fuel tank is in the rear.

Fig. 1. 1909 White Steamer Model "M.". **The engine** is considerably changed from 1908 as detailed in the text and develops 40 H. P. The high pressure cylinder is 3½-inch bore and the low 6-inch, the stroke is 4½ inches. The smaller car, Model "O" is very similar except for size. The engine is rated as 20 H. P., the high pressure cylinder being 2½ and the low pressure 4¼ inches bore with 3 inches stroke. The small car frame is pressed steel, heat treated and the large car is of armoured wood. The fuel tanks in both are at the rear.

36 x 5 inches. The car is regularly fitted with a straight-line, seven-passenger body. The engine is compound, of new design, described in full below. The high pressure cylinder is 3½ inch bore; the low pressure cylinder 6 inch bore, and the stroke 4½ inches. The frame is of armored wood, the reinforcing plates of nickel steel being fastened on both sides of the wooden sills. The front axle is of the tubular type; the front springs are 44 inches long and 2½ inches wide; the rear spring 55 inches long and 2½ inches wide. Both the foot brake and the hand brake act on drums on the rear wheels, the former being of the expanding type and the latter of the contracting type.

The smaller of the new White cars will be known as the Model "O". This car may be described more appropriately as a smaller edition of the new Model "M," rather than as a successor of any previous model. The Model "O" is rated at 20 horse power and sells for $2,000, f. o. b. Cleveland, equipped with oil lamps, horn and tool kit.

PRINCIPAL CHANGES.

The principal mechanical change in the new cars, as compared with previous White models, is in the engine. As previously mentioned the engines in the two new models differ only as regards dimensions and, therefore, the following description applies to both models. The new engine construction has been undergoing a thorough trying-out for two years, and both the Model "M" and the Model "O" engine have been subjected to tests of over 30,-000 miles of usage and, therefore, may be regarded as thoroughly seasoned products. The change in the engine may be summarized as follows: in the place of one standard type of valve mechanism, another standard type of valve mechanism is used. In former years, the engines used in the White cars were fitted with the Stephenson valve motion, which was actuated by eccentrics on the crank shaft, as were also the pumps. The new White engines are fitted with the Joy valve motion, which is actuated directly from the connecting rods

ENGINE SIMPLIFIED.

This new construction permits of a great simplification of the engine. The

draft of air between the condenser tubes is an important element in securing good condensation, which means good economy in water consumption.

ACCESSIBILITY.

The crank-case of the engine is made in

Fig. 2. Parts of the 1909 White engine. The two throw crank shaft owing to the new valve suction is now very short and runs on the two annular ball bearings shown. These bearings can be removed by taking off the two ring nuts shown on each side of the balance weight. Note the ball bearing connecting rods.

number of parts is reduced almost to a half of those formerly necessary, considerable weight is saved, all eccentrics are done away with and the cylinders are brought close together, permitting the use of a short one-piece crank shaft. The new crank shaft is a one-piece forging of tool steel with but two main bearings which is an advantageous construction because when three or more bearings are used in any shaft there is always a possibility that they may get out of alignment. The main bearings are of the annular type and may be removed from the crank shaft by taking off two lock nuts and lock washers. The two main bearings and the two connecting rod bearings are fitted with ball separators and the balls are of extra large size. The connecting rods are one-piece forgings.

In Fig. 3 are shown assembled all the working parts of the new White engine—pistons, cross-heads, connecting rods, crank, valve mechanism and pump levers. It will be seen that both the high pressure valve and the low pressure valve are piston valves. Steam is admitted through the center of the valves and exhausts at the ends. The pressure on the valve stuffing boxes is thus reduced to that of the exhaust from the respective cylinders. The small arm, A, on the end of the pump rocker-shaft is connected by means of a rod to a ratchet device which drives the oiler placed on the dash board. The sprocket on the forward end of the crank shaft is connected by chain to the fan-shaft and the ratio of the sprockets is such that the fan-shaft runs faster than the engine. The fan-shaft housing is mounted on eccentrics and the tension of the chain may be readily altered by turning these eccentrics. These improvements in driving the fan are of no little importance as a good

one piece, but ready access may be had to all the parts within by the removal of the side and bottom plates, and the crank shaft may be taken out through either end.

Fig. 3. Assembly of working parts of White 1909 motor showing the Joy valve mechanism which is now used in place of the Stephenson link motion. By shifting guide G. the engine is reversed or point of cut-off varied. VL and VH are the low and high pressure piston valves; PL and PH the pistons. Arm A drives thru a rod and ratchet drives the oiler on the dash. Note the ball bearing crank shaft and connecting rod ends. Arms D drive the pumps.

The new engine permits of a pleasing and symmetrical arrangement of the necessary piping and everything under the bonnet is easily accessible. Stuffing boxes are fitted to the upper end of the slides in which the cross-heads travel, so that no oil may be splattered out of the crank-case. The pumps are entirely enclosed so that they may be kept free from dust, yet they are readily accessible by removing hand hole covers. There are the most thorough provisions for keeping the pumps and all parts within the crank-case well lubricated.

The cylinders are provided with relief valves for getting rid of any water which

Fig. 4. Left side of 1909 White engine showing hand hole covers over pumps removed.

may be in the cylinders when starting the engine "cold" thus avoiding a water hammer. These valves are opened momentarily by a little lever on the dash, before admitting steam to the engine, and the entering steam quickly and effectually blows out the water.

The engine is so adjusted that it runs normally on "cut-off"—that is, the admission of the steam to each cylinder is stopped before the end of the stroke and the steam then works expansively for the balance of the stroke. In starting the engine, the pushing of the simpling pedal allows the engine to take steam during the full stroke. There is also a "cut-off" pedal which, when pressed, produces the same result. This "cut-off" pedal is used only when slow, hard pulling is required, as in climbing particularly steep grades or running over very heavy roads. An interesting feature of the Joy valve mechanism is that, when the "cut-off" is changed, the "lead" of the valves is unchanged and the engine thus runs more smoothly on "cut-off" than was possible with the Stephenson link motion. The engine is reversed and the "cut-off" is changed by simply changing the tilt of the guide, G, in Fig. 3.

DRIVE IS DIRECT.

The engine is supported on two cross-members of the frame which are so placed that the entire weight of the engine is behind the front axle. The engine is so hung that the driving shaft is perfectly horizontal and, as there is neither clutch nor transmission gear on the White, the drive is direct and positive from the engine thru the driving shaft to the rear axle.

EXHAUST FEED WATER HEATER.

The exhaust pipe from the engine to the condenser is located on the right side. Within this exhaust pipe there is a coil of piping, thru which the water from the pumps circulates on its way to the generator. This arrangement thus constitutes a neat and compact feed-water heater which performs the double function of heating the feed-water and of aiding the process of condensation.

The generator is of the same construction as in former years, consisting simply of a series of coils of steel tubing, placed one above the other, and connected in series. This generator is made of a single long piece of tubing. In operation, water is pumped into the upper coil and steam issues from the lower coil. There is but a very small quantity of water and steam in the generator at any given moment being in the larger car less than one-third of a cubic foot, but the process of making

Fig. 5. Rear view of White engine showing the complete housing of all working parts.

steam is so rapid that steam is always available in the quantity which the running conditions may make necessary.

RIGHT SIDE OF WHITE ENGINE, SHOWING THE AIR PUMP FOR SUPPLYING PRESSURE TO FUEL TANK AND THE PUMP FOR RETURNING WATER FROM CONDENSER TO TANK

1909

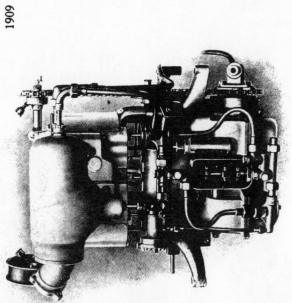

LEFT SIDE OF WHITE ENGINE, SHOWING THE FEED-WATER HEATER, THE PUMPS FOR SUPPLYING GENERATOR AND THE WATER REGULATOR

(The White Company)

1909

Lane Steamer, Model 7, 20 H.P.   Lane Motor Vehicle Co., Poughkeepsie, N. Y.

PRICE: $2,650
BODY: Touring with Victoria top
SEATS: 5 persons
WEIGHT: 2,350 pounds
WHEEL BASE: 97 inches
TREAD: 56 inches
TIRES, FRONT: 3¼x4 inches
TIRES, REAR: 3¼x4 inches
STEERING: Worm and sector and rear hubs
BRAKES: On transmission and rear hubs

SPRINGS: Semi-elliptic
FRAME: Steel
BORE: 3¼ and 5¼ in. STROKE: 3½ in.
CYLINDERS: Inclined under foot board
VALVE: Slide; link motion
BURNER: Lane tubular
CONDENSER: Vertical flattened tubes

FUEL REGULATION: Diaphragm controlled by pressure
LUBRICATION: Splash
MOTOR-CONTROL: Throttle lever
BOILER: Combination flash and fire tube
CHANGE SPEED CONTROL: Regulated by throttle
DRIVE: Center chain

Ross Touring Car, 25 H.P.   Louis S. Ross, Newtonville, Mass.

PRICE: $2,800
BODY: Wood; side entrance
SEATS: 5 persons
WEIGHT: 2,800 pounds
WHEEL BASE: 108 inches
TREAD: 56 inches

TIRES, FRONT: 34x4 in.
TIRES, REAR: 34x4 in.
STEERING: Irreversible
BRAKES: 2 sets
SPRINGS: Semi-elliptic
FRAME: Pressed steel

BORE: 4 in. STROKE: 5 in.
CYLINDERS: Two, in front
MOTOR SUSPENSION: Main frame
DRIVE: Shaft

Lane Steamer, Model 75, 30 H.P.   Lane Motor Vehicle Co., Poughkeepsie, N. Y.

PRICE: $3,400
BODY: Side entrance tonneau
SEATS: 7 persons
WEIGHT: 3,100 pounds
WHEEL BASE: 112 inches
TREAD: 56 inches
TIRES, FRONT: 36x4 inches
TIRES, REAR: 36x4½ inches
STEERING: Worm and sector
BRAKES: On transmission and rear hubs

SPRINGS: Semi-elliptic
FRAME: Steel
BORE: 3½ and 6½ in.
STROKE: 4 in.
CYLINDERS: Inclined under front foot board
VALVE ARRANGEMENT: Slide Stephenson link motion
MOTOR SUSPENSION: Lane patent
BURNER: Lane tubular

CONDENSER: Vertical flattened tubes
FULL REGULATION: Diaphragm controlled by pressure
BOILER: Combination flash and fire tube
LUBRICATION: Splash
MOTOR-CONTROL: Throttle lever
SPEEDS: Regulated by throttle
DRIVE: Center chain

White Steamer, Model G, 30 H.P.   The White Co., Cleveland, Ohio

PRICE: $3,500
BODY: Touring
SEATS: 5 persons
WHEEL BASE: 115 inches
TREAD: 56 inches
TIRES, FRONT: 36x4 inches
TIRES, REAR: 36x5 inches
STEERING: Worm and segment
BRAKES: 1 set expanding, 1 set contracting, on rear wheels

SPRINGS: Semi-elliptic
FRAME: Armored wood
BORE: Flash; pressure, 3 in.; low pressure, 6 in.
STROKE: 4½ inches
CYLINDERS: Two
VALVE ARRANGEMENT: Stephenson link
MOTOR SUSPENSION: On cross members

CONDENSER: Tubular
REGULATION: Automatic
BOILER: Flash
LUBRICATION: Force feed
MOTOR-CONTROL: Throttle alone
CHANGE-GEAR CONTROL: All speeds; direct
DRIVE: Shaft

STANLEY

L. S. Hertha went to Denver last Saturday and brought home with him a new thirty-horse-power Stanley steamer. The seats are detachable and the car can be quickly converted into an express or trunk car. Mr. Hertha's increasing business made it necessary for him to have a larger car.

The Mountain Wagon was used for many years to carry passengers from Loveland to Estes Park, Colorado. The three rear seats were removable, so that the car could be used as a truck. I believe this model was developed by the Stanley Company for use originally by the Loveland-Estes Park Transportation Co. — Clymer.

MODEL 810, THIRTY HORSE POWER MOUNTAIN WAGON, TWELVE PASSENGERS

Price, $2,300 F. O. B. Factory.   Equipment includes top; windshield; speedometer; headlights and Presto-O-Lite tank; "Long" horn; black-and-nickel finish.

Wheel base, 136 inches; tires 36 x 5, front and rear; quick detachable rims.

WHITE STEAMER

Goes Through the 2650-Mile

GLIDDEN TOUR

USING

Kerosene as Fuel

1910

The new fuel was publicly proven to be a complete success. Not a moment of delay and not a single penalty resulted from its use. Kerosene was purchased from 6 to 10 cents a gallon cheaper than gasoline; it was obtainable at any cross-roads store; and it could be hand.ed without any precautions. Finally, the new fuel was shown to be more efficient, gallon for gallon, than gasoline and it was proven to be absolutely smokeless and odorless.

Either kerosene or gasoline may be used as fuel in the 1910 White Steamers

THE WHITE COMPANY

New York City, Broadway at 62d St.
Boston, 320 Newbury St.
Philadelphia, 629 - 33 N. Broad St.
Pittsburg, 138-148 Beatty St.

860 East 79th St.
CLEVELAND
OHIO

Toronto, 170 King St , West

Cleveland, 407 Rockwell Ave.
Atlanta, 120-122 Marietta St.
Chicago, 240 Michigan Ave.
San Francisco, Market St. at Van Ness.

FLOYD CLYMER'S STEAM CAR QUIZ

HOW MUCH DO YOU REMEMBER ABOUT STEAM CARS?

1. What Steam Car had the same name as a famous piano?
2. There were 12 makes of Steam Cars with the same names as cities in the United States. Can you name them?
3. What Steam Car had the same name as a judicial court?
4. What Steam Car had the name of a dwelling?
5. What Steam Car had the name of a President of the U. S.?
6. What Steam Car had the same name as a one-time Secretary of State?
7. What Steam Car had the same name as the member of a train crew?
8. What Steam Car had the same name as a famous brand of silverware?
9. What man who made two makes of gasoline cars built an experimental steam car in 1897?
10. What make of Steam Car had the same name as a famous maker of cheese?
11. What Steam Car had the same name as a contest winner?
12. What Steam Car had the name of a famous watch?
13. What Steam Car had the name of a famous sewing machine?
14. In what year did a steam powered airplane fly at San Francisco?

(Answers are printed below)

10. Kraft.
14. 1933.
9. R. E. Olds, who built Olds and Reo.
13. White.
8. Rogers.
12. Waltham.
7. Porter.
11. Victor.
6. Kellogg.
5. Johnson.
4. House.
3. Federal.
2. Chicago, Malden, Mobile, Pawtucket, Reading, Toledo, Cincinnati, Milwaukee, Ormond, Prescott, Rochester, Waltham.
1. Baldwin.

ONE OF THE FIRST DOBLE STEAM CARS BUILT
This Model "A" 1911 Doble was photographed in Waltham, Mass., in 1912. John A. Doble is standing in front of the hood; Abner Doble is at the wheel; and Frank Lindstrom is at the rear.

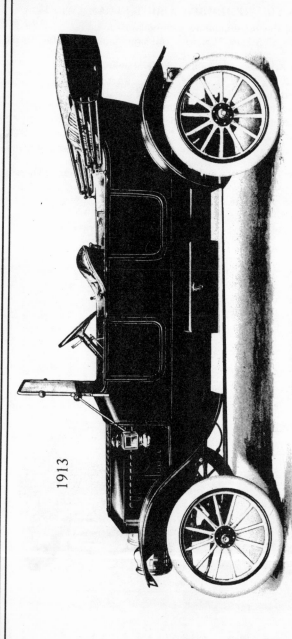

1913

Stanley Steam Car

MODEL 65, TEN HORSE POWER, FOUR PASSENGERS

Price, $1,300 F.O.B. Factory. Equipment includes top; windshield; speedometer; headlights and Prest-O-Lite tank; electric attachment for lighting gas headlights; electric gauge light; combination oil and electric side and tail lights; storage battery; "Long" horn; black-and-nickel finish. Wheel base, 112 inches; tires 32 x 4; quick detachable rims.

Price of Model 65 chassis including everything on the Model 65 except the body, top, windshield, robe rail, foot rest and the electric parts of the lighting outfit; $1,025 F. O. B. Factory.

A Power Plant Standardized One Hundred Years Ago

1916

It is in its power plant only that the Stanley is different. So far as general equipment is concerned, Stanley equipment is such as is used on the best types of internal explosive cars: Timken bearings and Timken front axle; Wyman & Gordon drop forgings; Warner steering gear; Mayo radiator; Silvertown cord tires; Warner speedometer; Klaxon horn; Apple dynamo and Willard battery for lights and horn; Aluminum body.

It is in its power plant that the Stanley is different—and it is in this difference that the Stanley is fundamentally superior. Because of this steam power plant the Stanley is called unconventional, and as compared with the internal explosive automobile it is unconventional—but in that sense only. As a matter of fact its power plant is the most conventional, the oldest, the most highly standardized, the most efficient, the simplest, the safest and the least mysterious that science has ever devised for driving a road vehicle.

Do You Know How Many Cylinders Are Necessary

properly to propel an automobile? One of the most successful manufacturers, having tried one and four and six, now says twelve is the proper and necessary number. The most successful manufacturer in the world says that four cylinders are enough. Who knows? Does any automobile engineer know? Does any automobile user know? Do you?

This problem arises from the fact that the internal explosive engine is essentially and normally a constant speed, constant load motor, and as such is fundamentally unsuited for a variable speed, variable load device like an automobile.

The number of cylinders necessary to drive a road vehicle was absolutely and definitely fixed nearly 100 years ago.

George Stephenson Laid Down The Principle

in 1820. And the principle he definitely fixed is that of a two cylinder engine, double acting (taking steam in each direction) simple (using the steam in one expansion only), with slide valves and link motion reverse.

Since Stephenson's time poppet valve engines have been tried, compound engines, multiple cylinder engines, rotary engines have been tried. All have been found wanting. In other words, Stephenson's principle has become definitely fixed, not because nothing else has been tried, but because EVERYTHING else has been tried.

To accomplish the result which you long for—which every automobile engineer is struggling honestly to give you—to deliver a smooth, continuous torque to the crankshaft without "impulses"—without even "overlapping impulses"—in other words, properly to propel an automobile—only two cylinders, and only thirteen moving parts are needed in the complete engine. As applied in Stanley construction, this fundamentally correct engine is geared direct and permanently to the rear axle, without "transmission" or gear-shift—

the engine speed is the car speed. The steam which supplies this engine is stored in the generating plant under the hood, which is nothing more than a kerosene stove boiling water, with no moving parts, no carburetor, no ignition system. The volume of steam entering the engine controls the speed of the car, and this is governed by the little finger throttle—the sole controlling device on the whole car. Thus the power from the liquid fuel is transmitted to the rear wheels with no carburetor, no ignition system, no clutch, no flywheel, no gear-shift, no "transmission," and with only thirteen moving parts.

What You Want Is Stanley Performance

You and your customers have been willing to try six, eight, and even twelve cylinders in searching for your ideal performance—for a smooth, continuous torque; a steady, uninterrupted flow of driving power; with power stored for the critical emergencies; without clutch or gear-shift; with all controlling devices limited to a single finger lever. You can now offer them this ideal performance.

Don't let the notion that the Stanley is "unconventional" deter you or your customers longer from riding it—from driving it yourselves—from experiencing for yourselves the relief from physical hardship and mental anxiety which this most highly standardized car in the world can alone give you. We shall be glad to hear from you and to send you our booklet.

The Stanley Touring Car is $1975 f. o. b. Newton, Mass. Wire Wheels $90 extra. Wheelbase, 130 inches—Tires 34x4½ Silvertown—Aluminum Body—12 Miles to the Gallon of Kerosene—200 Miles to a Tank of Water.

Founded 1898

STANLEY MOTOR CARRIAGE CO., NEWTON, MASS.

A CIRCULATION WITHOUT EQUAL
Perfect—Forced—Uninterrupted

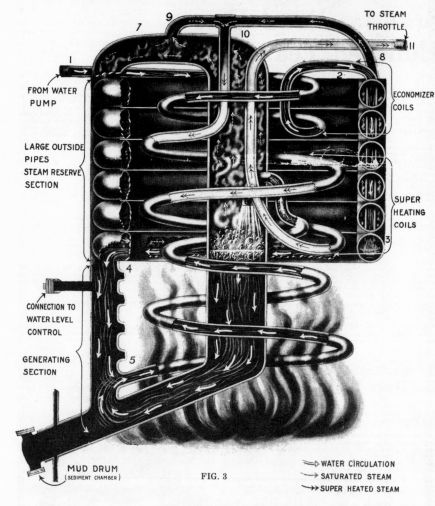

FIG. 3

THE BAKER BOILER

Several years ago the Baker Steam Car was built at Pueblo, Colorado. An illustration of the boiler used is shown here. Many steam car enthusiasts felt that the Baker Boiler was an exceptionally good one. It was a water-tube boiler, built in four sections—each section a separate and distinct unit which was assembled—yet each section functioned individually. Baker contended that with his boiler, efficiency was materially increased, proper separation of water and steam was assured, a constant water level was maintained ,and scaling and choking of tubes was eliminated, and the boiler was easily cleaned. The boiler was controlled by positive and dependable automatics. — Clymer.

The Literary Digest for November 17, 1917

DOBLE-DETROIT
STEAM CAR

The Ultimate Car

The World Will Find It, We Firmly Believe, In the Steam-Propelled Vehicle

Last January we introduced the Doble-Detroit Steam Motors Car. It was exhibited at the larger Motor Car Shows.

Its recognition was instantaneous — its endorsement almost universal.

In less than a month the Doble-Detroit Steam Car had "arrived" as no other car has ever arrived.

The ten months that have passed since the introduction of the Doble-Detroit have been months of constructive development.

Demonstrating cars have been built. They have been tested and proved. They have been exhibited in the larger cities of the country.

A new factory has been secured. The Sales organization has been perfected. Patent protection on the exclusive features of the Doble-Detroit has been supplemented and amplified.

And today more firmly than ever we are convinced that the ultimate car is the steam car.

And just as firmly do we believe that the Doble-Detroit is the nearest approach to the ultimate that has yet been achieved.

Today the Doble-Detroit is being manufactured in the new commodious plant of the Doble-Detroit Steam Motors Co. By early Spring demonstrating cars will be in the hands of distributors throughout the country and more extensive productions will be well under way.

Today—more than a thousand Doble-Detroit distributors and dealers constitute one of the strongest, most representative Sales organizations in the entire motor car field.

Today the Doble-Detroit Steam Motors Co. has entered upon the herculean task of filling orders for $20,000,000 worth of Doble-Detroit cars actually contracted for by Doble-Detroit dealers.

And of Equal Importance—

Today the revolutionary character of the Doble-Detroit achievement and the fundamental soundness of the principles involved in the development of the Doble-Detroit Steam Car are recognized by the United States Patent Office in the unusually sweeping patent protection that has been accorded them.

Doble-Detroit Steam Motors Co., Detroit, Michigan

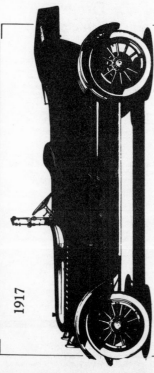

1917

STANLEY TOURING CAR
Five Passenger Twenty Horse Power
MODEL 725
Price, $2200 f.o.b. Newton, Mass.

SPECIFICATIONS—*Body:* Aluminum; stream-line, flush-side; concealed hinges; door opening, front 19 inches, rear 20 inches. Front seat 44 inches wide, 18 inches front to back, and cushions 8 inches deep. Rear seat 48 inches wide, 20 inches front to back, and cushion 10 inches deep. Tonneau space 30 inches from back of front seat to front of back seat.

Upholstery: Soft, bright finish, straight grain leather. Cushions upholstered with genuine horsehair. Seat sides and backs of same quality material and workmanship as cushions. Front seat not partitioned, but with divided cushion. Cushions in both front and back seats tilted for comfort, and with air outlets to get full benefit of spring.

Top: Improved one-man top, fastened to windshield. Close fitting bows with Bair bow-holders.

Windshield: Special Troy clear-vision, rain-vision ventilating windshield engaging with top; black enameled arms with nickel mountings; built into the body design.

Color: Body and wheel spokes Valentine's dark, rich blue, called Russian Body Blue, with fine gray striping. Running gear, except the wheel spokes, black without striping. Mudguards black enameled, without striping. Hood and radiator, header, Russian Body Blue.

Lighting System: Electric lights, Apple dynamo, geared direct to differential. Willard L. B. A. 6-80 storage battery; large

electric headlights in black and nickel with large and small bulbs; electric dash and tail lights; no side lights.

Horn: Klaxon electric under-hood type, button under driver's left foot.

Steering Gear: Warner steering gear of worm and gear type, with 18-inch wheel; on left side of car.

Wheel Base: 130 inches, with unusually small turning radius. Standard 56-inch tread.

Wheels: 34 x 4½, with Stanweld No. 60 Demountable rims with quick detachable clincher type rings. Wire wheels can be supplied at an extra cost of $90 for a complete set of five.

Tires: 34 x 4½ Goodrich Silvertown cord grooved. Provision for extra tire at rear of car.

Springs: Semi-elliptical front, full elliptical rear. All spring bolts lubricated by nickel-plated grease cups.

Mudguards: Heavy pressed steel crowned mudguards, with concealed rivets; mud-guards and aprons electrically welded. Running boards clear and covered with gray linoleum and bound with angle aluminum.

Chassis-Frame: Carefully tested channel section pressed steel, narrowed in front to give short turning radius.

Front Axle: Complete Timken front axle installation, incorporating tilted steering spindles which from the beginning have been a feature of Stanley cars.

Rear Axle: Stanley rear axle with the simple Stanley differential gear and with complete Timken bearing equipment.

Brakes: Service brake contracting on brake drum, operating from foot pedal. Emergency brake expanding internally on brake drum and operating from hand lever. Brake drums 14 inches in diameter, 2 inches wide.

Pumps: Driven from rear axle at one quarter engine speed with long stroke. All four pumps, the cylinder oil pump, the fuel pump, the service and emergency water pumps are driven direct and all four are actuated by but three moving parts.

Water Tank: Under the frame at the driver's seat; capacity twenty-four gallons, with gauge dial on dashboard.

Condenser Radiator: Mayo V-shaped, cellular type; giving a water-tank capacity of 150 to 250 miles.

Fuel Tank: Main fuel (kerosene) tank (fitted with quantity gauge) under frame at rear, behind axle. Pilot tank (fitted with quantity and pressure gauge) and cylinder oil tank under front seat. Baggage space under rear seat.

Boiler: Of regular Stanley type, lower head and shell pressed out of one piece of steel, top head welded in by oxyacetylene process. Three superheaters, heavily nickel-plated steel tubing. Extension water feed delivering the water to the boiler below the water level.

Burner: Improved drilled type. Our new combination burner takes equally well gasoline or kerosene, or any mixture of the two in the main burner. The pilot light takes gasoline and is fed from a separate tank under low pressure, the four-gallon tank supplying the pilot for about one hundred consecutive hours.

Engine: Engine equipped with oil-tight dust-proof case. Bolted rigidly to the rear axle and braced from the front of the engine back to the rear axle, thus making a unit of the engine, differential and rear axle, which run in an oil bath.

Chassis Price: The 725 chassis only, which includes everything but body and body-fittings, is offered at $1825 f.o.b. Newton, Mass.

A STEAM CAR ADVOCATE SUBMITS HIS IDEAS!

Of all my friends who are interested in steam automobiles, I know of no one having had more general experience with late model steam cars than Roland J. Giroux, of Big Pine, California. Roland is one of thousands who are confident the steam car will return. I therefore asked him to give his views as to the features that should be incorporated in a modern steam car. It gives me pleasure to present herewith his interesting ideas.—*Clymer*.

Specifications of the Modern Steam Automobile should include:

1. A two-speed axle, for the following reasons:
   a. Uses conventional axle.
   b. Having neutral point, would allow engine to idle without jacking up a rear wheel.
   c. Low speed gear to be used in city and on hills; high speed gear on open road.
   d. Allows engine to be mounted in front end of car, where it also drives auxiliary units, including a condenser fan, short steam pipe, and permitting sprung engine instead of dead weight on rear tires.
   e. Eliminates needing too much valve lead for high speeds, by using high gear for speed.

2. Coil type boiler, constructed similar to boiler built by Walter B. Kerrick, for the following reasons:
   a. Safety; no large steam drums to rupture in case of a road accident.
   b. Has forced circulation, using an injector inside tubes, fed by feed water pumps.
   c. Fast steamer, yet not a flash boiler.
   d. Has a steam dome out of the fire, to maintain water level, dry steam, and trap to prevent too high a water level.

3. Vertical, double acting, three-cylinder engine, similar to the Delling engine, for the following reason:
   a. With piston rods extending through cylinder heads, as in a marine engine, and marine-type copper piston rings, engine could operate with very little cylinder oil. Oil which otherwise would plug up small fins in condenser and shorten life of boiler is kept out of boiler feed water and condenser.

4. The boiler must have steaming capacity to maintain a speed of 60 miles per hour, or better, continuously.

5. The condenser must have capacity to condense exhaust steam for a mileage of 250 miles with a tankful of water, in the summer time. This means:
   a. A fan behind the condenser and a copper-finned condenser with a large cooling area. This in turn means that no oil in the exhaust steam gets to the condenser.

6. The burner (the biggest "bug" in steam cars so far) should be a gun-type, continuous ignition, pressure atomizing, forced draft type, with a suction fan on the flue pipe, for the following reasons:
   a. Burns No. 1 stove oil successfully.
   b. No pilot light required.
   c. With a time-lapse relay on the burner, motor, ignition and blower, the flue suction would always clear the firebox of unburned gases, to prevent backfire of the burner.

7. Engine reverse and cut-off should be a notched hand lever instead of a pedal, for the following reasons:
   a. Safety; never mistaken for a clutch pedal.
   b. All conventional cars use a lever, not a pedal, for reverse.
   c. More convenient to use to hold car back on down grade.

I have come to the above conclusions mainly as a result of my experience in driving a 1925 model Stanley Steamer, in which I installed a bus boiler and a 30-horsepower Mountain Wagon engine.

ROLAND J. GIROUX,
Big Pine, California.

DOBLE FOUR-PASSENGER STEAM CAR—SPORT TYPE
Mr. Doble in Rear Seat
Courtesy of Doble-Detroit Steam Motors Company, Detroit, Michigan

The following 67 pages appeared in "AUTOMOBILE ENGINEERING," published in 1918, and is reprinted here through the courtesy of the publishers, the American Technical Society, Chicago, Ill.

STEAM AUTOMOBILES

INTRODUCTION

Development of Steam Engines. That steam could be employed to produce mechanical motion was first noted in history about 130 B. C., but it was not until the seventeenth century that it found practical application in the industries. The developments were comparatively slow, however, until James Watt (1769) developed his engines to a point where they employed practically all the principles of the modern double-acting, condensing steam engine.

With these rapid inprovements came the idea of using the steam engine as a means of road locomotion, and in the opening years of the

Fig. 1.   Early Steam Carriage Built by Cugnot (France) in 1770

nineteenth century such machines were actually built and known as "road locomotives", Fig. 1. These machines might be called the forerunners of the steam automobile, although structurally they more nearly resembled the later traction engines. Bad roads, great weight, public opinion, and the development of railroads caused road locomotives to drop out of sight until the real coming of the automobile almost a hundred years later.

In the meantime the steam engine—both stationary and locomotive types—had reached a high state of development and hence many of the early automobiles carried this type of power plant.

STEAM AUTOMOBILES

Later improvements were made and are still being made along lines peculiar to steam automobile construction. Although during the last few years the steam car has not kept pace in numbers with other types of automobiles, it has certain characteristics, such as strong pulling powers at low speeds, capacity for big overloads, and ease in driving on the road, which make it especially useful under some conditions, the success of the London steam omnibuses being a good example.

CHARACTERISTIC FEATURES OF STEAM CARS

In the modern steam automobile the power plant is made up of the same general units as make up the stationary power plant, the only difference being the extreme compactness necessary and the development of the great flexibility required to meet the sudden changes in load conditions. With both plants there must be a supply of fuel, a means of burning it, a boiler or steam generator, a supply of water, an engine, and various means of controlling the amounts of fuel, water, and steam.

Location of Engine. With steam automobiles there is no uniformity of practice as to the placing of the different units in the

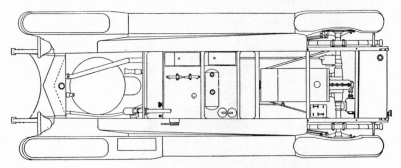

Fig. 2.   Plan View of Stanley Steam-Car Chassis
Courtesy of Stanley Motor Carriage Company, Newton, Massachusetts

running gear or chassis. For instance in the Stanley, Fig. 2, the boiler is under a hood in front of the driver and the engine is geared directly to the rear axle. In the case of the White cars, which were built in comparatively large quantities from 1904 to 1910, the engine was placed under the hood in front with a shaft running back to the rear axle. In the White car, a set of gears was also used in the

STEAM AUTOMOBILES

drive, by which the relation of engine to wheel speed could be reduced to one-half the usual amount, thus doubling the driving effort, or "torque". The White boiler was under the front seat. The new Doble, Figs. 3 and 4, uses the general arrangement of the Stanley. In

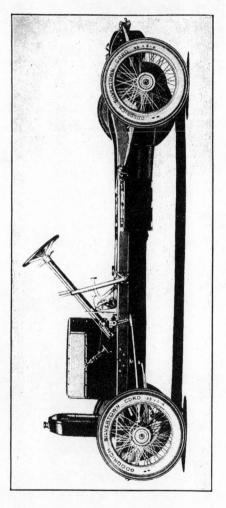

Fig. 3. Side View of Doble Chassis

Courtesy of General Engineering Company, Detroit, Michigan

the Leyland steam truck, Fig. 5, and the National busses, both of England, the boilers are in front, the engines are under the floor boards, with a countershaft and final chain drive, as in Fig. 5, or a shaft drive direct to the rear axle.

STEAM AUTOMOBILES

Boiler and Engine Types. Almost equal variation is found in the types of boilers and engines. The difference between fire-tube,

Fig. 4. Side View of Doble Steam-Car Chassis
Courtesy of General Engineering Company, Detroit, Michigan

water-tube, and flash generators is taken up in the section devoted to boilers, while the engine types are taken up in their respective section.

Fig. 5. Leyland Steam Truck with Chain Drive to Rear Wheels
Courtesy of Leyland Motors Company, Ltd., England

Some of the cars use the water over several times by condensing the steam in coolers, or "condensers", placed at the front of the car. The

STEAM AUTOMOBILES

White and Lane did this, and it is now done by the Stanley, Doble, and most of the English steam cars and trucks. The Stanley, up to 1915, had no condensers, allowing the steam to escape into the air after it had passed through the feed-water heater.

Simplicity of Control. As a general rule, the steam cars do not employ a transmission for giving various forward-gear ratios and a reverse. The extra heavy loads, as in starting, are taken care of by lengthening the cut-off and by "simpling", terms which will be more fully explained later. Instead of running the engine always in one direction and using a gearset for reversing the car, as is done on gasoline automobiles, the engine is itself reversed by means of changing the timing of the valves through the aid of the valve gear, or linkage.

This change of the valve-timing is used only at starting, reversing, or under very heavy load conditions, all ordinary running being accomplished with the cut-off in one position. The control of the speed of the car, therefore, is accomplished under normal conditions by changing the amount of steam going to the engine. The steam is turned on or shut off by a hand-operated valve, known as the "throttle valve", and this valve is turned by a lever, or second small wheel, just above or below the steering wheel. Thus the actual driving of a steam car consists of steering and operating the throttle. There are, however, numerous gages, valves, etc., which have to be worked upon when firing up, and which have to be given occasional attention on the road; these will be considered in detail in the following pages.

Having treated in a general way the different types of steam cars and their parts, the theory underlying the behavior of steam will be touched upon before taking up the details of construction and the operation of the various units.

HEAT AND WORK
HEAT TRANSMISSION

All forms of energy, such as light, sound, electricity, and heat, are believed to be different forms of vibration either of the molecules of material substances or of the ether which is believed to pervade all space.

Energy is indestructible, but any form of energy may be converted into any other form. Steam engines are classed as heat engines since they are employed to transform heat energy into mechanical work. Heat may be transmitted from one body to another in three ways, namely, by radiation and absorption, by conduction, and by convection.

Radiation and Absorption. Radiation is the transfer of heat from one body to another body not in contact with it. It takes place equally well in air or *in vacuo*. The rate of heat transferred depends partly on the distance separating the two bodies, and partly on the nature of their surfaces. In general, light-colored and polished metal surfaces radiate heat more slowly than rough and dark-colored surfaces. The laws governing absorption are the same as those governing radiation.

Conduction. Conduction is the transfer of heat through the substance of a body—solid or liquid—to other portions of the same body, or to another body in physical contact therewith. Metals are the best conductors of heat, but some metals, such as copper, are better conductors than others. Other solids, such as stone, wood, etc., rank after the metals. Liquids are very poor, and gases still poorer, conductors of heat. A vacuum is perfectly non-conducting, though radiation may still take place through it.

Convection. Convection is the term applied to the absorption of heat by moving liquids or gases in contact with heated surfaces. If a blast of air be directed on a piece of hot iron, the iron cools far more rapidly than it would in still air. The reason is that, as the air is a poor conductor, its molecules do not transmit heat readily from one to the next, but if each molecule on becoming heated is immediately replaced, heat is rapidly transferred. This property of air of taking up heat rapidly when blown over a hot surface is employed in gasoline automobiles to cool the so-called "radiators". In reality, the heat radiated cuts a small figure compared with that dispersed by convection.

What has just been said regarding air is equally true of other gases. It is also true of most liquids.

Relative Conductivity. Heat conducting qualities vary for different substances. Silver, copper, and aluminum conduct heat very rapidly, while asbestos is a poor heat conductor and is therefore used around the outside of automobile boilers.

Expansion. Another heat property which has to be con-

STEAM AUTOMOBILES

sidered in the selection of material for steam cars is that of expansion. Some metals expand much more than others for each degree of rise in temperature. Since brass and copper both expand under heat much more than iron they are used in preference to iron in the construction of expansion tubes, which are fully described later.

Temperature Measurement Scales. Temperature, which is the measure of the intensity of heat, is expressed by means of divisions called *degrees* on some thermometer scales. The two thermometers in most general use are the Fahrenheit and Centigrade; the former being the more common in America and England for both engineering and household use, while the latter is used exclusively on the Continent.

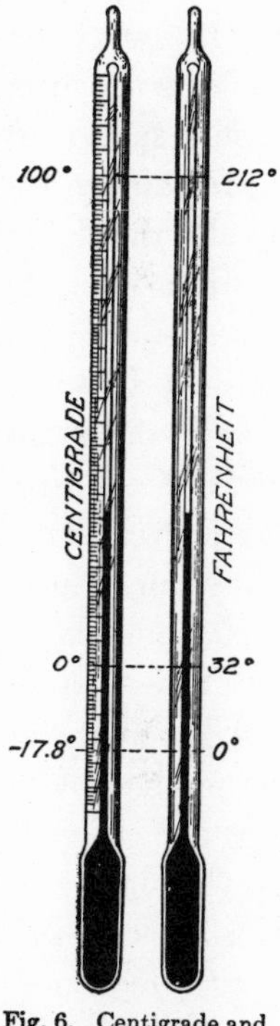

Freezing of water occurs at 32° F. (Fahrenheit) and boiling of water at 212° F. The scale between these two points is divided into 180 equal parts. On the Centigrade scale, the points of freezing and boiling occur, respectively, at 0° C. and 100° C., and there are, therefore, 100 equal divisions between the two points, Fig. 6. Thus it is seen that every 5 degrees Centigrade equal 9 degrees Fahrenheit.

Conversion of Scales. To convert readings in one scale to readings in the other, the reading given is substituted in the following equation:

$$\frac{°F - 32}{180} = \frac{°C.}{100}$$

Fig. 6. Centigrade and Fahrenheit Thermometers, Showing Comparison

Thus, if a temperature is given as −5° C. it is equal to 23° F ; 23° C. equals 73.4° F. Conversion tables over large ranges are given in engineering handbooks, such as Kent.

Absolute Zero. In engineering calculations the absolute zero and the absolute scale are sometimes spoken of. This absolute zero, which will be mentioned again, is taken as −270° on the Centigrade scale and −460.6° on the Fahrenheit scale. Thus −5° C. equals +265° on the C.-absolute scale and +483.6° on the F.-aboslute scale.

STEAM AUTOMOBILES

LAWS OF GASES

Almost all substances expand with rise of temperature. Solids expand least, and in some the expansion is imperceptible. Liquids expand about as much as solids, sometimes slightly more. Gases and vapors expand a great deal if free to do so.

Boyle's Law. Before considering the expansion of gases under changes in temperature, let us see how they act when the temperature is unchanged. A gas is perfectly elastic, that is, if not confined in any way it would expand indefinitely. The attraction of gravity is all that prevents the atmosphere surrounding the globe from dispersing into infinite space. When air is partly exhausted from a closed vessel, the remainder, no matter how small, expands so as to distribute itself equally throughout the vessel.

If a cubic foot of air at atmospheric pressure be compressed into one-half cubic foot without change in temperature, its pressure will be precisely twice what it was before. In speaking of gas pressures in this manner, it is customary to deal with absolute pressures, that is, pressures above a perfect vacuum. Thus atmospheric pressure at sea level is approximately 14.7 pounds per square inch, and a cubic foot of air reduced one-half in volume will have an absolute pressure of 29.4 pounds.

This relation of pressure and volume is expressed in "Boyle's Law", which states that, so long as the temperature is unchanged, the product of the pressure and volume of a given weight of gas is constant. That is

$$P V = C$$

This is the most important of all the laws of gases.

Curve Expressing Boyle's Law Relation. Fig. 7 expresses the relation between volume and pressure of a given weight of air starting at atmospheric pressure and compressed to a pressure of 500 pounds without change in temperature; also expanded to a pressure of one pound absolute. Horizontal distances represent volumes, the volume at atmospheric pressure being unity; and vertical distances represent absolute pressures. To find the pressure of the air for any volume greater or less than one, locate the given volume on the base line, then, from this point, read up to the curve and find the desired pressure by moving horizontally from the curve to the scale at the left.

STEAM AUTOMOBILES

Behavior of Gases with Changes of Temperature. As heat is a mode of motion, it follows that when all heat is withdrawn motion ceases, and the molecules, even of a gas, become fixed. From experiments and theoretical considerations the absolute zero, representing the absence of all heat, is believed to be $-273°$ C., or approximately $-460°$ F. In most theoretical studies of the behavior of gases, temperatures are reckoned from absolute zero instead of from the arbitrary zeroes of the conventional thermometer.

When a gas of given weight at an absolute temperature of 273 degrees—that is, 0° C. on the customary scale—is raised in temperature one degree without change in pressure, its volume is increased $\frac{1}{273}$. A second degree of added temperature increases its volume the same amount, and so on. In other words, for each degree Centigrade of added temperature its volume is increased $\frac{1}{273}$ of its volume at 273° A.

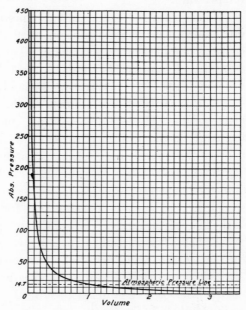

Fig. 7.   Curve Showing Relation between Volume and Pressure of Air

If degrees Fahrenheit are taken instead of Centigrade, the expansion is $\frac{1}{493}$ of the volume at 32° F. for each degree of rise in temperature. Five degrees C. equal nine degrees F.

If the gas thus heated is so confined that it cannot expand, it will suffer an increase in pressure in the same proportion, that is, $\frac{1}{273}$ of its pressure at 0° C. for each degree Centigrade. If the gas, instead of being heated, is cooled, its shrinkage in the one case or its loss of pressure in the other will follow the same rule as above. Theoretically it follows that at $-237°$ C.—absolute zero—the gas would have no volume at all. Of course that is impossible, but at ordinary temperatures the gases behave as if the assumption were true.

STEAM AUTOMOBILES

HEAT TRANSFORMATION

Specific Heat. The temperature of a body and the heat it contains are two different things. A gallon of water at 100° F. contains twice as much heat as half a gallon at the same temperature. That is to say, twice as much heat was imparted to it in raising it to that temperature.

Like quantities of different substances at the same temperature do not always contain the same quantity of heat. A pound of water contains more heat than a pound of oil or alcohol at the same temperature. It requires 7.7 times as much heat to raise a pound of water one degree in temperature as a pound of cast iron.

The quantity of heat required to change the temperature of a given weight of a substance one degree, compared with that required to change the temperature of the same weight of water a like amount, is called the "specific heat" of that substance.

Specific heat varies considerably for different substances, and for different temperatures and states of the same substance. Thus the specific heat of steam is much less than for water and varies slightly as the temperature and pressure of the steam is varied.

British Thermal Unit. The quantity of heat required to raise the temperature of one pound of water one degree F. is known as the "British thermal unit" (B.t.u.). Another unit is the "calorie", which is the quantity of heat required to raise the temperature of one kilogram (2.2046 lb.) of water one degree Centigrade. One calorie equals 3.968 B.t.u. The B.t.u. is the unit generally used in this country for engineering calculations. The latest investigations lead to slightly different and more complicated definitions of the B.t.u. from the one given above, but this is near enough for practical calculations.

Heat Value of Fuels. The number of heat units liberated by burning a pound of fuel varies for different fuels. The *heat value* for fuels is determined by experiment, and by calculation when the chemical composition is known. Due to the variation in the composition of commercial gasoline, different samples will give different results, but for most calculations the figure of 19,000 B.t.u. Kerosene has a slightly higher value.

Force. Force is defined as that which produces, or tends to produce, motion, and in practical work is usually expressed in units of weight, for example, pounds, kilograms, or tons. A force may exist without any resulting motion, and therefore without work being done. For example, the weight of any object represents the force of gravity attraction between the earth and that body. The atmosphere exerts a pressure or force of approximately 14.7 pounds per square inch at sea level.

Work. Work is done when force is exerted by or on a moving body, and is measured by the product of the force into the distance through which it is exerted. A convenient unit of work is the "footpound", which is the work done in lifting a weight of one pound against the force of gravitation a vertical distance of one foot, or exerting a force of one pound in any direction through a distance of one foot.

Power. Power expresses the rate at which work is done. If a foot-pound of work is performed in a minute, the power is small. If it is done in a second, the power is 60 times as great. The customary unit of power is the horsepower, which is 33,000 foot-pounds per minute. Whether a force of 33,000 pounds be exerted through one foot of distance, or one pound be exerted through 33,000 feet in the same time, the power is the same.

Mechanical Equivalent of Heat. Heat may be converted into work or work into heat. Experiments have been made in which water was agitated in a closed vessel by means of paddles run by falling weights and the resulting rise in temperature of the water carefully determined. From these and other experiments, it has been ascertained that one British thermal unit is the equivalent of 778 footpounds of work. That is, a weight of one pound falling 778 feet, or 778 pounds falling one foot, develops sufficient energy to raise one pound of water one degree F. in temperature. A horsepower, therefore, equals 42.416 B.t.u. per minute. The combustion of one pound of either gasoline or kerosene liberates approximately 19,900 B.t.u., but the kerosene is heavier for equal bulk. One U. S. gallon of gasoline weighs about 5.6 pounds; of kerosene, about 6.25 pounds. The combustion of a gallon of kerosene per hour develops theoretically about 49 horsepower but the actual amount of energy obtained falls far short of this. Owing to heat losses in the boiler and exhaust, and to radiation, etc., only a small fraction of this energy can be converted into useful work.

STEAM AUTOMOBILES

THERMODYNAMICS OF STEAM

Latent Heat. If water be heated in an open vessel it will reach a temperature of approximately 212° F. (100° C.) and will then boil away without further rise in temperature. The added heat is absorbed in converting the water into steam.

It takes far more heat to convert water into steam than to raise its temperature. A pound of water heated to boiling from 32° F. absorbs only 180 B.t.u., but in boiling away at 212° F. it absorbs 966 B.t.u. additional. At atmospheric pressure the volume of the steam is 1645 times the volume of the water whence it came. This bulk of steam must displace an equal bulk of air, and part of the heat energy represented by the steam has been spent in pushing back the air to give it room. This will be made clearer from the sketch, Fig. 8, showing a long tube open at the top and containing a little water at the bottom. On top of the water is a piston, supposed to be air-tight and without weight or friction. If the water be boiled into steam, the piston will be pushed upward against the atmospheric pressure a distance equal to 1645 times the original depth of the water. The work in foot-pounds thus done will be 14.7 times the area of the piston in square inches times the distance in feet through which it has moved. Approximately 7.45 per cent of the heat imparted to the steam represents work done against the atmosphere; the remainder is spent in overcoming the mutual attraction of the molecules of water. The heat which has been absorbed by the change in state from water to steam without change in temperature is called the "latent heat of vaporization".

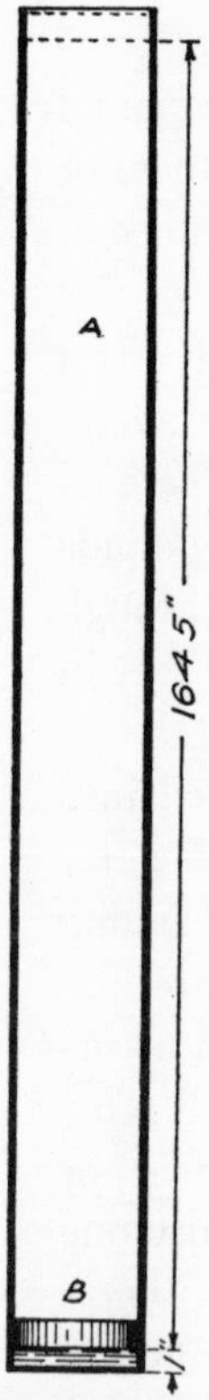

Fig. 8. Expansion of Water into Steam

If a vessel containing water at 212° F., which is the atmospheric boiling point, be put under the receiver of an air pump and the air partly exhausted, boiling will take place spontaneously without further addition of heat. At the same time the temperature of the water will decrease, because part of the heat contained in it has been absorbed by the conversion of water into vapor. If the air pump keeps on working, the water will boil continuously while its temperature steadily descends. If the experiment be carried far enough, with the vessel so supported that it can absorb little or no heat from adjacent objects, and if the vapor given off be rapidly absorbed, for example, by placing a tray of quick-lime or sulphuric acid adjacent, the water may actually be frozen by its own evaporation.

This experiment shows that the boiling point of water—and this includes other liquids also—is not a fixed temperature but depends on the pressure. All volatile liquids when exposed to partial or complete vacuum give off vapor; on the contrary, this vapor when subjected to pressure partly re-condenses and a higher temperature is needed to produce boiling. Under an absolute pressure of 147 pounds or 10 "atmospheres", the boiling point is 356.6° F. At 500 pounds absolute pressure the boiling point is 467.4° F. (242° C.).

The "total" heat of steam at the boiling point corresponding to a given pressure is the sum of its latent heat of vaporization and the heat contained at the same temperature in the water from which the steam was formed. The total heat of steam increases slowly, but the latent heat diminishes nearly in proportion as the boiling point rises. The space occupied by a given weight of steam diminishes approximately in proportion to the increase in pressure. In this respect the steam resembles a perfect gas without change of temperature in accordance with Boyle's Law. Tables showing the pressures, temperatures, latent heat, etc., of steam are given in Kent and other handbooks.

The experiment just cited of producing spontaneous boiling in water by exhausting the air above it, may be duplicated with hot water at any temperature and pressure. For example, the boiling point of water under 100 pounds absolute pressure is 327.6° F. If, in a boiler containing water at that temperature and pressure, the pressure be reduced to 50 pounds by the withdrawal of steam, the water will boil spontaneously, absorbing its own heat in doing so, until it reaches a temperature of 280.9° F., which is the boiling point for 50 pounds absolute pressure.

Cause of Boiler Explosions. Owing to the property of giving off steam under reduction of pressure, every steam boiler constitutes a reservoir of energy which may be drawn upon to carry the engine through a temporary period of overload. In other words, the boiler will give out steam faster than the fire generates steam, the difference being supplied from the heat stored in the water itself. This is an exceedingly useful feature of the ordinary steam boiler. At the same time, and for the same reason, it is a source of danger in case of rupture of the boiler shell. If a boiler explosion involved simply the release of the steam already formed it would not be so serious a matter; but when a seam starts to "go" the adjacent portions are unable to carry the abnormal strain put upon them, and the result is a rent of such proportions as to release almost instantly the entire contents of the boiler. The hot water thus suddenly liberated at high temperature bursts into steam until the whole mass drops to a temperature of 212 degrees, and this steam is many hundred times the volume of the water from which it came. It is to this fact that the violence of boiler explosions is due.

To take an extreme case, if a boiler bursts under 500 pounds pressure, approximately thirty-seven per cent of the water it contains will pass instantly into steam, and at atmospheric pressure the volume of the steam will be over 600 times the volume of the entire original liquid contents of the boiler.

Automobile boilers and steam generators are so designed as to minimize the danger of explosion, and only ordinary care is needed to insure entire safety.

Superheating. The foregoing paragraphs have dealt exclusively with steam at the boiling temperature due to its pressure. Such steam is called "saturated" steam. Steam will not suffer a reduction of temperature below this point; if heat be absorbed from it a portion will condense. On the other hand, steam isolated from the water whence it came may be raised in temperature indefinitely. It is then called "superheated" steam. The more it is superheated the more nearly does it act like a perfect gas.

Superheated steam is preferred for power purposes to saturated steam, for the reason that the latter condenses more or less, both in the pipes on its way to the engine and in the engine itself. Steam which condenses thus is a total loss, and it is more economical to add sufficient heat to it before it reaches the engine to replaces radiation losses, etc., without cooling the steam to the saturation point. To accomplish this in automobiles, the steam from the boiler is led through one or more pipes exposed to the maximum temperature of the fire. These pipes are called superheaters, or superheating pipes.

STEAM AUTOMOBILES

MECHANICAL ELEMENTS OF THE STEAM ENGINE

General Details of Steam Engine Parts. In Fig. 9 a plan view
of a stationary steam engine is given, with the cylinder and valve
chest shown in cross section, and with the various parts marked by
letters. A view of a stationary engine is used because it is not so
condensed as an automobile engine, and the parts are therefore
easier to mark and pick out. The relations and names of parts are
the same in an automobile engine.

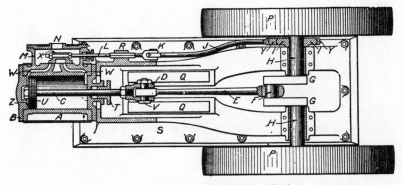

Fig. 9. Plan View of Typical Stationary Engine

A, Cylinder. *B*, Outer cylinder head. *C*, Piston rod. *D*, Crosshead. *E*, Connecting rod.
F, Crankpin. *G*, Crank. *H*, Crankshaft. *I*, Eccentric. *J*, Eccentric rod. *K*, Eccentric
crosshead. *L*, Valve stem. *M*, Steam chest. *N*, Steam pipe connection. *PP*, Flywheels.
Q, Crosshead guides. *R*, Valve stem guide. *S*, Engine frame. *T*, Stuffing box. *U*, Piston.
V, Wristpin. *WW*, Steam ports. *X*, Slide valve. *Y*, Eccentric strap. *Z*, Clearance space
between piston and cylinder head at end of stroke.

A is the cylinder to which steam is admitted through the passages, or ports, *WW*, which connect it with the steam chest *M*. The
opening and closing of these ports is accomplished by the movement
of the valve *X*. Because of its shape, the valve here shown is called
a **D**-slide valve. Other types of valves are piston valves and poppet
valves, names which explain themselves. The valve is attached to
the valve stem *L* and is guided by the valve-stem guide *R*. Motion
back and forth is given the valve by the eccentric *I*, which is a circular disk on the crankshaft, with its center offset from the center of
crankshaft *H*.

Returning to the cylinder, *U* is the piston, which is driven back
and forth by the steam. Connected to the piston is the piston rod *C*,

which passes through the gland, or stuffing box *T*. This gland is for the purpose of holding the packing which prevents the escape of steam around the piston rod. The end of the rod, or crosshead *D* slides back and forth in the crosshead guides *Q Q*. To the crosshead is attached the connecting rod *E*, by means of the wristpin *V*. In the lower end of the connecting rod is the crankpin *F*.

In steam automobile engines the flywheels *P P* are usually not needed and are consequently omitted. The rim of the gear wheel, when the engine is geared directly to the rear axle, has a slight flywheel action.

SLIDE VALVE

The leading mechanical elements of the steam engine have been briefly described. It remains now to show the precise manner in which the steam is used.

Elementary Slide Valve. Fig. 10 represents an elementary slide valve. In order to indicate the movements of the crankpin and the valve eccentric on one drawing, the crankshaft center is located at

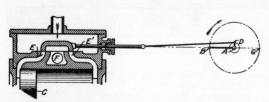

Fig. 10. Elementary Slide Valve—Valve in Mid-Position

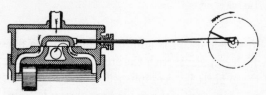

Fig. 11. Elementary Slide Valve—Inlet and Exhaust Ports
Partly Uncovered

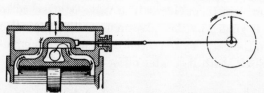

Fig. 12. Elementary Slide Valve—Inlet and Exhaust Ports
Fully Opened—Piston in Mid-Position

A. *B* represents the crankpin center with the piston *C* at the inner end of its stroke. The larger dotted circle is the crankpin circle, and the small circle is that in which the center *D* of the eccentric moves. With the crankpin traveling as the arrow shows, the valve is in mid-position when the piston starts to move, and the first effect of its movement is to uncover the steam port *E*, at the same time establishing com-

STEAM AUTOMOBILES

munication between port E' and exhaust port F, Fig. 11. At half-piston stroke the ports are wide open and the valve starts to return, Fig. 12. When the crankpin reaches the outer dead center G the ports are again closed.

Use of Steam Cut=Off. A steam engine with valve arranged as above would take steam through the entire stroke, and would exhaust at boiler pressure. It would develop the maximum power of which it was capable at that pressure, but no use would have been made of

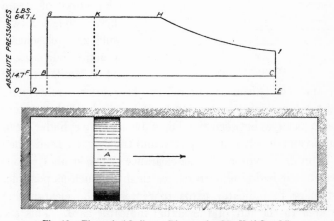

Fig. 13.   Theoretical Indicator Diagram for One-Half Cut-Off

the expansion force of the steam. For this reason, all practical steam engines are made to admit steam only for the first portion of the stroke, that is, about one-half stroke or less, the remainder of the stroke being devoted to expansion. In Fig. 13, suppose A represents the position of a piston moving from left to right. The horizontal distance $B C$ represents the stroke, and vertical distances represent steam pressures. $D E$ is the line of zero pressure, and $F C$ that of atmospheric pressure. Suppose steam is admitted at 50 pounds gage pressure during the first half of the stroke from G to H; the steam port then closes and the steam expands with diminishing pressure along the curve $H I$. Since work is the product of force into distance traveled, it follows that for each fraction, such as $B J$ of the piston travel, the included area $B G K J$ will represent the work done during that portion of the stroke, and the area of the entire card $B G H I C$ will represent the work done during the whole stroke.

In the case under consideration, the area of the whole diagram is
84.4 per cent of that which would have been produced if the steam
had entered during the entire stroke, yet only half as much steam
is used.

Indicator Diagrams. A diagram such as Fig. 13 is called the
"indicator diagram" or "indicator card", and is employed to study

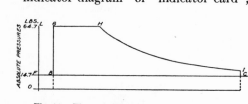

the internal action of
the engine. The expan-
sion curve of steam fol-
lows Boyle's Law with
sufficient closeness for
practical purposes. Fig.
14 is similar to Fig. 13

Fig. 14.   Theoretical Indicator Diagram for One-
Quarter Cut-Off

except that the steam is cut off at one-quarter stroke, point *H*.

In the foregoing, no mention has been made of the contents of
the steam passages between the slide valve and the cylinder, or of the
clearance volume between the piston and the cylinder head when the
crank is on dead center. These clearance spaces cannot wholly be
avoided, but it is desirable to reduce them as much as possible. It
is customary in indicator cards to represent the clearance space
by an area to the left of the actual indicator card. This area is
F L G B in Fig. 13 and Fig. 14. Its volume averages about 5 per
cent of the volume swept by the piston. Owing to the necessity

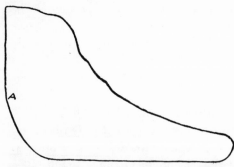

of taking the steam in
the clearance space into
account, the actual steam
consumption in Fig. 14 is
a trifle more than half
that in Fig. 13.

**Effect of Compres=
sion on Indicator Card.**
The objectionable influ-
ence of the clearance

Fig. 15.   Actual Indicator Card, Showing Compression

may be neutralized by
closing the exhaust port

before the piston has finished its return stroke, thereby trapping
the remaining steam at atmospheric pressure and compressing it to
boiler pressure. If this is done, none of the entering steam is wasted

merely in filling the clearance space. Fig. 15 shows the effect of compression on an actual indicator card. It is not carried to boiler pressure, but only to point *A*.

Another reason for using compression is to cushion the reciprocating parts at the end of their stroke and prevent the shock which may otherwise occur on suddenly admitting live steam.

Effect of High Pressure and Early Cut=Off. As Fig. 14 shows, no great advantage is gained when working with steam at 50 pounds by cutting off earlier than one-third stroke. If higher pressure is used, however, the cut-off can be considerably shortened. Fig 16 is a theoretical indicator diagram for 200 pounds gage pressure (214.7 absolute). The clearance is 5 per cent of the piston displacement, and cut-off occurs at one-tenth stroke. The weight of steam per stroke is about the same as in Fig. 14, but the work done by the higher pressure is nearly two-thirds greater. This shows strikingly the economic advantage of using high pressure, provided the cut-off is shortened to correspond.

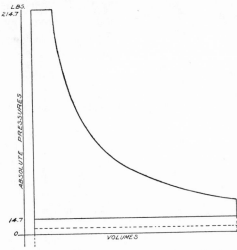

Fig. 16. Theoretical Indicator Card for One-Tenth Cut-Off

Effect of Adding Steam Lap. To produce a short cut-off, what is known as outside lap or steam lap is added to the edges of the slide valve *A A*, Fig. 17. To produce compression inside exhaust lap *B B* is also added. Figs. 18 and 19 show how the valve mechanism is affected by these changes. In

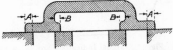

Fig. 17. Section of Slide Valve, Showing Steam and Exhaust Laps

Fig. 18 the piston is about to begin its stroke, but the valve is no longer in mid-position. Instead, the eccentric has had to be advanced through an angle, known as the "angle of advance", in order to open the port as the piston starts to move. The necessary travel is also increased in order to accomplish the idle movement when all ports are closed. As the diagrams show, the valve reaches the end of its movement, returns, and closes the steam port while the piston is in the first quarter of its movement. It then continues to move, but with only the exhaust open.

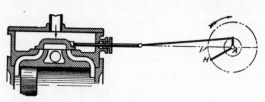

Fig. 18. Elementary Slide Valve, Showing Effect of Adding Laps

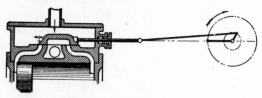

Fig. 19. Elementary Slide Valve, Showing Adjustment of Lead

It is customary, as Fig. 19 shows, to open the steam port a trifle before the piston begins its stroke in order to avoid wire drawing of the steam before the port goes fairly open. If this were not done, there would be an appreciable drop in pressure at the beginning of the stroke. The amount of this premature opening of the valve is called its "lead".

SUPERHEATED STEAM AND COMPOUND EXPANSION

Superheating to Avoid Cylinder Condensation. When steam expands its temperature drops by reason of expansion, causing the cylinder walls to assume an average temperature which slightly increases from contact with the hot steam and slightly diminishes at the end of every stroke. The hot entering steam condenses on the walls, and re-evaporates near the end of the stroke. This is very undesirable, and is avoided by superheating the steam sufficiently to compensate for the initial loss of heat to the walls. In addition, heat loss by radiation is minimized by lagging the cylinder walls and heads with asbestos, magnesia, or other non-conducting coverings.

When steam is used at pressures above 100 pounds, compound engines are preferable, although not always used.

Compound Engines. In a compound engine the work done by expansion is divided as nearly equal as practicable between two

STEAM AUTOMOBILES

cylinders, called respectively the high-pressure and the low-pressure cylinder. The high-pressure cylinder is the smaller in diameter, and it exhausts into the low-pressure cylinder instead of into the atmosphere. In the diagram, Fig. 20, showing the elements of a compound engine, the steam is being transferred from the high-pressure cylinder to the low-pressure cylinder. The steam expands by reason of the difference in the areas of the two pistons.

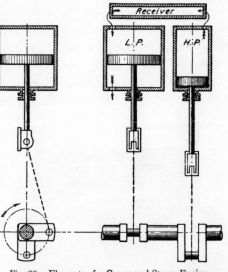

A compound engine may be considered as though the steam were expanded wholly in the low-pressure cylinder, and the indicator diagrams of the two cylinders may be combined to show the total work done, by shortening the horizontal distances of

Fig. 20.   Elements of a Compound Steam Engine

the high-pressure card in proportion to its smaller piston area.

Comparison of Indicator Diagrams for Stationary and Automobile Engines. Fig. 21 is a combined diagram from the high- and low-pressure cylinders of a stationary compound engine. Both cards are drawn to the same scale as regards stroke, but the low-pressure card reads from right to left. F is the point of admission to the high-pressure cylinder. The slight peak at A is due to the inertia of the in-rushing steam. At B the admission valve closes. At C the steam is released and goes into the receiver between the cylinders. DE is the

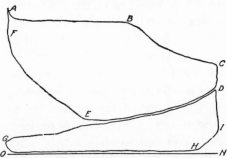

Fig. 21.   Indicator Diagram of a Stationary Compound Steam Engine

exhaust line, and $E\,F$ the compression line.. From D to E steam passes from the high- to the low-pressure cylinder, the difference between the two lines being due to frictional resistance of the passages. At G the exhaust valve opens. $H\,I$ is the compression line of the low-pressure cylinder.

Use of Condensers. In the foregoing paragraphs steam is supposed to be exhausted at atmospheric pressure. In other words, the steam in the working end of the cylinder must overcome a back pressure of 14.7 pounds per square inch in the exhaust end. If the exhaust steam were discharged into a closed vessel and condensed, a vacuum would be formed containing only water vapor at a pressure

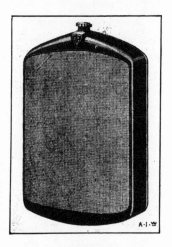

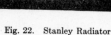
Fig. 22. Stanley Radiator

Fig. 23. Doble Radiator

proportionate to its temperature. This would mean the addition of 5, 10, or even 12 pounds to the height of the indicator card without having to increase the heat units put into the steam. To do this requires considerable apparatus—condenser, vacuum pump, etc., all of which it has been found inadvisable to install on an automobile.

Condensers on steam cars are not for the purpose of increasing the total expansion by dropping below atmospheric pressure, but to condense the water at atmospheric pressure so as to be able to use it again and avoid having to fill the water tank so often.

As shown in Figs. 22 and 23, both the Stanley and the Doble use condensers of the same general construction and appearance as

STEAM AUTOMOBILES

the radiators used on the ordinary gasoline car. The exhaust steam from the engine enters at the top of the radiator and is forced downward by the steam which is following. As it passes down the radiator, the air going through the spaces between the water passages cools it, until, by the time it reaches the bottom, it has been condensed into water.

VALVE GEARS

Throttling and Reversing. Steam engines are regulated partly by the cut-off and partly by throttling. As has been pointed out above, it is impracticable to use a cut-off so short as to expand the steam to, or below, exhaust pressure. Beyond this point reduction of power must be had by throttling the steam on its way to the engine. The shortening of the cut-off, and the complete throwing over of the valve timing to the other side of the dead center to reverse the engine, may be accomplished by shifting the angular position of the eccentric on the crankshaft or by the use of one of several valve gears or linkages.

Types of Gears. Up to the last few years the most common gear was the "Stephenson Link", developed by Robert Stephenson and Company, in 1842. In locomotive work the Stephenson gear has been largely displaced by the Walschaert gear. Practically all the earlier steam automobiles used the Stephenson, but later some changed to the "Joy Gear", which is one of a number of radial gears employing linkages without the use of eccentrics.

Stephenson Link. The Stephenson link is shown in Fig. 24. It consists of two eccentrics A on the crankshaft—one for the forward motion and the other for the reverse. The two eccentric rods are pinned to the link B, in which there is a curved slot. In the slot is carried the block C, which is a sliding fit and is pinned to the valve stem.

By means of the hanger rod D and the reverse lever arm E, the link is moved up and down, so that the slide is in different positions from the center of the slot. When the block is on one side of the link center it partakes of the motion of one of the eccentrics, and when on the other side of the motion of the other eccentric. Thus the valve timing is changed from the forward running position to the reverse by changing the position of the block in the curved slot.

STEAM AUTOMOBILES

It is a feature of the Stephenson link motion that by rocking the link toward (but not to) its mid-position the valve travel and cut-off are shortened, and this feature is utilized to improve economy. At the same time the lead is increased, that is, steam is admitted before the piston begins its new stroke. This is not a disadvantage

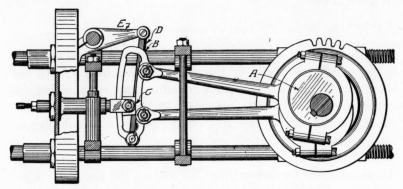

Fig. 24. Stephenson Link Motion Used on Stanley Steam Cars

at high speeds, as the fresh steam has a cushion effect on the reciprocating parts. At low speeds, however, the engine runs jerkily, and consequently the cut-off is shortened only at medium to high speeds.

Joy Gear. The Joy gear is a well known English development, which is used on a number of steam automobiles. Its operation may

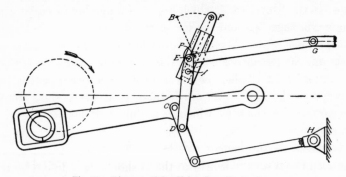

Fig. 25. Diagram of Joy Valve-Gear Mechanism

be understood by referring to Fig. 25. A link is pinned at one end to the engine at *H* and at the other end to a link, which in turn is pinned to the connecting rod at *C*. To this second link is pinned the link

D E, to the upper end of which is attached the rod *E G*, which moves the valve. At *A* on *D E* is pivoted the block *A*, which slides in the slotted guide, the guide being slightly concave on the side toward the valve. This guide is pinned to the engine frame at its center point *P*. In the position of the guide, as shown, the valve is in full gear for forward running, but if the guide is swung about the point *P*, by means of a connection at *F*, until it is in the position *B F*, the engine will then be in full reverse.

As with the Stephenson, the moving of the Joy toward the half-way point shortens the cut-off. This gear has an advantage over the Stephenson in that the lead is not increased and the distribution of steam to the two ends of the cylinder on short cut-off is more nearly equal. The Joy gear also gives a rapid opening and closing to the valve.

ENGINE TYPES AND DETAILS

Although makers have their individual preferences in engine types as regards the placing of the cylinders, compounding, and other features, the practice of using two cylinders has become almost universal.

Stanley. An example of the two-cylinder type is the Stanley engine, which, in the present models, is made in three sizes of the following bore and stroke: $3\frac{1}{4}$ by $4\frac{1}{4}$, 4 by 5, and $4\frac{1}{2}$ by $6\frac{1}{2}$ inches. This engine is geared directly to the rear axle by a spur gear mounted on the crankshaft, as shown in Fig. 26, and the frame rods are attached radially from the axle housing. The cylinder end is attached to the frame of the car. The rear-axle gear ratio in the small light runabout model is 30 to 56, and in the heavy delivery car is 40 to 80. With a gear ratio of 40 to 60 in one of the touring cars the engine turns over at 447 r.p.m. when the car is running 30 miles per hour.

Both cylinders take high-pressure steam at both ends, the engine being of the double-acting, simple type. The steam chest, Fig. 27, lies between the two cylinders, with the D-slide valves driven by the eccentrics lying next to the drive-shaft gear. In Fig. 26 is shown the Stephenson link by which the cut-off is hooked up and the reversing of the engine accomplished. This valve gear has been described in detail on page 23. The cross shaft, working the link, and the hook, for holding it in the normal position, are shown just to the left of *A*.

STEAM AUTOMOBILES

The hooking up is done by the left pedal, which can be released by a pedal beside it called the clutch pedal.

Roller and ball bearings are used extensively in the Stanley motor. The crosshead bears on a plain crosshead guide, and the

Fig. 26. Stanley Two-Cylinder Steam Engine, Showing Link Motion and Balanced Shaft

connecting-rod and eccentric-strap bearings are of the ball type. The counterweights are also shown in Fig. 26.

Lubrication of the outside parts is effected by enclosing the gears, crankshaft, and other parts in a sheet-metal case, which is kept about half full of moderately thin mineral oil. The lubrication of the cylinder walls is accomplished by feeding the oil into the steam line, and the special superheated steam-cylinder oil recommended is given fully in a later section.

The Stanley power pumps for water, fuel, and oil, shown in Fig. 46, are driven from the rear axle.

Doble. The Doble engine, shown in full length section in Fig. 28, is made up of two cylinders of the same size. It is of the simple-expansion double-acting type, and the interesting feature is that the

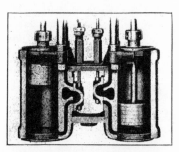

Fig. 27. Cylinder Construction of Stanley Steam Engine, Showing Steam Chest in Center

uni-flow principle is employed. The cylinder bore is 5 inches and the stroke is 4 inches.

On top of the cylinders are the valve chests. Each valve is made up in two pieces so that it may lift when the compression pressure exceeds the steam pressure, as sometimes happens in slow running. This construction allows the use of high compression, which is desired at the higher speeds. The gear used to control the valve motion is a modification and simplification of the Joy gear, Fig. 25. In the Doble gear the connecting and anchor links are done away with, and a straight rocker guide is employed. In starting, the cut-off is five-eighths stroke, and this same position is used for heavy pulling. For ordinary running, one-fifth stroke cut-off is used, while for economy and high speed it is reduced to one-eighth stroke.

By the uni-flow principle is meant that the steam moves in but one direction within the cylinder. It enters through the inlet passage at the extreme end of the cylinder, expands against the piston head, and passes out of the exhaust ports, which are uncovered by the piston a little before it reaches the end of the stroke. It is claimed for this system that the thermal conditions are so good that the use of superheated steam, with its attendant troubles, is unnecessary.

Aluminum is employed for the crankcase, with large cover plates, top and bottom, for easy access to the

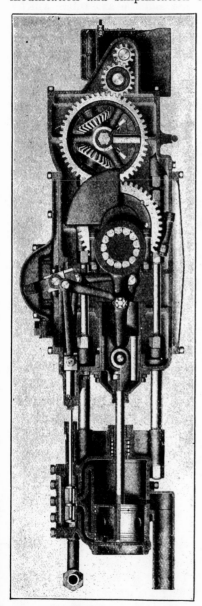

Fig. 28. Section of Doble Engine
Courtesy of General Engineering Company, Detroit, Michigan

moving parts. The accessibility of the valve gear is very well shown in Fig. 29. The case, which has its cover removed, contains all the moving parts of the engine with the exception of the valves and pistons; and, since the case and the axle tubes, which are bolted to it, are oil-tight, all these parts are kept in a bath of

Fig. 29. Rear Portion of Doble Chassis, Showing Easy Access to Moving Parts
Courtesy of General Engineering Company, Detroit, Michigan

Fig. 30. Piston and Crosshead Guide of Doble Engine

oil. This oil keeps comparatively cool and as there is no combustion, it does not deteriorate as in the gasoline car.

A special design of long cast-iron gland is used for the piston rod at the cylinder, and there is a stuffing box where the rod passes into the crankcase. The crosshead guide is part of a cylinder, as shown in Fig. 30, giving a large bearing surface. Annular roller bearings are used for the big end of the connecting rod, for the crankshaft, and for the differential. Hardened steel, running in hardened steel bushings, is used for all the other bearings.

Being geared at practically a 1 to 1 ratio to the axle shafts, the engine always runs at comparatively slow speed. A 47-tooth pinion is carried on the engine crankshaft and to this is fastened the counterbalance. This gear meshes with one of 49 teeth on the differential spider. The dif-

Fig. 31.   Top View of National Power Plant for London Steam Omnibuses
Courtesy of Society of Automobile Engineers, New York City

Fig. 32.   Separate Engine and Dynamo for Lighting National Busses
Courtesy of Society of Automobile Engineers, New York City

ferential is of the three-pinion bevel-gear type. Meshing with the axle gear is an idler, and then a gear on the electric generator, which furnishes current for the combustion system and the lights.

National.   In the National steam omnibuses of London, England, the engines are placed under the floor boards, Fig. 31, and, unlike any of the American engines, the two cylinders lie across the chassis. The drive is taken by a shaft to worm gearing at the rear axle. These engines have a Joy gear, and the pumps for the water and kerosene are driven from a cross shaft, which in turn is driven by a worm gear off the extension of the crankshaft, as is shown in the illustration. An interesting feature of the National chassis is the use of an entirely separate steam engine for driving the electric-lighting generator, which supplies the large number of lights used inside the busses. This auxiliary engine is shown in Fig. 32.

From what has been said it must not be supposed that all automobile steam engines use two-cylinder engines with either **D** or piston valves. The Pearson-Cox steam truck of England has a three-cylinder vertical engine with poppet valves in chambers at each side of the cylinders, and the whole engine looks very much like a vertical poppet-valve gasoline motor.

A number of very heavy English trucks, or "lorries" as they call them, are driven by steam, and are very popular in England. These carry from 3 to 10 tons, and the boilers and parts of some of them are very large.

FUELS AND BURNERS

Gasoline and Kerosene as Fuels. Energy for driving steam engines is derived, of course, from the fuel burning and forming steam from the water, the steam in turn doing mechanical work by its expansion in the engine. In an automobile it is of prime importance that the fuel be as easily handled, carried, and purchased as possible. Of the commercial fuels, gasoline and kerosene come the nearest to these ideals and are, therefore, the most popular. Kerosene is less expensive than gasoline, but does not vaporize at as low a temperature while, as a rule burners are specially designed for kerosene, many modern burners will handle either of these fuels or a mixture of them.

To burn either of these fuels the vapor must be mixed with air, which supplies the necessary oxygen for combustion. Either of these vapors, if mixed with the right amount of air, is highly inflammable and explosive, and therefore, care must be taken in storing and in filling the fuel tank, not to have open lights about—not even lighted cigars.

STEAM AUTOMOBILES

Burner Principles. *Bunsen Burner.* The purpose of the burner is first to vaporize the liquid fuel by heating it and then to mix it with enough air to produce the hottest possible flame under the boiler. In principle the burner is the same as the ordinary Bunsen burner, Fig. 33, in which the gas passes under moderate pressure through the small opening *b*. In going up the tube *a* it draws in a certain amount of air through the openings *o*, the fuel gas and air becoming well mixed in the tube before reaching the flame. In case either too much or too little air is mixed with the gas, the flame will run back through the tube *a*, and will burn at *o*. This is called "popping back", and not only takes away the effect of the flame but will ruin the burner if allowed to continue in operation in this way.

Modifications for Automobile Work. In automobile work the burner is somewhat modified in order to act over a large area and to give a flame of more intense heat. For the purpose of feeding more gas, and to mix it more quickly with the air, the fuel is fed under considerable pressure.

The correct mixture of air and fuel gas gives a blue flame, just slightly tinged with orange at the top, and burning rather close

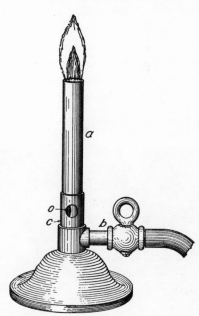

Fig. 33. Typical Bunsen Burner

to the burner. If too much air is given the mixture, the flame will start a considerable distance above the burner and will be very blue. The excess air tends to cool the flame. Too little air is equally bad, for the combustion will then be incomplete and, since gasoline and kerosene are hydrocarbons, soot will be deposited on the surfaces above the flame. Such a flame is indicated by a yellow color. As in the ordinary Bunsen burner, poor mixtures are apt to pop back. When this happens the operator must turn off the burner and relight it. The popping back is indicated by a roaring sound.

STEAM AUTOMOBILES

Pilot Light. As the demand for steam is not constant in an automobile, it is desirable to have the main burner come on and off automatically. In order to light the main burner whenever it may come on, a small light is kept burning continuously while the car is in use, whether running or standing still. It is even the practice of some owners to keep this pilot light, as it is called, lighted over night. Besides relighting the main burner when the car is running, the pilot is lighted first when firing up a cold boiler. The burning of the pilot serves to heat the vaporizer of the main burner as well as to light the main fire. The handling of the pilot in firing up will be taken up later.

Due to its easier vaporization, gasoline is always used for the pilot-light fuel even when kerosene is used for the main burner. It is also quite general to have the two fuel systems separate, although both may be using gasoline. In starting up a cold system the pilot vaporizer must be heated by some outside means. This is done in several ways: one is to use a separate gasoline torch; another is to use an acetylene torch instead of a gasoline torch; and a third method is to light a little pool of gasoline below the vaporizer, similar to the method used in many gasoline cook stoves and plumbers' torches.

Fig. 34.   Stanley Burner, Showing Vaporizer and Mixing Tubes
Courtesy of Stanley Motor Carriage Company, Newton, Massachusetts

Types of Burners. Different makers, of course use somewhat different constructions for their burners, but in all cases the fuel gas is vaporized by heat and mixed in a burner of the Bunsen type. As a fair example of all the burners, that of the Stanley will be described in detail, while short descriptions will also be given of other makes.

Stanley. Either gasoline, kerosene, or a mixture of the two can be burned in the Stanley main burner. The burner, Fig. 34, consists of a corrugated casting with a large number of slots cut across the peaks of each parallel corrugation. Vaporization of the fuel takes place in the two coiled tubes *A A* which lie directly over the fire. From the vaporizing tubes the gas flows at high velocity through the nozzles *B B* into the mixing tubes *C C* drawing with it the air necessary for good combustion. The mixing tubes lead under the burner, and combustible gas issues through the fine slots, where it burns with an intensely hot blue flame tipped with orange. No air currents are present to blow or cool the flame, for the burner casting excludes all air except that drawn in and mixed with the gas through the tubes *C C*. To adjust the amount of air to give the correct color to the flame, bend the nozzles closer to the opening of the mixing tube for less air, and *vice versa*.

Between the two main-burner vaporizer tubes is located the pilot light, which is a small independent casting. The pilot burns gasoline, supplied from a separate tank, irrespective of whether the main burner uses gasoline or kerosene. Due to the position of the pilot, it keeps the main-burner vaporizer warm when the main burner is shut off by either the automatic or hand valve controlling it. When the main burner is turned on, the pilot flame ignites the gas. Since the pilot is independent of the main-burner valves, it remains lighted until turned off by its own hand-operated valve. The heat from the pilot is sufficient to hold steam in the boiler for several hours after the car is stopped and the main burner shut off.

In starting up the pilot of the Stanley when cold, an acetylene torch is played on the pilot vaporizer to vaporize the first gasoline, after which the heat from the pilot light itself keeps the pilot vaporizer warm. The acetylene is carried in a "Prest-O-Lite" tank and turned on by a valve at the tank. The torch lights by simply applying a match, and should be played on the pilot vaporizer until it is sizzling hot, which takes between 15 and 30 seconds. The torch is then moved so that the flame enters the peek-hole, lighting the pilot, after which the torch is played upon the upper part of the vaporizer for 15 to 30 seconds, until the main burner nozzles are sizzling hot.

After closing the acetylene-tank valve the main-burner valve is opened and closed quickly several times until the gas from the main nozzles is dry. It is then left open, being lighted by the pilot flame. The pilot nozzle is provided with a wire which is filed off on one side to allow the passage of the gas. If the pilot light does not seem to burn strongly, it can be cleaned while burning by turning the outside screw back and forth with a screwdriver. If this does not suffice, the wire should be taken out and cleaned; it is good practice to do this every day before firing up. The color of the flame can be adjusted by bending the nozzle tube to bring the nozzle in or out from the mixing tube, the same as is done in adjusting the main burner.

In the older models of Stanley cars, which used only gasoline as the main-burner fuel, the pilot fuel system was a branch of the main system, and the pilot vaporizer was heated by a gasoline torch.

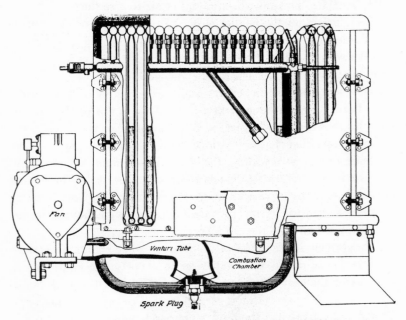

Fig. 35.   Section through Combustion Chamber and Boiler of Doble Car
Courtesy of General Engineering Company, Detroit, Michigan

Doble. Very radical departures from the long-established Bunsen type of burner have been made in the combustion system on the new Doble car. The fuel is ignited by electricity and there is no pilot light. Kerosene is used for both starting and running and is fed from the main fuel tank to a float chamber by an air pressure of three pounds per square inch. From the float chamber, which is of the standard gasoline-carbureter type, the fuel passes through a spray nozzle, which is located in the throat of a Venturi tube leading to the combustion chamber.

STEAM AUTOMOBILES

Air for the support of the combustion of the fuel is drawn through the radiator by means of a multiple-vane fan driven by a small electric motor. It passes the jet with sufficient velocity to draw out the fuel and atomize it. Owing to the enlarging of the passage directly beyond the throat, the velocity is decreased in order to give time for the complete combustion of the gas by the electric spark, which takes place at this point.

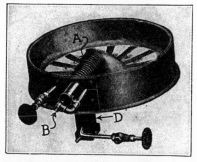

The combustion chamber, Fig. 35, is completely closed and lined with a highly refractory material. As soon as the combustion has been started, the electric spark is automatically shut off, and the burning of the gas is continuous until it is

Fig. 36. Ofeldt Blue Flame Kerosene Burner
*Courtesy of F. W. Ofeldt and Sons,
Nyack-on-the-Hudson, New York*

stopped by the action of the automatic steam control, as described later. The lining of the chamber not only has the property of resisting high heats, but it holds and gives back the heat so as to assist in completely burning the gases. The combustion chamber is also well illustrated in Fig. 41, page 40.

Ofeldt. The Ofeldt burner, Fig. 36, is designed especially for the use of kerosene as a fuel. Forming the foundation of the burner is

Fig. 37. Kerosene Burner, Used on National Busses with Starter
Courtesy of Society of Automobile Engineers, New York City

a galvanized iron pan, lined around the sides with millboard asbestos. In the bottom of the pan are drilled rows of small holes. Since these holes are in straight lines under the burner pieces, and of equal size, they admit even amounts of air throughout the lengths of the burner pieces.

Cast iron is used for the burner pieces, which radiate from a central gas-distributing chamber, into which they are screwed. The gas flows through fine slots cut in the burner pieces. Surrounding the mixing tube is the main vaporizer A, which passes through the outside of the pan, ending in the nozzle B at the opening of the mixing tube. The mixing tube is a part of the central gas-distributing chamber.

Attached below the burner pan is the pilot D, where its flame heats both the main and the pilot vaporizers and the mixing tube. By means of a hand valve the pilot flame can be adjusted to keep up steam when the main burner is out, or it can be turned down so as to keep only the main vaporizer warm.

Fig. 38. Stanley Fire-Tube Boiler

A comparatively low pressure is used on the Ofeldt system, the fuel being kept under about 60 pounds per square inch.

National. Kerosene is used as the fuel in the National busses. These burners are quite different in appearance from those described above, as is shown in Fig. 37.

AUTOMOBILE BOILERS

Classification. In stationary steam-power plants there are two distinct classes of boilers, the fire-tube and the water-tube. These two types are also used in automobile work, together with a third type, the flash boiler, which is a development of the water-tube type.

Fire-Tube Boilers. In principle the fire-tube boiler is like a big tea-kettle filled with vertical tubes, which run from the bottom to the top for the purpose of carrying up the flame and hot gases. This construction gives a very large surface on one side of which are water and steam and on the other flame and hot gases.

Stanley. One of the simplest of the fire-tube boilers is the Stanley, Fig. 38. This is made up of a pressed-steel shell, which includes the lower head, the upper head being a separate piece.

STEAM AUTOMOBILES

Between these two heads run a large number of tubes of $\frac{33}{44}$ inch outside diameter, which are expanded into the heads by a taper expanding tool. Stanley boilers are made in three sizes, 20, 23, and 26 inches in diameter and 14 and 16 inches in height, respectively. The number of tubes is 550, 751, and 999, giving 77, 104, and 158 square feet of heating surfaces. To keep down the radiation losses, the boiler shell is lagged with asbestos, and the strength of the shell is greatly increased by winding it with steel piano wire.

To keep a reserve of steam, and to have the steam free from particles of water, the boiler is kept only about two-thirds full of water, the upper space being filled with steam. To further insure dry steam at the engine the steam is led by a pipe from the top of the boiler down to a superheating coil directly over the burner.

Fusible Plug. As a warning against too low water the side of the boiler is provided with a fusible plug, held in a fusible-plug tube which, in turn, screws into a steel fitting. The elbows on this fitting are made on a taper and are driven into two short tubes in the boiler. As long as the water level is above these tubes the circulation prevents the plug from melting. If the water gets below the plug and about 3 inches from the bottom of the boiler, the plug will melt and the noise of the escaping steam will warn the operator of the danger—not danger of an explosion of the boiler, but danger of doing the boiler damage by heating it without water. There are other means by which the operator may know that the water is getting low before it gets low enough to blow out the plug, and these will be taken up in detail later, together with the causes of unexpected low water and other points.

The fusible plug may melt out, not only from low water but also because of dirt or something retarding the circulation of water around the tubes or fittings. The blowing off of the steam will usually remove the obstruction. If the escaping steam is dry, it is a sign that the melting has been caused by low water, but if it is wet the trouble is due to faulty circulation. It is good practice to replace the fusible plug once every two or three weeks, doing this when the boiler is cold.

Since the addition of the condenser to the Stanley in 1915, these boilers have been made without the fusible plugs. Among other improvements in these boilers is the brazing, or welding, of the tubes in the lower heads. This is to prevent any trouble from oil, which might be carried over into the condensing system. Before the boilers are turned out from the factory, they are tested by a water pressure of from 1500 to 1800 pounds per square inch.

Water=Tube Boilers. Water-tube boilers also are made up of tubes, but in this case the tubes carry the water and steam *inside* and the fire and hot gases pass over the tubes. The metal hood over this type of boiler carries no pressure, but merely serves to keep in and direct the hot gases. In stationary practice the tubes are often straight or only slightly bent, but to economize space the automobile boiler has the tubes coiled to give the most surface to the fire in the least possible space.

Fig. 39. Ofeldt Safety Water-Tube Boiler

Ofeldt. The Ofeldt safety water-tube boiler, Fig. 39, is built about a central standpipe of 5 inches or more in diameter, with a bottom of $\frac{1}{2}$-inch metal welded in. Threaded into the upper end of the standpipe is a steel cap with three arms, to the ends of which the sheet-metal hood, or cover, is fastened.

The object of the standpipe is to hold a reserve of water at the bottom and of steam at the top, and to distribute the water to the coils. In the coils and standpipe the reserve of water varies from 3 gallons in the small sizes to 8 gallons in the 24-inch size.

Water is fed to the bottom of the standpipe, from where it flows into the coils. As it passes up the coils it turns into steam. A pipe from the center of the standpipe carries the steam down to the superheater, which lies under the boiler directly over the burner, as shown in Fig. 39. From the superheater the steam is carried by the second straight pipe back to the top of the boiler and then to the engine.

These boilers are supposed to supply steam at 250 pounds pressure but are tested up to 1000 pounds per square inch.

Doble. Almost as great a departure from ordinary practice has been made in the Doble boiler as in the combustion system previously described. The generator is of the water-tube type, with the tubes arranged in rows, which are really separate sections, Fig. 40. There are 28 of these sections in the generator part of the boiler. The tubes are made from seamless drawn-steel tubing of about ½-inch diameter and are swaged down to a diameter of about ⅜ inch at the ends. These ends are welded into the top and bottom headers, thus making each section a continuous piece of steel.

Besides the 28 sections of tubes in the generator portion, there are 8 more sections in the economizer or feed-water heater. The

Fig. 40. One Section of Doble Boiler
Courtesy of General Engineering Company, Detroit, Michigan

arrangement of all these sections is clearly shown in Fig. 41, the view being cut across each of the 36 sections, similar to Fig. 40. The picture does not show all the details but has been arranged to give an idea of the general layout and the direction of flow of the hot gases and of the water and steam. The boiler sections are completely covered over, except at the bottom, by a ¾-inch wall of heat-resisting and insulating Kieselguhr material. Over this is a planished iron jacket.

All of the sections are connected together by headers, which run along the sides of the boiler. One of the features of the construction is that if anything should go wrong with a section of tubes, it can be very easily cut out of operation by means of the side headers, until such time as it is convenient to replace the section.

In Fig. 41, the direction of flow of the hot gases of combustion is shown by the heavy arrows, while the flow of the water and steam is indicated by the small arrows. From the combustion chamber at the bottom of the boiler, the gases pass upward and then over the top of the fire wall between the generator proper and the economizer. Here they turn and pass downward in order to escape through the

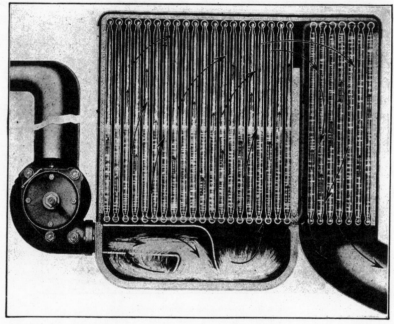

Fig. 41.   Section through Doble Boiler, Showing Combustion Below and Economizer Section at Right

exhaust at the bottom. It should be noted that the power-driven feed pump forces the water in an upward direction in the economizer tubes, exactly opposite to that of the gas flow outside of the tubes.

From the top headers of the economizer sections, the water overflows through a manifold to the lower headers of the generator sections. An automatic valve controls the feed water, so that the water in the boiler, under normal conditions, stands about half-way to the top. On the road, the usual pressure is around 600 pounds per square inch, which is maintained by an automatic valve controlling the fuel supply. Each section of the boiler is tested to a water pressure of 5000 pounds per square inch. The actual bursting pressure is said to be over 8000 pounds. As a precaution against any danger, however, a safety valve is attached to the boiler.

Flash Boilers. Flash boilers differ from the fire- or water-tube types, both of which have a reserve of steam, in that the steam is generated only in the quantity demanded each moment by the engine. These boilers consist of a continuous metal tube in one or more coils lying over the burner. As the water from the reservoir passes along the tube it gets hotter and hotter until at some point in the tube it bursts into steam. During the rest of its travel the steam is superheated.

As practically no steam is kept in reserve, the capacity of the boiler and burner must be great enough to supply at once the maximum demand for hill climbing. The relations of water and fire must be nicely balanced at all times to prevent too much superheat on one hand and wet steam on the other.

Safety against a dangerous explosion is the leading argument for the flash type of boiler. Since there is no reserve of steam or hot water under pressure, there is no large amount of energy to be liberated in case of a rupture of any part of the boiler.

Serpollet System. In the early days of steam automobiles a Frenchman named Serpollet reduced the amount of water in a boiler to an extremely small amount. To give the maximum of heating-surface area together with a minimum of cross-sectional area, the tubes were made a U-section instead of circular; this type, however, was abandoned later.

With the Serpollet system the fuel and water were fed simultaneously, one lever varying the strokes of both pumps. To avoid trouble from extreme superheat, single-acting pistons and poppet valves were employed. The valve cut-off was variable and worked in conjunction with the fuel and water supplies. Since there was no reserve of energy to the system, it took a great deal of skill to handle it smoothly, especially in hilly country.

White. A great improvement over the Serpollet system was the flash generator of the White Company. Although the White steam cars were discontinued in 1911, they were the leading example of the flash system in this country.

STEAM AUTOMOBILES

In the White generator there was a sufficient supply of water to serve as a reserve in cases of sudden demand. Referring to Fig. 42, it will be noted that the boiler was made up of several rows of tubes, each coiled in a horizontal plane, and each connected to the row below by a tube which first passes to the top of the boiler. Unlike the ordinary fire-tube or water-tube boilers, the water entered the White boiler at the top, through the pipe *128*. The upper coil was in the coolest portion of the gases from the burner. After passing through the top coil, the water flowed through the tube at the end of the coil, being carried up and over the top of the boiler and then down to the second coil, and so on down from coil to coil. Being nearer the burner, each coil was hotter than the one above, and,

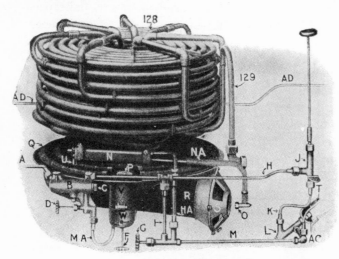

Fig. 42. Generator, Burner, and Fuel Connections Formerly Used on White Steam Cars

since the vertical pipes at the ends of the coils kept the hot water from circulating back to the coil above, there was some point in the lower coils where the water burst into steam. The steam became superheated during the remainder of its travel through the coils and left the boiler by the pipe *129*.

These principles of construction were held to in all the White steam cars from 1904 to 1911 inclusive. Because of the strength of the small-diameter tubes and the small amounts of steam and water

STEAM AUTOMOBILES

in the boiler at any one time, it was possible to carry a working pressure in these generators of 600 pounds per square inch.

Special Types. *Lane.* The Lane boiler, Fig. 43, was a combination of the fire-tube and flash systems. The main part of the boiler was of the fire-tube type, with very large tubes. Above this were several coils of brass tubing, the water entering the top and getting hotter as it passed down the tubes until it was partly converted into steam by the time it passed into the main part. The water was here separated from the steam, falling to the bottom of the boiler, while the steam was superheated by coming in contact with the hot upper portion of the fire tubes.

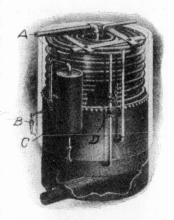

Fig. 43. Lane Boiler

National. For the National London busses a water-tube boiler is used, and these stand a great deal of abuse, often being run dry by the carelessness of the drivers. As is shown in Fig. 44, these boilers are

Fig. 44. Water-Tube Boiler Used on National London Busses
Courtesy of Society of Automobile Engineers, New York City

built around a central steel drum, which is pressed from a single piece of metal.

STEAM AUTOMOBILES

BOILER ACCESSORIES AND REGULATION

Besides the main units of burner, boiler, and engine on the steam automobile, there have to be many other small units, most of them automatic in their operation, for the control of the fire, water feed, and engine to meet the conditions of the wide variations in road and driving conditions. These are the power pumps, the hand pumps, valves, feed-water heater, condensers, and others.

Check Valves. In the lines where it is desired to have the fuel, water, or steam pass in but one direction there are placed valves which allow only this one-way passage and are known as check valves. There are several types, including poppet, hinged, and ball checks. The latter, Fig. 45, is very largely used and consists of a ball which

Fig. 45. Crane Ball Check Valve

rests on a seat forming a ground, fluid-tight joint. When the fluid is passing in the desired direction it lifts the ball off the seat. The body of the valve is so made that it keeps the ball from being carried on down the line with the fluid. As soon as the direction of flow or pressure changes to the opposite direction the ball drops onto its seat, closing the valve against this opposite flow.

Check valves are used in many places in the fuel, water, and steam lines, as is indicated by the diagrams further along. For instance, there are check valves on the inlet and outlet sides of the water pumps. When the piston is on the suction stroke, the inlet check is open while the outlet check is closed, keeping the water already pumped from being drawn back. As soon as the piston starts on the delivery stroke the inlet check closes and the outlet valve opens. This action applies to all the types of check valves.

If dirt lodges on the seats of a check it will leak and, if the dirt cannot be forced off by vigorous action through the valve, the valve must be opened up and the seat cleaned and possibly ground. In most check valves this can be done without removing the whole valve from the line.

Fuel System. Considerable fuel-carrying capacity is always provided in automobiles, and for this reason there should always be enough in the car for more than one run. Before starting out it is

STEAM AUTOMOBILES

always well to see that there is plenty of fuel in the main and pilot
supply tanks. Not only is running out of fuel on the road very
inconvenient, but the running-dry of the tanks may air-lock the
pumps and cause a loss of considerable extra time in getting the

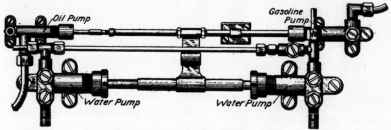

Fig. 46.   Power Pumps of Stanley Engine

system back into smooth action. The above applies equally well to
the water supply.

As mentioned in the section on burners, the fuel is fed under
pressure. In some cases the pressure is carried on the main tank,
while in other cases it is carried by air or spring pressure on small
auxiliary tanks. The power and
hand pumps on steam cars are
of the plunger type.

Due to the interrelations between the demands for steam,
water, and fuel and the automatic devices, one controlled by
the other, it is difficult to deal
separately with the various
units. For this reason one complete fuel, water, and steam system will be discussed and then

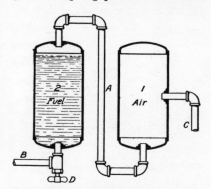

Fig. 47. Fuel Pressure Tanks on Stanley Cars

descriptions of other makers' units and methods of operation will be
taken up. The Stanley system will be used to show the relation and
operation of the various units.

Stanley Fuel, Water, and Steam Systems. *Fuel System.* On the
Stanley cars the main fuel tank is carried under atmospheric pressure
and the fuel is drawn from the tank by the power-driven pump
Fig. 46. In series with the power fuel pump is a hand pump for us.

when the engine is not running or if the power pump should be out
of order. The *small pressure tanks* on the Stanley are shown in
Fig. 47. The fuel does not flow through the left tank, marked *2*, but

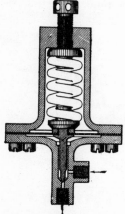

merely rises and falls in it, the tank acting
as a pressure equalizer between the strokes
of the power pump, similar to the standpipe
in many city waterworks systems. Tank
number *1*, on the right, is filled with compressed air, which is supplied by the power-
driven air pump or by the hand air pump. A
pressure gage on the dashboard shows the
operator what the pressure is on the tanks.
From the auxiliary tanks the fuel passes to
the vaporizer.

Since the fuel power pump has a capacity
greater than that usually demanded by the
burner an *automatic by-pass valve*, called the

Fig. 48. Stanley Gasoline
Automatic Valve

fuel automatic relief, Fig. 48, is placed in the line. When the fuel
from the pump is at a higher pressure than is being carried on the

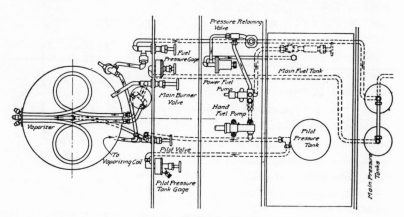

Fig. 49.   Stanley Fuel System
Courtesy of Stanley Motor Carriage Company, Newton, Massachusetts

pressure tanks, the needle valve of this fuel automatic relief is raised
and part of the fuel is returned to the main tank, as shown in the
layout of the fuel system, Fig. 49.

Should this needle valve fail to seat properly, it is probably due

STEAM AUTOMOBILES

to dirt between the needle and the seat. This can often be removed by taking the tension off the spring by unscrewing the adjusting nut and then pumping fuel with the hand pump. If this does not cure the trouble the whole valve should be taken apart and cleaned and, if necessary, the needle ground into the seat.

Beyond the pressure tanks there is a *fuel filter* which should be watched for leaks and cleaned every once in a while. Near the tanks is also a pressure-retaining valve, which may be closed by hand when the car is left standing, the purpose being to keep the pressure on the tanks, as it might otherwise be lost, due to slow leaks in the lines, and thereby necessitate the pumping-up of pressure by hand.

Actual fuel supply to the vaporizer, and hence to the burner, is governed by the steam automatic regulator, or "diaphragm regulator", as it is sometimes called, Fig. 50. This regula-tor governs the relation between the steam pressure and the fuel supply to the burner. It consists of a metal diaphragm, clamped between the cap and the body. When the steam pressure rises above the predetermined amount, the pressure against the diaphragm causes it to bulge and thus move the rod attached to it so as to keep the ball valve from leaving its seat, thereby shutting off the fuel to the boiler.

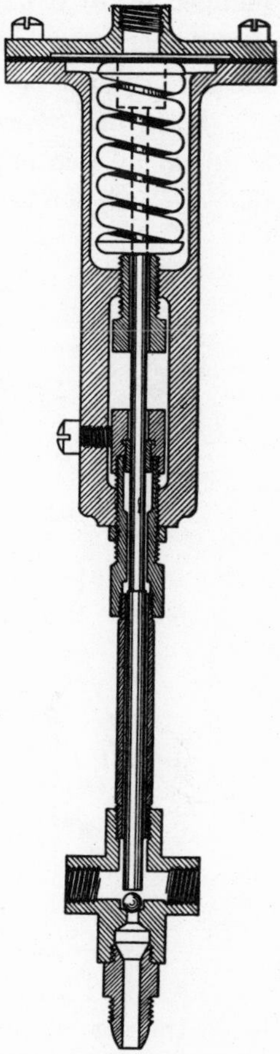

The strength of the spring determines at what steam pressure the fuel is shut off. To

Fig. 50. Stanley Steam Automatic Valve

regulate the strength of the spring the adjusting screw is moved in or out. The valve stem is provided with a stuffing box which can be tightened up to stop leaks through the gland. The screw locks the gland in place after the adjustment is made. Care must be taken not to get the gland too tight.

Upon the older Stanley models, in which gasoline was used for the fuel of the main burner as well as for the pilot light, the line for the latter was a branch of the main fuel line. In the newer models, the pilot system is entirely separate, so that kerosene may be used for the main burner. The pressure on the separate gasoline tank is pumped up by a hand pump and should be kept at from 20 to 30 pounds per square inch. In leaving the pilot burning over night the pressure will not fall over 5 to 10 pounds.

Water and Steam System. From the main water tank the water is drawn by two opposite *power-driven pumps*, Fig. 46, and follows the course shown in Fig. 51. A *hand pump* is also provided for use

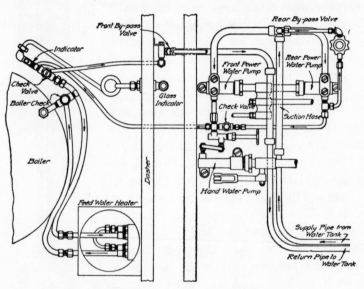

Fig. 51. Diagram of Stanley Water System
Courtesy of Stanley Motor Carriage Company, Newton, Massachusetts

when the car is standing still or in case of a failure of the power pumps. Beyond the pumps are by-pass valves, the opening of which allows the water to return to the supply tank. The rear by-pass is operated by the usual type of handle, while the one in front is controlled by a lever on the steering post. The handling of these by-pass valves will be taken up in relation to the general operation of the car.

On the way to the boiler, the water passes to the water-level indicator, which is explained in detail in the following paragraph, and then to the *feed-water heater*. Over the water pipes in the feed-water heater the exhaust steam from the engine is passed. In this way

STEAM AUTOMOBILES

much of the otherwise waste heat of the exhaust is given back by heating the water before it reaches the boiler, resulting, of course, in a saving of fuel. The feed-water heater also serves as a muffler for the sound of the engine exhaust.

The *water-level indicator* is for the purpose of showing the operator the amount of water in the boiler. It consists of three tubes, Fig. 52, *M, N, O*, which are brazed together. The middle one *N* is a part of the water column, that is, its lower end connects with a pipe leading

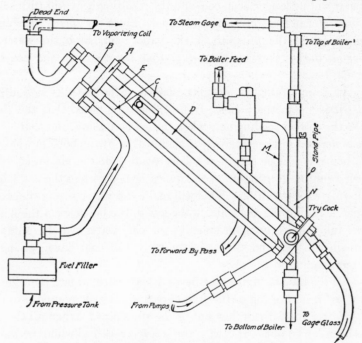

Fig. 52. Diagram Showing Stanley Low-Water Automatic Valve with Three-Tube Indicator Body

to the bottom of the boiler and its upper end is in communication with the top of the boiler, so that the water stands in this column at the same height that it does in the boiler. At the lower end of tube *N* is the low-water try cock.

Tube *M*, at the left, is part of the water system from the pumps to the boiler and, when the car is running, water is constantly passing through it. The standpipe *O* is closed at its upper end and at its lower end is connected by a copper tube to the glass water glass on

the dashboard in front of the driver. The standpipe, tube, and glass
form a U-tube which is filled with water, the level of which, when cold,
stands about an inch above the bottom of the glass.

If the water level in the boiler, and therefore in the tube N, is
above the top of the standpipe O, the cold water passing through M
on its way to the boiler will keep the standpipe O comparatively
cool, and the water in the glass will show about an inch above the
bottom; but if the water in the boiler falls below the top of the standpipe, it will no longer keep cool and the resulting heat will turn some
of the water in the standpipe into vapor. Since the end of the standpipe is closed, the pressure of the vapor will cause the water in
the glass to rise, showing the driver that the water in the boiler is
getting low.

It is important to remember that when the water is *high* in the
glass it is *low* in the boiler. It should also be noted that the glass
gives the correct reading only when the car is running, and that when
the boiler is cold the water in the glass will be at the bottom whether
the boiler is full or empty. A false reading of the glass may also
occur from the heating-up of the indicator body when the car is left
standing with steam up. This will make the water rise in the glass,
apparently showing the water to be low in the boiler even though it
were full. Directly upon starting the car, water will be pumped
through tube M and the indicator body will cool down, giving a
correct reading in the glass.

To fill the standpipe, U-tube and glass with water, the plug is
removed from the top of the standpipe and water is poured into the
glass faster than it can flow out of the standpipe. When all the air
has been forced out in this way, the screw is replaced while the water
is still running, but is screwed down only lightly. The water is then
shut off and, when the level in the glass has gone down to about an
inch above the bottom, the screw in the top of the standpipe is
tightened up.

In freezing weather an anti-freeze solution should be used in the
U-tube and glass. This can be made of equal parts of glycerine and
water or of alcohol and water. A test of the indicator can be made
when steam is up by opening the low-water pet cock until the water
rises in the glass and then pouring cold water over the body of the
indicator, which should cause the water in the glass to fall.

STEAM AUTOMOBILES

When the boiler is cold the amount of water in it is determined by opening the low-water pet cock. If water flows it shows that there is enough in the boiler to allow firing up. If no water comes and a wire run in the pet cock shows that it is not stopped up, water should be pumped in the boiler by hand. When trying the water level by the pet cock the water should be allowed to run several seconds so as to be sure that it is not merely the condensation which may have gathered.

If dirt or incrustation should stop up the lower end of the water column, it would cause false readings of the indicator and try cock. It is therefore important that this be guarded against by *blowing down* the boiler regularly. The procedure in blowing down will be referred to later.

Another protecting device of the Stanley is the low-water automatic valve, which in its action and location is closely connected to the water-level indicator. The purpose of this valve is to shut off the fuel supply in case the water becomes low in the boiler. As shown in Fig. 50, it consists of a valve B in the fuel line, an expansion tube D and two rods C, the latter forming a framework or support.

When the water in the boiler and water column gets below the try cock, the expansion tube D fills with steam and the heat of this steam causes the tube to become longer. This expansion moves the valve stem E, connected to the end of the tube, and this closes the valve, shutting off the fuel to the burner.

In case the low-water automatic valve closes, first make sure that there is water in the main tank, and that the pumps are working properly. Then with both by-pass valves closed run the car as far as it will go. By this time the pumps probably will have delivered enough water to cover the bottom of the expansion tube, allowing the fuel valve to open again. If not, the engine can be run with the wheels jacked up or water can be pumped by the hand pump.

There are four other accessories to the Stanley and other power plants, which have not yet been mentioned: the safety valve, steam gage, siphon, and oil pump.

The *safety valve* is connected to the boiler and will blow if the steam pressure exceeds the amount for which the valve is set. The *steam gage* is placed on the dash and indicates the steam pressure in pounds per square inch. The steam itself does not actually enter the gage, but the pressure in the system is communicated to the gage by means of a tube filled with oil, which will not freeze in winter.

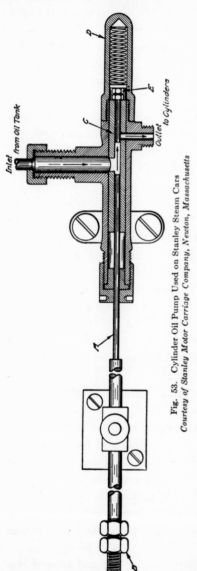

Fig. 53. Cylinder Oil Pump Used on Stanley Steam Cars
Courtesy of Stanley Motor Carriage Company, Newton, Massachusetts

When it is desired to draw water from a water trough or some other place from which it cannot be run into the tank from a faucet, the *siphon* is used. This is a hose, a branch of which is connected to the steam system by a hand valve. One end is placed in the tank-filler opening and the other end, which is provided with a screen, is put in the supply of water. The steam is turned on and, due to an injector action, draws the water up into the tank.

Driven by the same mechanism which drives the Stanley fuel and water pumps, is the *oil pump*, Figs. 46 and 53. From the oil tank the pump forces the oil through the sight feed on the dash, from which it is led into the steam line to the engine.

In the oil pump, Fig. 53, the plunger A is set in its extreme foreposition, so that the end will just come to the outlet. This is done by removing the delivery stub cap and delivery check ball and inserting a small wire in the outlet. When the driving crosshead is in the extreme position, the plunger should come to a point where it will strike the wire; the lock nut B is then tightened. This adjustment should be looked to if the position of the driving crosshead becomes changed.

STEAM AUTOMOBILES

To vary the amount of oil pumped, the distance between the end of the adjusting piston C and the pump inlet is varied. The shorter this distance the less the amount of oil pumped. The adjustment is made by removing the cap D and adjusting the set nut E. If the oil tank is allowed to run dry the pump may become air-locked, and it is then necessary to disconnect the copper pipe and work the pump until the air is expelled.

All ordinary steam-cylinder oil is not suitable for use in these engines because of the high degree of superheat. The Stanley Company recommend either the "Harris superheat steam-cylinder oil" or the "Oilzum high-pressure superheated steam-cylinder oil". Other makers recommend different classes of oils best suited to their particular engines and these will be noted later.

Now that a general idea of the make-up and operation of the power-plant accessories has been given in the description of the Stanley layout, attention will be turned to the characteristics of the accessories offered by other makers.

Doble. The details of construction of the Doble combustion chamber and boiler have already been shown in Figs. 35 and 41, and discussed on pages 34 and 40. The water level in the boiler is kept at the half-way point by an automatic by-pass valve, which is operated by the expansion of a regulator tube. As the water rises in the boiler, the tube is filled from an outside pipe with comparatively cold water. The decided change of temperature causes the tube to contract again, and the water is by-passed to the supply tank. The steam pressure is maintained around 600 pounds by another automatic device, which controls the fuel system.

From the upper headers of the generator sections, the live steam passes into a manifold which leads it through the throttle valve and then to the engine. From the engine, it passes back to the condenser, being forced along by the following steam.

A non-rusting alloy is used for the seats of the throttle valve. The valve, shown in Figs. 28 and 29, is a compound design, being a combination of a poppet and piston valve. The piston portion regulates the flow of steam, while the poppet serves to keep the valve in a tight, or non-leaking, condition.

The force of the steam constantly coming from the engine causes the steam to pass from the top to the bottom of the radiator condenser and, under normal conditions, the steam has been completely condensed to water before it reaches the bottom. This water of condensation enters the water tank very near the bottom, so that any steam which still remains will be condensed as it bubbles up through the tank. Rapid acceleration from a slow speed or very hard slow pulling are the two conditions under which some steam may remain uncondensed in passing through the radiator. As a safety measure, in case of a very long stretch of slow heavy pulling, the water tank is provided with a vent at the top. With this condensing system, it is said that a car will run 1500 miles on one filling of water.

Doble Lubrication. Another one of Doble's departures from standard steam-automobile practice is in the matter of lubrication. The throttle, engine valves, cylinder walls, water pumps, and interior of the generator are all lubricated by regular gasoline-engine oil instead of the heavy steam-cylinder oil used in power plants.

This comparatively light mineral oil at once forms an emulsion with the water, due to the shaking up from the roughness of the road and the agitation of the feed water as the condensation enters the tank from the radiator. The oil, therefore, is sent into the generator along with the feed water and gives the interior of the tubes a very thin coating of lubricant. How thin this is may be judged by the statement that the generator temperature is 485° F. at the working pressure of 600 pounds. This coating not only prevents the tubes from rusting, but keeps scale from forming as it cannot stick to a greasy surface. The oil in the water also prevents scale from forming in other places and pipes, for it coats each particle of lime, etc., which may be thrown down and keeps it from sticking to any other particle and building up a deposit. It is this same oil that is carried over with the steam that lubricates the throttle valve and cylinder parts. The condenser saves the oil supply as well as the water, so that the lubricant is used over and over again, and a car is said to run 8000 miles on one gallon of oil.

Steaming Test. One of the main features claimed for the Doble design is the short length of time required to raise steam to a working pressure, that for ordinary running being 600 pounds per square inch. The following test was recently given out by the company.

The generator had approximately 150 square feet of surface and contained, when the water was at its normal level, $8\frac{1}{2}$ gallons. Com-

STEAM AUTOMOBILES

bustion started with the water in the generator at 66° F. The first
trace of steam came in forty seconds.

Pressure lb. per sq. in.	Elapsed Time	Pressure lb. per sq. in.	Elapsed Time
Trace.........	40 sec.	700...........	3 min.
100...........	1 min., 20 sec.	800...........	3 min., 10 sec.
200...........	1 min., 45 sec.	900...........	3 min., 15 sec.
300...........	2 min., 10 sec.	1000...........	3 min., 20 sec.
400...........	2 min., 25 sec.	1100...........	3 min., 25 sec.
500...........	2 min., 40 sec.	1200...........	3 min., 30 sec.
600...........	2 min., 50 sec.		

Ofeldt. *Fuel, Water, and Steam Connections.* Fig. 54 gives a
clear idea of the fuel, water, and steam connections of the Ofeldt

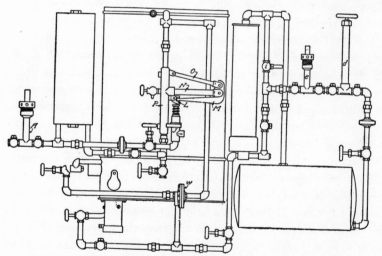

Fig. 54. Diagram of Connections for Ofeldt Boiler Feed and Fuel Systems
Courtesy of F. W. Ofeldt & Sons, Nyack-on-the-Hudson, New York

system, the burner and boiler of which have been described previously. The feed-water pump *A* and the fuel pump *e* are usually
on opposite crossheads of the engine, but to make the two systems
clearer they have been separated in the diagram.

The Ofeldt Company makes these accessories either for use as a
complete system, as shown in the diagram, or for use with other
units. The company does not make a complete automobile.

An expansion tube N is the basis of the Ofeldt water regulator. This tube stands at right angles to the middle point of the boiler water column P, and when the water becomes low enough in the boiler and column for the tube to fill with steam, the expansion causes the closing of the water by-pass valve through the movement of the linkage O, M, L. When used with the Ofeldt water-tube boiler it is claimed that a water-level glass is unnecessary.

Fuel regulation is accomplished by the diaphragm valve, w. This is made up of two concave discs with a steel diaphragm fastened between them. Combined with the upper disc is the valve controlling the fuel supply. When the steam pressure on the lower side reaches the point for which the valve has been adjusted, the diaphragm pushes upward, shutting off the fuel. Upon the decrease of the steam pressure, the natural spring of the diaphragm again opens the fuel valve. Where used with a pilot light the closing of the valve completely shuts off the fuel to the main burner, but where no pilot is used just enough fuel is allowed to pass to keep the fire burning.

Automatic Fuel Feed. Possibly the most interesting of the Ofeldt accessories is the automatic fuel feed i, in which a spring is used to keep the fuel under pressure. It consists of a brass cylinder, 18 to 36 inches long and 4 inches in diameter, which is plugged at one end and capped at the other. Running the length of the cylinder is a coil spring with a piston at one end. The engine fuel pump e, or hand pump d, forces the fuel into the tank, pushing back the piston and compressing the spring. This spring keeps the pressure on the fuel the same as is done by the air tanks in the Stanley system. As part of the pressure layout is a safety or by-pass valve J, which can be set for the desired pressure on the fuel, the excess fuel from the by-pass valve and from the leakage past the piston in the regulator are returned to the fuel tank.

MANAGEMENT AND CARE OF STEAM CARS

In the preceding description considerable has been said as to the management and care of the units, but in this section some further hints will be added on the operation of steam automobiles.

Management on the Road. As will be understood from the foregoing, the operator's part in managing the power plant—other than attention to the throttle—is ordinarily limited to watching the water-

STEAM AUTOMOBILES

level indicator and managing the by-pass valve—if not automatic—in accordance with the water level. When the level drops, the by-pass valve must be closed, thereby causing all the water pumped to enter the boiler. When the water level exceeds the proper height, the by-pass valve is opened and water ceases to enter the boiler. It is not practicable to open the by-pass valve part way, as this would cause the water to go through the valve at boiler pressure and, in time, the scouring action due to the pressure would make the valve leak.

Blind adherence to the above rule will not always give as good results as may be obtained through manipulation. For example, if one sees a hill ahead, he can fill the boiler somewhat higher than its usual level and give the added water time to get hot before the hill is reached. This affords a reserve supply for surmounting the hill. In the average hilly country, one can make a practice of pumping water on down grades when little or no steam is being used and the heat of the fire is available to heat the incoming water. Near the bottom of the hill the by-pass valve is opened and the ascent taken in good style. If the accumulated pressure has caused the fire to shut off, the throttle may be opened just before the bottom of the hill is reached, and the drop in pressure will bring the fire on while impetus is being gained. It is a general rule for all classes of steam cars that *the fire should, if possible, be "on" before an up grade is begun.* By proper management the fire may be kept burning continuously in a hilly country, while power is used only on the up-grades.

In applying the above principles it should be remembered that only the wetted inside surface of the boiler is available for making steam. If the water is low, steam cannot be raised as rapidly as when the boiler is full, assuming that the water is hot in both cases. On the other hand, if the boiler is worked too full one may get wet steam despite the superheater, with loss of power due to condensation. In an extreme case, enough water might even be carried through to choke the clearance spaces at the cylinder ends. This would probably result in a head being knocked out or a connecting rod or crank bent, as the water could not be ejected quickly enough by the lifting of the slide valve to save the engine from severe shock when the piston reached the end of its stroke. A boiler of the Lane type, in which the water is partly converted into steam in coils above the boiler proper, and in which the fire tubes are large enough to permit combustion to take place inside of them, is an exception to the above, in that superheating takes place chiefly in the "boiler".

The more rapidly fuel is supplied to the burner, the hotter will be the fire. Where ample power is desired, therefore, the burner is worked under more than ordinary pressure. In the Stanley cars, which carry pressure only in the auxiliary tank, 120 to 140 pounds is recommended.

Firing=Up. The following remarks apply particularly to cars with the Stanley type of burner and boiler. In the case of the Doble car, the constructions are so different that many of the instructions will not apply. The Doble system has been described in detail in the preceding pages, and the reader is referred back to these paragraphs for the firing-up of the boiler, etc. As will be explained later, it is customary at the end of a run to *blow down* the boiler for the purpose of ridding it of whatever sediment may be present. The blow-off valve is shut when a few pounds of pressure still remain, and the condensation of this remaining steam should suck the boiler full of water, *provided* the by-pass valve is closed. The presence of this water is desirable to protect the superheating coil when the fire is started. Therefore, if the car has a conventional fire-tube boiler with superheating coil beneath, the first step is to ascertain whether the boiler is actually full. Close the by-pass (if open), open the upper try cock, and if no water comes out, work the hand pump. See that the water tank is full. Open the throttle and the drip valve on the steam chest and continue pumping by hand till water comes out. Leave them open while starting the fire, to allow the water to expand.

If there is no pressure in the fuel tank, pump it up to the minimum working pressure by hand. Heat the pilot, either by burning gasoline in a cup, by an alcohol wick, or by the modern acetylene torch, as the case may be. When thoroughly heated, slowly open the pilot-light supply valve. If a blue flame does not result, close the supply valve and admit more gasoline to the cup.

After starting the pilot light, allow it to burn till the vaporizer is hot, then open the main-burner valve carefully. If it fires back into the burner, shut it off, wait a minute or two and try again. Turn the burner to full height gradually. If the flame is yellow or smoky, it is not getting enough air, if it is noisy and lifts off the

STEAM AUTOMOBILES

burner, it is getting too much air. Once adjusted for a given fuel pressure, the nozzle or air shutter should not need changing.

While the water is getting hot, the oiling up can be attended to. As soon as the pressure begins to rise, water will issue from the drip cock on the steam chest. Close this cock and the throttle valve as soon as clear steam comes out.

When pressure reaches 100 or 200 pounds, get into the car, throw the reverse lever to its full forward or backward position, open the throttle slightly and then close it at once. Repeat till the engine starts. With some yards of clear way, work the reverse lever back and forth with the throttle open only a crack, so that the car "seesaws" slowly. This will work the water out of the engine and warm up the cylinders till the entering steam ceases to condense. This process must not be hurried. An attempt to cut it short is likely to result in damage to the engine. As long as water is present the engine will run jerkily. When it runs smoothly the car is ready to start.

On starting, the first few blocks should be run slowly to complete the warming-up process. If the air pressure is below normal the air pump should be kept going.

At the End of a Run. On finishing a run, the boiler should be blown down with the fire turned off. This should be done by opening the blow-off valve near the bottom of the boiler. The escaping water will carry with it all the mud and precipitate that have accumulated. Close the blow-off valve at about 100 pounds, and the subsequent condensation will fill the boiler by suction from the tank. If the water in the tank is covered with oil, the end of a hose should be inserted and the tank flushed out to get rid of the oil. It is a good plan to put a cupful of kerosene into the tank. It will not only loosen whatever oil may be clinging there, but will help loosen the scale liable to form from hard water.

A thermostat water-level indicator operates only when steam is up. When the boiler is cold it indicates high water whether water is present or not. When the car is running, a faulty reading of the water level is usually soon noticed, and if it is overlooked there is still protection of the fusible plug. If, however, the boiler should be fired up with no water in it, the fusible plug would melt without the fact being heralded by escaping steam. Therefore, the fusible plug, like the water-level indicator, is useful only when steam is up.

STEAM AUTOMOBILES

Engine Lubrication. For the older cars not using superheated steam, the regular power-plant steam-cylinder oil is usually recommended. This is a mineral oil mixed with tallow to make it hold on the wet cylinder walls. It often contains graphite. This type of oil will not stand the high temperatures of superheated steam, and special oils must be used. As an example, the Stanley Company has recommended either "Harris superheat steam-cylinder oil" or "Oilzum high-pressure superheated steam-cylinder oil". The Doble uses the same kind of gasoline-engine oil as is used by the ordinary motor-car driver. Other engines use different grades of oil to the best advantage, and it is best in each case to find out the maker's recommendations.

The Fusible Plug. If the fusible plug blows out when the car is running, the escape of steam may be shut off by closing a valve usually interposed between the boiler and the plug. The fire should be shut off at once and, if possible, the car should be run to reduce the pressure, thereby allowing the boiler to cool somewhat. When the drop in pressure compels a halt, close the by-pass valve and pump water in by hand till it shows in the lowest try cock. Then, after replacing the fusible plug, the fire may be relighted and the water level restored while the car runs.

If the plug blows simply because the by-pass valve has been open too long, the by-pass can be closed, the main fire shut off, and the engine run by jacking up the rear wheels, till water shows in the lowest try cock.

Causes of Low Pressure. Low pressure is generally due to insufficient fire. If the burner pressure is low, steam will not be made rapidly. If the burner pressure is all right, the burner nozzle may be clogged or the vaporizing tube may be choked with carbon. The nozzle may usually be poked out with a bent wire without turning off the fire. If, however, the vaporizer is clogged it will have to be removed when the car is cold and cleaned, with a drill or otherwise, as the makers direct.

Occasionally the valve controlled by the diaphragm regulator may be choked, and rarely the main-burner valve. Either can be cleaned by disconnecting and running a wire through.

Occasionally the pilot light may clog in the same way, usually at the nozzle. The remedy is the same as for the main burner.

If the air pump fails to raise the pressure on the fuel tank to the required degree, it is probable that the intake or outlet check valves leak. If, as is likely, they have oil on them, the oil may have gathered dust. The valves should be taken out and cleaned, and a drop of oil put on them to make them tight.

The various packings about the engine and auxiliaries require occasional tightening, and once in a while new packing is necessary. If the new packing is soft, like wicking, it may be put on top of the old, otherwise the old must be removed. The packing should not in any case be tighter than necessary to prevent leakage, for unnecessary friction would thereby be caused. A slight leakage about the water and air pumps may be permitted to save friction. As the hand pumps are rarely used their packings can be looser than those of the power pumps.

Scale Prevention and Remedies. In sections where hard water is used, the subject of scale is a serious one, and its treatment will depend on the character of the mineral contained in the water. Frequently it is possible to precipitate the mineral before putting the water into the tank. Sometimes the addition of a small quantity of lime will do this, sometimes carbonate of soda or "soda ash". Still other waters are successfully treated by adding caustic soda. Sometimes the simple addition of kerosene to untreated water will loosen the scale as above indicated. If these remedies are not successful, the user is advised to send a sample gallon of water to a maker of boiler compounds and have it analyzed, after which a suitable compound can be recommended. Scale allowed to accumulate by neglect is not only very detrimental to the boiler by interfering with the free flow of heat, but it also seriously reduces the steaming power. Instances have been known of the steaming capacity of boilers being reduced fifty per cent or more by scale. At the same time the shell and tubes get hotter than they should, resulting in unequal expansion and leakage.

Filling the Boiler. Before firing up, be sure that the boiler and superheaters are full. To be sure of this, open the throttle valve and steam-chest drip, close the by-pass valve and work the hand pump until water comes from the steam-chest drip. If more convenient fill the boiler from the town supply by means of the coupling furnished for this purpose, connecting to the blow-off valve. Never light the fire until you are sure that the boiler is full.

STEAM AUTOMOBILES

At the end of a run open the blow-off valve at the front of the boiler, and blow down to about 100 pounds. Fill the water tank and close the by-pass valve, and the condensing steam in the boiler will siphon the boiler full. Before blowing down, see that the pilot light is out, as well as the main burner. It can be extinguished by blowing into the pilot mixing tube.

Raising Gasoline Pressure. If the pressure tanks are empty and the pressure zero, proceed as follows:

Open the hand gasoline-pump valve and work the pump till the air gage registers 10 or 15 pounds. Tank 2, Fig. 47, is now full of gasoline, and tank 1 is full of compressed air. Attach the hand air pump to air valve and pump air into tank 1 till the gage indicates 80 or 90 pounds, which is the working pressure for the burner.

If now the fire is lighted and the car stands still, the pressure will gradually drop, but may be raised in a moment by working the hand gasoline pump. When the car runs, the power pump maintains the supply.

The air in tank 1 is gradually absorbed, and additional air is required. This is indicated, first, by the vibration of the air-pressure-gage needle when running; second, by a rapid drop of pressure when the car stands still. In case of doubt whether the drop is due to lack of air or to a leak in the automatic or pump valves, close the pressure-retaining valve. If the pressure still falls the air is insufficient.

Occasionally empty the pressure tank by opening valve *D*, and refill in order to determine definitely the amount of gasoline in it.

If the car is to stand some time with pilot burning, close the pressure-retaining valve to prevent the gasoline from leaking back through the valves and automatic. Be sure to open again on starting.

General Lubrication. On page 60, are mentioned the different grades of oil suitable for cylinder lubrication in the various types of engines. The lubrication of the cylinder walls and valves, however, is not the end of the subject, for, wherever there are two moving surfaces in contact, there must be lubrication in order to keep the friction losses at a minimum. Useless friction in the running parts of the engine and chassis of the car means an increased consumption of fuel. This, however, is often of secondary consideration in comparison with the wear and resulting repair bills, often caused by lack of lubrication. When a bearing becomes dry, it usually heats up and expands, and

STEAM AUTOMOBILES

in case this is continued to the point of "freezing", the car may be completely disabled on the road.

Of course all parts of the car do not have the same amount of motion and, therefore, do not require the same amount of lubrication. All makers of cars issue instruction books for each model and, when possible, the operator should provide himself with a copy and follow the oiling instructions. This, however, is often impossible, and it is then a matter of good judgment based on the known requirements of other cars. Outside of the power plant there is no particular difference between the construction and care of a steam- and a gasoline-engine driven car, and the lubrication chart of any of the later makes can be safely followed.

In the modern Stanley and Doble types, the crankshaft, cross-head, and other moving engine parts, other than piston, together with the rear-axle bearings, are all lubricated by splash, the crankcase being thoroughly oil-tight. The level of this oil should be inspected every two months, although it will probably not need renewing that often. Some of the older cars require that the eccentric be given a squirt of oil daily, by a hand gun. It is a good habit to give all grease cups a turn-down each day.

Water Pump. If the water pump fails to work, first see if the tank is empty. In addition to this there are three other causes to which failure is mainly due, viz, (1) *The pump may be air-bound.* To remedy, open the by-pass valve and run the engine. The air will work out readily, since there is no pressure against it. (2) *The check valves may leak.* There are three check valves, one on the pump intake, another on the outlet, and the third at the boiler. The intake valve is the most likely to leak. Remove the valve cap and clean the valve ball and its seat, being careful not to scratch them. If the boiler check valve is leaking, it will permit steam to escape into the water tank when the by-pass valve is open. This valve can only be examined when there is no pressure. (3) *The pump packing may leak.* Tightening the packing nut generally suffices, but occasionally repacking is necessary. Do not screw the packing nut tighter than is necessary, as it causes needless friction; a slight leakage may be tolerated. In case the power pump fails, use the hand pump, first running with the main fire off till the pressure is reduced to about 100 pounds. After pumping, close the valve with the pump plunger in.

Gasoline Pump. In most respects the gasoline pump resembles the water pump. If it becomes air-bound, it can be primed by using the hand gasoline pump, which is much larger and, drawing through the power pump, will suck out the air.

The gasoline pump packing should not leak at all, as it is both wasteful and dangerous. The pump is so small that adjusting is seldom needed.

If the hand gasoline pump becomes air-bound, unscrew the valve, which is open when the hand pump is used, till it comes out. Press the thumb over the valve-stem hole when the pump plunger is pulled out, and lift it off when the plunger is forced in. Repeating this several times will expel the air.

If the hand gasoline pump and hand water pump work together, the packing nut on the gasoline pump should be just tight enough to hold the gasoline, and the water pump should have its packing so adjusted that the pump will run perfectly free.

To pack the gasoline pump, put in first a thin leather washer, then three of the special packing rings supplied by the makers, then another thin leather washer, and screw the stuffing-box nut only hand tight. Do not use a tool to tighten it, otherwise the plunger will cut out the packing.

Care of Engine Bearings. If the engine is regularly lubricated the bearings will seldom require adjustment. If the bearings show the slightest discoloration from rust they have been insufficiently oiled. Adjustments are made as follows:

The crosshead guides are taken up by screwing down the nut on the bolt holding the frame rods together. The crosshead balls must be under sufficient pressure to keep them from slipping.

The wrist pins are taper and are adjusted with a screw held by a lock nut. First loosen the lock nut, turn up the screw till it stops, then back it one-eighth turn and tighten the lock nut.

The crankpin ball bearings are adjusted by removing the bolt, taking out the plug, and reducing it slightly by filing. When correctly adjusted the bearings should have no perceptible play.

The main bearings and eccentrics can only be adjusted after the engine is taken out of the car. They are adjusted to take up lost motion by filing or grinding down the face of the bearing cap, which must be very carefully done.

STEAM AUTOMOBILES

Be sure the engine-frame hangers are properly adjusted. Should the nuts work loose, the front end of the engine will sway, to the damage of the engine case and gears. In adjusting the engine-frame hangers do not set them up so tight that they will not swivel around the rear axle. If necessary insert shims of paper or thin brass, removing the rear engine case to gain access.

Operating the Cut=Off and Reverse. In the more recent Stanley cars the cut-off is variable from one-quarter to one-half stroke. On the engine is a quadrant from which the reverse lever works in connection with the reverse pedal. The quadrant has one notch, into which a dog attached to the reverse lever drops when the engine is "hooked up", that is, operating on short cut-off. To hook up the engine, press on the reverse pedal only. To release the dog, press a pedal beside the reverse pedal, called the *clutch pedal*. This releases the reverse pedal and a spring pulls it back, allowing the engine to cut-off at half-stroke. The car should always be started with the reverse pedal released, and the cut-off should not be shortened until the engine attains good speed. If it operates jerkily, release the reverse pedal by pressing the clutch pedal.

Care of the Burner. If the car does not steam well, look at the fire first. See that the gasoline pressure is not below 100 pounds.

If the pressure is right, the gasoline line may be clogged in the automatic valve, vaporizer, burner nozzle, or main-burner valve. If the burner has two mixing tubes, see if both sides are affected; if so, the trouble is probably in the automatic valve. If the two burner flames are unequal, the trouble may be in the vaporizing tubes or the nozzle, more likely the latter. Clean the nozzles by running a small wire through them with the screw out, or by using a bent wire without removing the screw.

If the vaporizing tubes are clogged, uncouple at the back of the burner, take out the bundle of wires from the tubes, and clean the tubes and wires thoroughly, using the bundle as a swab. Extinguish all fire before beginning.

If the pilot-light nozzle becomes clogged, use a screwdriver to turn the horizontal nozzle screw back and forth. A wire projects from this screw through the nozzle orifice and turning the screw causes the wire to clean the nozzle. Do this only with the pilot burning.

STEAM AUTOMOBILES

To regulate the air received by the pilot, bend the pilot vaporizer tube slightly away from the mixing tube for more air, or inward for less air. The pilot should burn with a blue flame slightly tinged with yellow, and may be adjusted while lighted.

Never use a reamer for cleaning either the pilot or main-burner nozzle, as it is likely to enlarge the hole, which is that of a No. 62 drill.

Sometimes after the automatic valve closes, the gas pressure at the nozzles will reduce gradually, causing the burner to light-back. When next the automatic valve opens, the fire will burn inside the mixing tubes with a roaring sound. This sound should be the instant signal for closing the main-burner valve and allowing the mixing tube to cool.

If the burner should fire back frequently and with a sharp explosion, it would indicate either a leak in the burner or a leak of steam in the combustion space. To test for a steam leak, first get up steam pressure, then take off the burner and examine the boiler, then run the front wheels against something immovable and open the throttle valve to see if steam escapes from the superheaters.

To Adjust the Throttle. If the throttle valve leaks it must be reground or a new valve substituted. It may, however, appear to leak owing to improper adjustment. There should be some tension on the valve stem when the lever is locked in the closed position. There is a distance rod running from the body of the throttle valve through the dashboard close to the throttle-valve stem. To increase the tension on the throttle, adjust the nuts on the distance rod.

To Adjust the Automatics. To carry a higher steam pressure, screw the adjusting screw on the automatic valve further in; for a lower pressure, screw it out. The same regulation of the gasoline relief valve will produce similar variations of the fuel pressure.

To Lay Up for the Winter. Run the car, on the road or with the rear wheels jacked up, till everything is hot, then extinguish the fire and blow off the boiler. While steam is escaping, open the safety and siphon valves and take out the fusible plug to clear them of water. Empty the tank, take off the caps of the check valves, and blow into the suction holes to clear the water from the checks ahead. Take off the water indicator and empty it, unless it is filled with non-freezing mixture.

STEAM AUTOMOBILES

General Remarks on Operating. The commonest fault of Stanley operators is opening the throttle too abruptly on starting. This is bad enough if the cylinders happen to be clear of water; if they are not clear, the results may be destructive. Always start slowly, and do not come up to road speed till the engine runs smoothly.

Never open any of the valves more than two or three full turns. They are screw valves, and if turned a dozen or more times they will come clear out.

Practice reversing where you have plenty of room. The ability to look and steer backward while operating the reverse pedal and throttle is not a natural gift. After reversing, be sure that the pedal has been released, by pressing the clutch pedal before giving steam.

THINGS YOU "AUTO KNOW" ABOUT STEAM CARS
By Floyd Clymer

There was once a Hudson — and a Jaxon Steam Car . . . R. E. Olds once built a steam automobile, a 3-wheel horseless carriage at his father's machine shop in Lansing, Michigan, in 1887 . . . The Stearns Steamer was built in Syracuse, New York, in 1889 . . . Steam cars were in use long before gasoline automobiles appeared . . . If Henry Ford, Walter P. Chrysler and Charles Kettering had been steam engineers, we might be using steam automobiles today instead of gas cars . . . Webb Jay, renowned early-day racing driver, won many spectacular racing events in the famous White Steam Car Racer, "Whistling Billy" . . . Fred Marriott, in a Stanley Steamer, was the first human being to ever travel over two miles per minute when he established the world's speed record of 127 miles per hour at Ormond Beach, Florida, in 1906 . . . A steam car called the Delling had a 3-cylinder steam engine . . . The Stanley and Doble engines were mounted on the rear axle, while the White Steamer had the engine located under the hood . . . An airplane powered by a steam unit was flown in 1933 at San Francisco.

THE IMPROVED "LIGHTNING" KEROSENE BURNER

It lights with a match.

As quick or quicker to start than any gasoline burner.

Makes more steam than you can use. Absolutely safe; can not be flooded. Indestructible, odorless, noiseless; will not carbonize.

Makes your steamer as economical as a gasoline car. Pays for itself. Ask for catalog A.

E. C. WALKER CO.
New Albany, Ind.

FROM ORIGINAL STANLEY STEAMER LITERATURE

QUESTIONS AND ANSWERS

1. Why is the Stanley car a Steam car?

Because steam is one of the only two powers which will meet the demands of a variable-speed, variable-power device.

2. What is a variable-speed, variable-power device?

A machine that must operate under conditions of speed and power that are not constant. An automobile, for instance, is a variable-speed, variable-power device because it should run smoothly and efficiently at any speed from one mile an hour to 60 miles per hour. And it requires variable power even without variable speed, because it needs more power on a grade, or for acceleration in traffic, than it does on a smooth, level road.

3. What power besides steam meets these requirements?

Electricity can be adapted to the work. But in an automobile it must have a battery which is limited in stored power and radius of action, and rapidly loses its maximum power.

4. Why not an internal-explosive engine?

Because it is a constant-speed, constant-power device that operates efficiently only at a certain speed. That is, in order to get its rated power it must run at a certain constant speed. If it runs faster or more slowly than this, its rated power falls off. So an engine that gives 60 H.P. at 2500 R.P.M. can only produce about 5 H.P. at 500 R.P.M. and at very low speeds it has a "stagger point" at which it has just power enough to turn itself. Below this speed it cannot run smoothly, or may even refuse to run at all.

5. How, then, are so many internal-explosive or gas engines driving cars today?

Simply because automobile engineers have *made* the internal-explosive engine operate under these conditions. By the addition of extraneous devices that make up for some of the shortcomings of the engine itself, and have thus adapted it to an automobile even though it is not well-suited for the work.

6. What are these extraneous devices?

Carburetors, gear-shift sets, clutches, starting motors, jointed drive shafts.

7. Why do you call them extraneous devices?

Because they are not a part of an internal-explosive engine; but have to be added to it in the attempt to apply it to an automobile.

8. Could not an internal-explosive motor drive an automobile without these devices?

No, because it is a constant-speed, constant-load engine and has no starting effort, no stored power; nor can it be placed on the rear axle where the engine should be, and where the power is used.

9. But is it not true that some gas cars have reserve power?

Reserve power, yes — but not in the sense of stored power. A gas car can have any amount of power by using a large enough engine. But an engine large enough to handle the heavy demands, or "peak" loads, is larger than necessary, and therefore inefficient under the light demands of good, level roads.

10. Then what do you mean by "stored power" in a power plant?

Power which is generated in advance and is instantaneously available for use in any desired quantity when the driver wants it. Steam and electric power plants are the only ones that can have stored power.

11. Why has a gas engine no stored power?

Because in any engine the only source of energy is the fuel. And the internal-explosive engine cannot burn or explode its fuel without instantly converting it into rotative motion in the crank shaft. To have stored power, the fuel must be burned independently of the engine, and the energy taken from it in advance. When an internal-explosive engine is at rest there is not an ounce of power available — that is the reason it must receive an initial impulse from the outside by hand-cranking or from a starting motor, before it can turn itself. It cannot even start alone. And that is why the clutch is always put into an internal-explosive automobile. The engine must be started before it can deliver power, and it must be disconnected from the load till it is turning at a good rate of speed. Then the connection between power and load may be made, by "slipping in the clutch."

12. Are the gears absolutely necessary with a gas engine?

In an automobile, yes. This is the service where a maximum variation in speed and power is necessary. There have been times when you wanted a high power with a low car speed — as on hills, or for acceleration. At such a time the gear-box is absolutely necessary to permit a change of ratio between engine and axle, from say four to one, to seven to one, or to twelve to one. Were it not for this gear shift, which permits the engine to turn faster than the axle, the engine would run more and more slowly, and, of course, with less and less power, until it reached the "stagger point," and finally "stalled." This is not only inconvenient, but often dangerous. But by using the gear shift, the engine speed can be increased, and more power delivered, without increasing the car speed.

13. Doesn't that make a satisfactory solution?

No. It is a most unsatisfactory solution. Every motorist is demanding a better solution, and every manufacturer is trying to find it.

14. What would be a satisfactory solution?

Stored power. Power built up in advance, and the ability to apply that power in any desired volume to the rear wheels without gears to shift or clutch to pedal, and with only a finger-throttle control. Power that doesn't have to wait to build itself up in the speed of a fly-wheel, but is there all the time. Power that can be applied in maximum volume to the rear wheels, no matter how low the car speed.

15. What uses is an internal-explosive engine fit for, then?

It is perfectly adapted for purposes where only a constant power is wanted at a constant speed. The two most conspicuous examples of this are the aeroplane and the motor boat. These are constant-speed, constant-power devices. Land vehicles are not in this class. But the best example is a stationary plant, in a loft building, for instance, where not only the power and speed are constant, but the temperature and humidity as well.

16. How did the internal-explosive engine ever acquire such general use if it is not suited for land vehicle work?

As a matter of fact, it is not generally used in land vehicles. True, it has been used generally in automobiles,

STANLEY STEAM CARS

but that is only one type of land vehicle. Railroads have never been able to adapt the internal-explosive engine to their work, although it has been tried repeatedly. And railroads demand the best performance they can get in a power plant.

17. *Then why such general use of internal-explosive engines in automobiles?*

Because years ago an engineering fashion set in around the internal-explosive engine, and around the idea of getting "power direct from fuel." And the problem of adapting the gas engine to the automobile so absorbed the attention of the engineers of the day, they soon conceived their problem to be, not the perfection of a power plant that was fundamentally suited to the work, but the adaptation of the internal-explosive engine to the automobile.

18. *If the gas engine gets "power direct from fuel," is it not more efficient than the steam engine?*

That would be true if it always ran at its rated speed and power. But efficiency rapidly falls off if these depart from the narrow middle range. Even with the same fuel-cost, and with constant speed, the advantage would be slight, and is secured at the expense of long life, reliability and convenience. But when you consider that kerosene is used in the Stanley, the efficiency per dollar is about two or two and a half to one in favor of the steam car.

19. *Why is the gas engine short-lived as compared to a steam engine?*

It must run at much higher speeds, making lubrication uncertain and difficult, and because of this high speed there is increasing wear and strain. At 3000 R.P.M. each piston travels up and down the cylinder fifty times per second, which is an almost incredible situation. Another reason is because in exploding (or burning) the fuel in the cylinder, the most delicate parts of the engine, —the valves, pistons and cylinder walls,—are exposed to the terrific heat of combustion and the action of the burning gases at these high temperatures. It is no exaggeration to say that the cylinder is actually used as a fire-box.

STANLEY STEAM CARS

20. *Why is the gas engine more **unreliable** than a steam engine?*

Because it depends upon so many delicate devices and adjustments for its operation, any one of which can make trouble. These are such devices as carburetors, magnetos or generators, and distributors, cam shafts, timing gears, poppet valves, spark plugs and valve springs, etc. Not only are these devices themselves delicate, but the processes or functions they perform are even more so. There are no correspondingly delicate processes or devices on the Stanley car.

21. *Why is the gas engine not so **convenient** in an automobile as a steam engine?*

Because its successful performance in an automobile is contingent upon the manipulation of spark and throttle levers, transmission gears and gear shifting, and throttle and it must have a highly-refined, semi-precious fuel like gasoline. The steam engine can use any fuel: crude oil, kerosene or gasoline; and such a refined power plant as the Stanley can burn either kerosene or gasoline or any combination of the two, without adjustment.

22. *You spoke, a minute ago, of getting "power direct from fuel." Why doesn't that make things simpler than in the Stanley? You have two conversions to make. You burn your fuel in one place, and use the power in another.*

Yes, that is what is called the "two-stage" system. And if getting the power out of the fuel were the whole of the problem, then the "single-stage" might be better. But the whole problem consists of getting the power from the fuel to the rear wheels of the automobile. And engineers have found that all the mechanisms which have been necessary to do that with the gas engine, are far more complicated and unsatisfactory than the "two-stage" system which they set out to get around.

23. *Why do you say more complicated?*

Because the clutch, the gear shift, the jointed drive shafts, the fly-wheel, the bevel driving gear which is necessary to make the power turn a right angle, altogether make a far more complex system than the steam generating unit which has no moving parts whatever.

STANLEY STEAM CARS

24. *Then the power-processes of the steam car and the internal-explosive car are not the same?*

No. Any automobile must have means of generating power from fuel; of controlling the power; and of applying it to the rear axle. But while these functions are distinct and independent in the steam car, in the internal-explosive car they overlap so that they cannot be separated. In an internal-explosive car no power can be generated without either using it instantly or wasting it. It cannot be stored as steam can be stored in a Stanley.

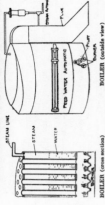

BOILER (cross section)   BOILER (outside view)

25. *How is the steam generated in the Stanley car?*

By heating water in a small boiler over a kerosene burner. The boiler, which is 23" in diameter and 14" deep, and contains the water, is under the hood of the car. Directly beneath it is the burner which supplies the heat.

26. *Where is the steam stored?*

Right in the boiler itself, which is kept about one-half full of water. With steam up, it holds enough stored power to drive the car two or three miles even if the fuel is shut off. There is only one type of boiler that can store power this way,— that is the kind we use,— a fire-tube water-level boiler.

27. *Just what is a fire-tube water-level boiler?*

One that is built like a drum and holds the water inside it. Through it run vertical tubes, open at each end so that the heat from the burner can pass up through them. The object of these tubes is to give additional heating surface; so this boiler, which has only about 3 square feet of surface on the bottom, has a total heating surface, with the tubes, of 104 square feet.

28. *Why is this large heating surface so desirable?*

Because it makes rapid steam generation possible. The objective in boiler design is large heating surface in the smallest possible boiler, with water and steam capacity sufficient to give stored power. A Stanley boiler generates steam very rapidly and at the same time carries a quantity of hot water and steam. This is a combination that cannot be had in the so-called "flash" or "semi-flash" boilers, which can steam rapidly but have no stored power capacity.

29. *What prevents too much steam from being generated?*

An automatic valve governs the fuel, so when the correct pressure of steam is secured, the fuel is shut off till enough steam has been drawn from the boiler to lower the pressure. This device is called the "steam automatic."

STEAM AUTOMATIC

30. *Is not an automatic device of this kind rather delicate?*

Not at all. Like the other devices on the Stanley, it is one of the oldest principles in engineering,—rugged and simple. It contains only one movable part.

31. *How does the fuel come on after it has been shut off?*

As soon as the steam pressure drops, this steam automatic opens the fuel line and admits the kerosene to the burner. This is ignited by a small pilot light which is not controlled by the automatic, but burns continuously.

32. *What is this pilot light?*

It is a tiny burner at the mouth of the main burner, and is made so small that it requires very little fuel, even though it burns constantly. It is supplied with fuel from a tank separate from the main burner and is entirely independent of it. This pilot also keeps the main burner hot so the kerosene lights instantly when the steam automatic turns it on.

33. *Isn't this pilot troublesome?*

No. Why should it be? It burns steadily, under constant conditions. A twelve-cylinder engine has 12 pilots, each expected to ignite and go out by mechanical operation 25 times a second — a total of 18,000 times a minute. Ours is not mechanically operated, it is not electric, and burns steadily. This is another instance of the simplicity of our problems, as compared with internal-explosive problems.

34. *How is the fuel supplied to the main burner?*

By air pressure automatically kept up by a small plunger pump. A feature of this system is the pair of small quart pressure tanks which make a pressure feed possible without pressure in the main fuel tank. With this arrangement fuel can be taken in the main tank without losing the air pressure every time the filler cap is removed. The system has all the advantages of the old, reliable pressure system without the disadvantages.

35. *Does not the water-level in the boiler drop as steam is used for driving the car?*

Yes, surely,— so it is necessary to supply it with water to replace that which is drawn off as steam. This is done mechanically by a pair of plunger pumps.

FEED WATER AUTOMATIC

36. *How is the amount of this "feed water" to the boiler controlled?*

By a valve which automatically regulates the feed water as it enters the boiler. The two pumps mentioned are driven from the rear axle and work whenever the rear axle turns. Therefore, there is a constant flow of water from them, while it is always greater than is required by the boiler. The automatic valve on the boiler admits just the right amount of this water to replace that used as steam, and the balance is returned to the tank. By this arrangement the pumps can be ordinary plunger pumps and run at a low speed and still furnish the boiler just the right quantity of water.

37. *How much attention would I have to give the fuel and water systems while running?*

None at all. They are entirely automatic. When you start, you open your main burner fuel valve. After that, the automatic valve will open and close itself without your attention, and in fact even without your knowledge.

38. *Isn't there danger that the boiler will explode?*

None at all. It is provided with these automatic fuel and water devices, and with a safety valve.

39. *But what if all these should fail to work?*

Then it is no exaggeration to say that the boiler itself consists of 750 safety valves. There are 750 tubes. Since the shell as well as many, many times stronger than the tubes, the tubes would first yield to excessive pressure. The weakest one would yield first, and begin to leak like a safety valve. Then the next, and the next, until the leakage was greater than the generation. To cause an explosion, every one of the 750 tubes would have to go at once; which is just as impossible as to pull a chain with 750 links, and make them all break at once.

40. *Does not the fresh water pumped in tend to chill the steam and hot water in the boiler?*

It would if it were cold, but this water is heated before it enters the boiler, by the feed water heater, which thus utilizes the heat of the exhaust steam.

41. *What becomes of this exhaust steam?*

As it is exhausted from the engine it passes through the feed water heater and is then led into the radiator where it cools and condenses into water again. From there it returns to the water tank.

42. *The water then makes a complete cycle through the car and is used over and over again?*

Yes, it makes the circuit about ten times, before it is lost through surplus exhaust and dissipation. That is why present Stanleys use so much less water than the older cars that exhausted the steam into the air and used it only once.

STANLEY STEAM CARS

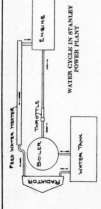

WATER CYCLE IN STANLEY POWER PLANT

43. *What do you use for a condenser?*

An ordinary Mayo radiator.

44. *What mileage does a tank of water give?*

One filling is sufficient for from 150 to 250 miles; it varies considerably according to the road, the load and the speed.

45. *Why is the Stanley engine on the rear axle?*

Because that is the ideal place for any engine,—right where the power is used. All cars would undoubtedly be built that way if the engine design would permit. Even electric trolley cars have their motors right down on the axles.

46. *Just why is this location the most efficient one?*

Because no jointed drive shaft is needed to carry the rotative power back to the rear axle. A drive shaft requires at least two and sometimes four universal joints, with double that many bearings, and every one of these added devices uses up power in friction, and requires attention and lubrication. Besides, the drive shaft must always be at right angles to the rear axle in a gas car, and bevel gears are required to turn right angles to divert the direction of rotation. Making rotative energy turn right angles is in itself bad practice. This crank shaft of the Stanley engine is parallel to the rear axle, geared right into it, and within 9 inches of it.

47. *How does it compare to a gas car crank shaft?*

It is only 8¼ inches long, and runs on only two main bearings. Yet it performs the function of cam shaft as well as that of a crank shaft. Furthermore it delivers its power from the middle, between two closely associated bearings, and not from the extreme end.

STANLEY STEAM CARS

48. *Why are gas engines not on the rear axle?*

For many reasons, but chiefly because they are too bulky and heavy to fit under a car. This is especially true of the big multi-cylinder engines such as the sixes, eights and twelves.

49. *What are the other reasons?*

Because they have so many moving parts that they must be accessible for adjustment and repair. The accessibility of a gas engine is a serious consideration, and is widely advertised by different manufacturers.

50. *But doesn't the Stanley engine ever require attention?*

Very little. About as much as the gear-box does in your car. The Stanley engine has only two cylinders and only 15 moving parts and has no carburetor, ignition, starting motor, spark plugs, cam shaft, poppet valves, timing gears, etc. Nor can it ever have carbon troubles.

51. *Why no carbon troubles?*

Because in the Stanley the fuel is not burned in the engine. Nothing but steam enters the cylinders.

52. *You say the Stanley engine has only two cylinders?*

Only two, with 4 inch bore and 5 inch stroke. It is, however, a double acting engine. That is, the steam works against either side of the piston. This gives as many impulses as an 8 cylinder internal-explosive engine.

53. *Why does a gas engine have so many cylinders?*

Owing to the fact that the gas explodes violently, it is desirable to divide this destructive force up into as many smaller explosions as possible. Then too, by getting more impulses to the revolution it is possible to reduce the size of the fly-wheel, or as it is often called, the "balance wheel."

54. *Why does the gas engine have to have a balance wheel if the Stanley engine does not?*

To absorb and smooth out the sharp explosions, and steady the turning of the shaft. In addition to this the heavy balance wheel carries the gas engine over the three idle strokes, one of which is the compression stroke, which would otherwise stall it. The Stanley, on the contrary, exerts a *continuous pressure.* This pressure

STANLEY STEAM CARS

expands, instead of exploding, and does not have to swing a heavy weight to turn the shaft smoothly. And there is no compression stroke to a steam engine, nor is there any "stalling,"—so a fly-wheel would be superfluous.

55. *If four or eight or twelve cylinders are better in a gas car, why not in a Stanley, too?*

Because the whole object is accomplished in a Stanley with two. That is, a smooth continuous flow of power. We spoke of impulses a minute ago. That is a misnomer, as applied to the Stanley engine. They are not impulses, but a uniform, continuous flow of power. Any number of additional cylinders could not make the "push" on the crank shaft any more uniform and continuous.

56. *You say you do not have any poppet valves, or valve springs, or cam shaft. How do the valves operate, then?*

Only two valves are used, one for each cylinder. They are not mechanically lifted, and do not depend upon valve springs, but merely slide back and forth over an opening or port which connects the cylinder with the steam chest. There are several well-known methods of operating these slide valves, but we employ the oldest and simplest, the "Stephenson link motion."

57. *What do you mean by the steam chest?*

That is a chamber in the engine through which the steam passes to the cylinder. The valves operate in this chamber.

58. *What is the function of the Stephenson link?*

It is this action that makes it possible to reverse the car without reverse gearing. It is an arrangement by which the motion of the slide valves is reversed, changing the entrance of steam into the cylinders and turning the axle the other way.

59. *How is this valve action controlled?*

By a pedal at the left foot of the driver. When the foot is released a spring returns the pedal to normal.

STANLEY STEAM CARS

60. *What other pedals are there on the car?*

Only the service brake. The Stanley has no clutch pedal because it has no clutch.

61. *If the engine and axle are direct connected how is the speed and power of the car controlled?*

By a throttle lever which controls the flow of steam. This little lever does it all, and is so small in size and easy to handle that it is placed right on the steering post under the wheel. To get more speed or more power it is only necessary to advance the lever. This opens the throttle valve in the steam line and lets more steam to the engine. The steam is controlled like the water in a faucet, —in fact, the functions of faucet and throttle are identical.

STANLEY STEERING WHEEL AND THROTTLE LEVER

62. *How can the car climb a steep grade without gears to shift?*

Because the Stanley is powerful enough to slip the rear wheels, which is all the power that can possibly be used in a car.

63. *How about steep hills at low car speed?*

Power does not depend upon speed in a steam engine. A gas engine, on the other hand, must be turning fast to deliver its rated power. Gears in a gas car simply provide a means of getting high engine speed with low car speed. In some gas trucks the engine turns forty times as fast

STANLEY STEAM CARS

as the rear axle. This gear reduction is necessary to get power out of the engine at low car speeds.

STANLEY ENGINE (stripped to show moving parts)

64. *What is the ratio between the engine and the rear axle in the Stanley?*

The engine gear has 40 teeth and the differential ring-gear 60, so the ratio is 1½ to 1.

65. *What is the differential ring-gear?*

The big gear on the rear axle. This gear is present in any car around the differential, but in a shaft drive car it is a bevel gear driven by the drive shaft. In the Stanley, it is a straight spur gear and meshes directly into the engine gear.

66. *What is the engine gear?*

The gear on the crank shaft which the engine pistons turn.

67. *Why are these gears necessary?*

Because the pistons and connecting rods have to work on a crank shaft. These two gears, and there are only two, permanently connect the crank shaft and the rear axle direct.

68. *What takes the rear axle torque in a Stanley car?*

The engine acts as a torque arm. It is bolted solid to the rear axle housing and hung flexibly at the front end. So, little if any, of the torque is on the springs.

69. *What kind of springs are on the Stanley?*

Full elliptic in the rear. Semi-elliptic in front

STANLEY STEAM CARS

70. *What takes the drive?*

All four springs. This method has all the advantages of the Hotchkiss drive, but instead of the rear springs taking the entire driving strain, the load is distributed through both front and rear axles by tie rods which connect the front and rear axles. This is an exclusive Stanley feature and is one reason the cars are so comfortable to ride in.

71. *What are the other reasons?*

The steam power itself, smooth and noiseless, is the main reason; but the absence of gear-shift, clutch, starting motor, controls,— in a word, the simplicity of Stanley control is one of its greatest charms. Especially in traffic or on bad roads the Stanley control is a real comfort. Drivers soon learn instinctively that it is no effort to change the car speed — no shifting of gears, no pedalling of clutch, no separating the power from the load. So the Stanley owner slows down for bad spots in the road more often than the driver of a gas car. This, we think, is the principle reason why Stanley cars have the reputation of being the easiest riding cars in the world. Then there is no vibration or consciousness of mechanical forces at work.

72. *What tire mileage do you get on Stanley cars?*

Excellent. Five thousand miles is regarded as good mileage on the average car, but the Stanley under the same conditions gets 10,000 miles from the tires.

73. *How do you account for this tire economy?*

By the smoothness of the steam power plant. It is the internal strains on tires which cause them to give out. In a gas car a violent strain is put on the tire every few minutes; especially when starting or shifting gears. When the clutch engages, no matter how gently, there is a point at which it takes hold and the hard, inflexible, rotative force of the drive shaft must be transmitted through the tire on the road surface. Then the car moves, but for the instant during which the inertia of the car was being overcome, the tires had to absorb and cushion the jerk on the axle. This is so hard on tires, as compared with the smooth, flexible pressure of steam, that one tire manufacturer was on the point of giving a special long mileage guarantee with tires that were to be used on steam cars.

74. *Isn't the Stanley uncomfortably warm in summer?*

No. There is no more heat to be felt than in any gas car. In fact, there is less than in those where the exhaust pipe comes close under the floor boards.

75. *How about cold weather? Will Stanley cars freeze in cold weather?*

The Stanley is the best car in the world for winter going, because it has more stored heat than any other. It will freeze if you don't look out for it, just the same as your car will — just the same as your fingers or your ears will freeze, if you don't take care of them. But the precautions necessary to protect a Stanley car are less than with a gas car.

76. *What do you do if you are to leave your car in the street for two or three hours in zero weather?*

Nothing, just leave it there. Or if you leave it in an unheated garage over night, just leave it there. If you are going to leave it a week or so, in zero weather, then turn out the pilot and drain it, just as you would your present car.

77. *What did you mean by stored heat?*

Hot water. Eight gallons in the boiler, 20 gallons in the tank. You are more careful to have your radiator full in the winter than in the summer, because you want this stored heat, so your engine won't chill so quickly. The more stored heat you have, the better. In the Stanley, by the way, the radiator contains not a particle of water while the car is standing. It all goes back to the tank.

78. *How about starting up after a stop — say a two hour stop?*

The pilot will maintain two or three hundred pounds of steam. The car is ready to go instantly. There is no "ten minute fight with your engine," as one manufacturer advertises it.

79. *What would happen if it did freeze in a cold garage?*

Nothing. Stanley cars have been left all winter in unheated garages, undrained. They have frozen and thawed a dozen times. There is no harm done, beyond bursting a pipe or two — nothing critical or expensive.

80. *How much time is required to get up steam in the morning?*

Steam is already up in the morning if the car has been used the day before. With just the pilot burning, two or three hundred pounds of steam will be maintained over night, and the pilot will burn several days without attention.

81. *How long will it take when the pilot has been turned off a week?*

About seven or eight minutes. Experienced drivers do it in six minutes, but eight minutes would be a good average for Stanley owners. A beginner would, undoubtedly, require a little more time.

82. *Isn't steaming up a slow, difficult process?*

Not at all. You turn a switch and the pilot vaporizer is heated electrically and the pilot is lighted electrically. Then you turn on the main fuel.

83. *But isn't seven or eight minutes' delay inconvenient when starting?*

Yes, it would seem so, but as a matter of fact, it is this very time which gives you the stored power that is essential to good performance, so the time is well worth spending. There is scarcely a gas car owner who would not gladly stay in his garage, behind closed doors, and shift gears steadily for even fifteen minutes, if he knew that when he got his car on the road he would have stored power, and would not have to shift another gear all day. But most Stanley cars are not steamed up oftener than once a month or so. They are left every night with the pilot burning.

84. *Can't a steam car be made that would get up steam in a minute or two, even when cold?*

Yes, easily, but that would mean a flash or semi-flash boiler, that could not possibly have the hot water and steam reserve that gives the Stanley its stored power and ideal performance. Quickly lift up power is quickly spent, and such a change would reduce the Stanley (as far as flexibility and stored power are concerned) to the level of the internal-explosive car.

85. *What about fire? Can I get a Stanley car insured?*

Certainly. Insurance rates are just the same as on internal-explosive cars. The fire risk is less, in fact, since we use kerosene fuel.

86. *If steam cars are so superior, why so many gas cars?*

That's a very proper question, and at the same time a very broad one. The motives that govern mankind in the aggregate are usually as varied as the number of individuals concerned and cannot be ascribed to any single reason. There are four general reasons for the prevalence of gas cars.

First: At first the internal-explosive engine, by getting "power direct from fuel" seemed the best for the very moderate standard of performance required. The self-propelled vehicle was, even then, so superior to horse-drawn vehicles, that no one seemed to mind cranking, occasional balking, vibration and noise, complicated control and indirect transmission. The gas power plant, as then conceived, seemed simpler than the steam plant, as then conceived, and was consequently adopted.

Second: Automobile engineers were largely recruited, not from the engineering profession, but from those who first became interested in the sport of automobiling. For the reasons set forth above, their entire environment and habit of thought was solely gasoline-propelled vehicles,— in other words, they accepted without question, as a habit, that the only motive power was the internal-explosive engine.

Third: Automobile manufacturing is a commercial enterprise, following the path of least resistance, desiring quick sales, and like any other industry, fearing radical innovations. As a result of the habit of thought alluded to, it continued to adhere to the internal-explosive engine.

Fourth: The standard of performance has steadily risen. The car that was satisfactory a few years ago would not be tolerated to-day. The effort to meet the demands has resulted in such great elaboration of the internal-explosive power plant, that it has long since lost its imaginary initial advantage and has become far more complicated and burdensome to maintain and control than the steam plant, and even then, is inferior in performance, since it cannot have stored power.

New Standard Steam Car

Automatic Controls—High Pressure Condensing Are Features of Car—Operates 300 Miles on One Filling of Water

IT is generally recognized by all engineers that the steam power plant offers a means of readily burning low grade fuels with an ease that has not as yet been approached in the motor car type of internal combustion engine, and we are finding therefore that there is an increased amount of attention and study being given the steam plant and its possibilities; one of the latest entries to the steam car field being the Standard Engineering Co. of St. Louis, bringing out a steam car, on which all controls are automatically operated, it being necessary for the driver to only sit in the seat, press a button, and start off after a thirty second wait.

Two-Cylinder Engine

The car is powered with a two-cylinder double acting engine supported at its front end on a cross-member in the frame and at the rear, by the axle. The boiler is of the water-tube type, and its position in the chassis is just behind the radiator, which in this case serves as a condenser, making it possible to use the boiler water over and over again, obtaining about 350 miles per filling.

Following is a description of the car as given by the builders of the car, L. L. Scott and Dr. E. C. Newcomb, St. Louis.

"The boiler is of the continuous flow type, consisting of frustro conical coils connected in series so as to form a continuous tube through which the water fed to the boiler and the steam discharged from the boiler must pass. These coils are arranged one within the other around a central combustion chamber. Water enters the bottom of the coil most remote from the fire, and steam is discharged at the lowest point of the coil next to the fire. Nickel-steel tubing ½ in. I. D. by ¾ in. O. D. is used. This tubing will stand a pressure of 35,000 lb. per sq. in. Freezing does not affect it. All joints—which are very few—are welded. Circulation of water through this boiler is dependent upon action of the water pump, and the velocity of the steam through boiler approximates 450 ft. per second. Owing to this high steam velocity and to the use of deflocculated graphite mixed with kerosene for lubricating the engine, scale and deposit trouble have been eliminated. This boiler has about 72 sq. ft. of heating surface and can produce 500 lb. of steam per hour, at an average efficiency of over 80 per cent. The car will run one mile on the stored steam in the boiler, after the fire has been shut off.

Combustion System

"We use kerosene fuel, which is ignited cold by an electric spark. The spark plug circuit after two seconds operation is cut off by a switch operated by the kerosene gage. No pressure is carried on the fuel tank. When the fire is on, the fuel is pumped by a small electric motor —this motor also

Scott Steam Car Specifications

ENGINE.....................Two-cylinder double acting
BOILER..............................Water tube type
STEAM PRESSURE............................600 lb.
FUEL AND WATER SUPPLY..Automatically controlled
CONDENSING SYSTEM...........................
..............Gives 300 mile operation on one filling
FUEL USED..............................Kerosene

runs the water pump and air blower—to a mechanical atomizing nozzle and is discharged in a very fine spray at 35 lb. pressure, and directed downward from the top of the boiler into a combustion chamber. This chamber is entirely surrounded by pipe coils. In a fire of the atomized type, it is necessary to have a long space in which to burn the fuel. Great difficulty has been experienced by others in the past with refractory linings breaking down under this type of fire. It is also necessary to complete combustion before the fire touches the boiler tubes or sooting will take place. With the combustion chamber as shown in the cut, the fire cannot play on any coil, the heat is gradually absorbed over a large area, with the result no trouble is experienced in burning boiler coils or breaking down refractory lining.

Method of Control

"Great difficulty has been experienced with the continuous flow of type of boiler (in motor car use) in maintaining an even pressure and temperature; pressure and temperature were either too high or too low which lead to burnt boilers, burnt-out packing, and irregular running of the car. Control systems of the past included numerous by-pass valves, steam automatics, flow motors, etc. Our control consists of a steam gage which operates an electric switch; said switch controls the operation of an electric motor. As the water and fuel pumps are driven by an electric motor these liquids are pumped in definite quantitive relation. The length of time that the motor is 'on' depends on the demand for steam. If the car is running at 25 m.p.h. on level road, the motor will be 'on' about one-third of the time. If running at 60 m.p.h. on a level road the fire would then be "on" all of the time.

Airplane view of Standard steam car, showing the round boiler at the front with the condenser at the front, which to all appearances is similar to a radiator. The engine is at the rear, suspended on the frame and partly on the axle

(Continued on next page)

(Continued from preceding page)

It is a very easy matter to see the advantage of using an electric motor of constant speed in place of driving the pumps from the engine. This drive also has the advantage of locating all parts containing water, right at the boiler. By driving the water pump by electric motor, it is not necessary to use a cushion in the water line to prevent water hammer. We also eliminate the safety or blow-off valve by a fuse in the motor circuit.

The starting and stopping of the motor is controlled by the steam pressure gage. This gage operates a small switch which is set to open the circuit at 600 lb. steam pressure and to close the circuit when the steam pressure has dropped to 500 lb. It is absolutely necessary to break the circuit at one steam pressure and close the circuit at a lower pressure.

Steam Temperature Control

The back of duplex gage is shown in the cut. Small pins are attached to the Bourdon tubes of these gages, which project out through the back of the gage and operate the small electric switches. The kerosene gage controls the time of operation of the spark plug. This circuit is closed from 0 to 25 lb. pressure and open above 25 lb. pressure. The normal pressure on delivery side of fuel pump (when motor is running) is about 35 lb. To avoid handling the motor circuit, we use a magnet switch which operates in the motor line. The magnet switch takes half an ampere to operate it and this is the current carried by the gage switch. A steam temperature gage is used to indicate the temperature of the steam, which runs from 600 to 750 deg. F. This gage has an electric switch which closes at 800 deg. F., at which time the fuel will be automatically cut off from the combustion chamber. The closing of this switch causes a little magnet by-pass valve in the fuel line to open. This switch seldom comes into action in the normal working of the system, but it is a safety means to shut off the first in the event that the water tank is empty.

"As common with most gas cars, we use an electrical motor, a storage battery and a dynamo; our motor and dynamo are connected in series. The dynamo furnishes all of the current to the motor direct, when the motor

The engine of this steam car has two cylinders. The double acting principle is used together with poppet valves

shuts off, due to pressure being up to 600 lb., the series field of the dynamo is automatically cut out, thereby reducing the dynamo output to a current suitable for charging the battery. For tractor work —where the speed of the engine is nearly constant—it is possible to eliminate the dynamo, motor and storage battery, but it is necessary to have hand-starting devices, a dry battery for ignition and con-

trol of small magnets which act on suction valves of pumps. We feel that the motor and storage battery is the most direct and simple arrangement.

Throttle Valve

"The throttle valve is made of non-rusting material. Steam cannot pass the seat of the valve until the valve seat has a full opening, thereby preventing wire drawing which tends to destroy the valve seat. The throttle valve will close automatically when the brake is applied.

Water Pumps

"One of the sources of trouble, on automotive steam systems of the past, was the water pump. The valves on our water pump are made of special non-rusting material that has very long life. The lift of the valve is limited to 1-16 in. Due to small lift and special design of the valve and to the fact that the pump always runs at the same speed regardless of the speed of the car we absolutely eliminate all pump noises. As our pump has practically no clearance space it cannot get air-bound. We use no stuffing-box whatsoever and the entire pump is inclosed in a case and submerged in oil. The pump plunger is made of hardened stainless steel; it is so designed that there can never be any sidethrust on it or the pump cylinder and consequently there is absolute alignment at all times. By making the pump cylinder long and making the bore absolutely round and straight, and no possibility for wear of plunger or cylinder, we avoid the use of stuffing-boxes and get a minimum amount of friction between plunger and cylinder. Our pump does not leak. It may be interesting to add that these pumps have been built to work successfully against 5000 lb. pressure although our pressure never exceeds 600 lb. The engine of the Standard steam car is of the semi-uniflow two cylinder double acting, poppet-valve type. Valves and piston rods are made of non-rusting material. The valves never need to be reground. The metal in the cylinder is absolutely uniform in section, so as to insure even expansion of the metal when hot. The cam box, which carries the cam and tappets for operating the valves, is thoroughly insulated from the cylinder to avoid heating of the oil in the cam box. Different points of 'cut-off' and reverse are obtained by simply shifting the

(Continued on next page)

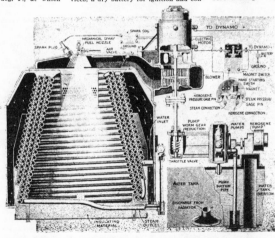

The steam boiler is composed of a number of sections of steel tubing built up into the shape of a cone

(Continued from preceding page)

cam. The cam is of special shape to permit easy shifting and to allow an infinite number of cut-offs.

Low Steam Consumption

By the use of short cut-off, tight valves, small clearance space, free exhaust, uniform section in cylinder metal, we get very low steam consumption. The mechanical efficiency of our engine is about 95 per cent. We use no stuffing-boxes on valve-stems or piston rods; it is simply a question of proper non-rusting material, proper design and workmanship and means to maintain perfect alignment. In passenger cars we mount the engine partly on the rear axle and partly on the frame; the major part of the weight is carried by the frame. The unsprung weight on the axle is very small. By this drive we eliminate the driveshaft, and universal joints and get a smooth-riding job.

Pleasure Car Differential

"Where the engine is mounted partly on the rear axle and partly on the frame, we carry the differential spur gear in the engine case, which case is an aluminum casting very carefully designed to take care of all conditions of the service. There are many unique features in our differential. The principal one being the means of adjusting the differential spur gear to the engine spur gears. This adjustment is brought about by having the bearing for the axle mounted in the aluminum frame on an adjusting axis of rotation, eccentric to the axis of the axle. This arrangement allows a very fine adjustment between the engine driving gear and differential gear and maintains concentric alignment of the entire axle.

Condensing System

"It is possible to obtain a water mileage of from 100 to 350 miles on a 25-gal. tank of water by simply running the exhaust steam from the engine into the top of a radiator similar to a gas car radiator and connecting the bottom of the radiator with the water tank, this without the use of a radiator fan.

Weather and road conditions greatly affect the water mileage. It is very desirable to get a long water mileage because aside from the general convenience the amount of foreign matter brought into the system is greatly reduced.

Long water mileage will also permit the use of alcohol in the water to prevent freezing in cold weather. One of the first things to look after in this matter is to have an engine that is efficient. The efficiency of the engine not only saves fuel and water but it regulates the size of the boiler, etc. The exhaust steam from the engine must be properly distributed at the top of the radiator and the discharge from radiator to water tank must be distributed to prevent noise. It is also very desirable to have a radiator fan that is driven by the exhaust steam from the engine. If we drive the fan from the engine mechani-

Three-quarter view of new Standard steam car. The condensing system gives 300 mile operation on one filling of water

cally it will not do very much good on long hills or on heavy pulling where the car is moving slow and the steam consumption is large. The ordinary exhaust turbine will not do for this work on account of the constantly changing load.

If the turbine nozzles are set so that the turbines will run at average road speeds, when we run at higher speeds or in heavy pulling, the back pressure on the exhaust line will be so high that the engine horsepower will be materially reduced. If the nozzle area is set to keep down the back pressure, the turban will not run except in very heavy going. We have experimented with an exhaust act-

Boiler is of continuous flow type, consisting of frustro conical coils

uated turbine which is provided with automatic means for increasing the nozzle area as the volume of steam increases thereby keeping the steam velocity approximately constant irrespective of variation in steam volume. While we have obtained some very interesting results in condensing steam, we have not

as yet completed our experiments in this and therefore we would prefer to withhold information on this until a later date.

Comparative Efficiency

It is probably not generally known that a properly designed automotive steam plant using steam at 600 lb. pressure and 700 deg. F. temperature, has a total efficiency at the rear wheels of around 15 per cent. or more. While this is slightly below the full load efficiency of the average gasoline power plant, it must be kept in mind that the efficiency of the internal combustion engine is at its maximum only at full engine power.

This is not true with the steam engine, in fact the steam job is almost the opposite. Most automobile engines run at about one-fourth load the greater part of the time and under these conditions the efficiency of the steam job is way above the gas engine plant. We have obtained from 12 to 15 miles from a gallon of kerosene with seven passengers in a car, which weighed 4200 lb. without the passengers, and this over average road conditions.

DENBY TO HEAD FULTON TRUCKS

New York, March 11—At the auction sale to-day conducted by the receiver, stockholders of the Fulton Motor Truck Co., of Farmingdale, L. I., combined with Garvin Denby and other financial interests purchased the factory and property for $290,000.

A new company to be known as Fulton Motor Corp. and to be headed by Denby, who was president and general manager of the Denby Motor Truck Co. of Detroit before its reorganization a year ago, is being formed with Denby as president and general manager. It is announced that the capital of the new company will be $1,500,000 of Class A stock at $10 par value and $350,000 of Class B stock of no par value. Through ownership of a majority of the Class B stock Denby will have control.

*T*HIS AUTOMOBILE is a 1922 Stanley Steamer, converted by us to burn any type of coal to produce steam at a pressure of 150 lbs. up to 500 lbs., which operates the car. The car weighs 6000 lbs. Has been operating with coal as the motive power for several years. We carry our coal and water Actually a power plant on wheels. ... By means of this car we have demonstrated the efficiency you can obtain by burning any type of coal on Mershon Shaking Grates. ... We have been manufacturing Grates since 1830 —114 years, and are in a position to make proper recommendations for grates to burn coal properly and efficiently.

MERSHON PATENT SHAKING GRATE WORKS

58th and Westminster Avenue, Philadelphia, Pa.

This American Steam Car is owned by W. B. Lewis
of Scotia, New York.

STANLEY STEAM MOTOR

This attractive, special built Stanley Steamer is owned by Harry W. McGee, Sr., of Milwaukee, Wisconsin. The car weighs 4460 lbs., and cruises at 55 to 60 miles per hour. Mr. McGee built this car in his spare time with the help of a good sheet metal worker. Hood and grill were especially designed by Mr. McGee. The car has a special under-draught system from condenser to condense all steam under any road conditions. Water capacity is 24 gallons — sufficient for approximately 100 miles. — Clymer.

Do You Know These Facts About the STANLEY?

IT HAS NO GEARS to shift.

* * * *

IT HAS NO CLUTCH to pedal.

* * * *

IT HAS NO STARTER to depend on.

* * * *

THE STANLEY MOTOR can start itself.

* * * *

THE STANLEY MOTOR can reverse itself.

* * * *

THE STANLEY MOTOR has only fifteen moving parts.

* * * *

THE STANLEY MOTOR can drive the car at 1 mile per hour, which is an engine speed of only 15 R. P. M.

* * * *

THE STANLEY CAR has only 37 moving parts.

* * * *

THE STANLEY CAR heats its own garage?

* * * *

THE STANLEY knows no "anti-freeze" solutions.

THE STANLEY fights cold with heat? (A natural endowment which nature gave it).

* * * *

THE STANLEY BOILER cannot explode.

* * * *

THE STANLEY BOILER is safer than the tires.

* * * *

THAT JUST COMMON every day intelligence IS ALL that is needed, to understand AND DRIVE a Stanley car.

* * * *

THE STANLEY CAR can run 200 miles without stopping for fuel or water.

* * * *

THE STANLEY can use Kerosene or gasoline and go 12 miles on a gallon.

* * * *

THE STANLEY does not have to take a run for a hill. It can stop in the middle without the brakes, and start on again.

* * * *

THE STANLEY drivers do not "raise" steam. They keep it up. THE PILOT LIGHT does that for them.

* * * *

That the Stanley concern WAS THE first one TO EQUIP all models WITH GENUINE flexibility.

Reproduced from advertising circular issued by Mr. H. W. McGee, Sr., of Milwaukee.

1922

Three Big Plants Now Producing
COATS STEAM CARS

Plant Number One

The [Y.F.] Stewart Motor Car Co. Plant at Bowling Green, Ohio. Engine and Boiler Assembly of Coats Steam Cars.

Plant Number Two

Executive offices of [Y.F.] Stewart Motor Car Co., and Final Assembly and delivery Plant of Coats Steam Cars at Columbus, O. Coats bodies are made and painting, trimming and finishing are done here.

Plant Number Three

At Louisville, Kentucky, manufacturing the Cumberland Cord Tires with which all Coats Steam Cars are equipped.

Any one wishing to see George A. Coats will find him either at the Columbus, Ohio, Plant No. 2, or at the Chicago address below. All Dealers and Prospective Dealers are invited to visit this fine plant.

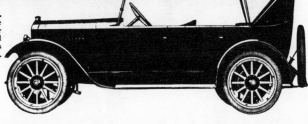

$1085

Coats Steam Car Co., *Exclusive Selling Agents*
2337 Michigan Avenue, Chicago, Illinois

170

MacDonald

offers

Steam Bob-Cat

Cars and Units

1923

Models Now Available:

CHASSIS

COMPLETE CAR
(All Body Styles)

PATENTED DIRECT DRIVE
ENGINE-REAR AXLE

BOILER-BURNER UNIT

A new thrill awaits the American motorist in the MacDonald Steam Bob-Cat Car. Here is a car that will change your every conception of motoring comfort and convenience; a car that responds to every touch of the throttle with a smooth flow of power that takes you over the steepest hills at any speed desired or through the mazes of traffic at two miles an hour or less.

For it is powered by steam; the source of power that many experts contend will ultimately replace gasoline. The MacDonald Steam Bob-Cat Car is flexible to a degree never possible in a gasoline-propelled automobile. There is no changing of gears; there is none of the inconveniences of the gasoline motor; nothing but a smooth flow of power whenever you want it.

And the Patented Direct Drive Engine-Rear Axle with Boiler-Burner Unit will also solve the transportation problems of many industries. Firms operating fleets of small delivery trucks will find these units of unusual economic value and the change of power plant is quickly and easily made. The heavier Steam Units are ideal for converting gasoline-propelled Motor Busses, Delivery Trucks and Pleasure Cars into Steamers.

Inquiries are invited from firms and individuals relative to this new idea in the utilization for steam.

MacDONALD STEAM AUTOMOTIVE CORP.
Office and Factory
GARFIELD   OHIO

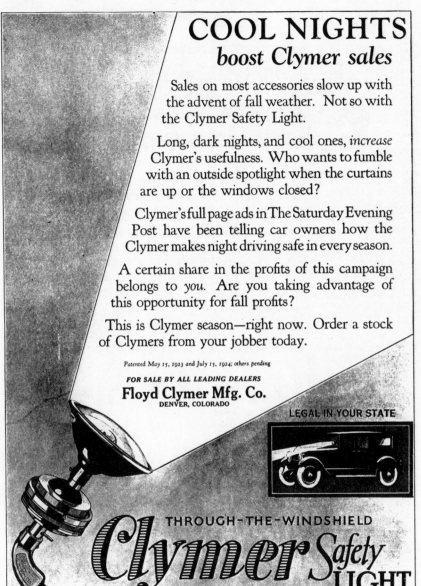

COOL NIGHTS
boost Clymer sales

Sales on most accessories slow up with the advent of fall weather. Not so with the Clymer Safety Light.

Long, dark nights, and cool ones, *increase* Clymer's usefulness. Who wants to fumble with an outside spotlight when the curtains are up or the windows closed?

Clymer's full page ads in The Saturday Evening Post have been telling car owners how the Clymer makes night driving safe in every season.

A certain share in the profits of this campaign belongs to *you*. Are you taking advantage of this opportunity for fall profits?

This is Clymer season—right now. Order a stock of Clymers from your jobber today.

Patented May 15, 1923 and July 15, 1924; *others pending*

FOR SALE BY ALL LEADING DEALERS

Floyd Clymer Mfg. Co.
DENVER, COLORADO

LEGAL IN YOUR STATE

THROUGH-THE-WINDSHIELD

Clymer Safety LIGHT

For several years I manufactured the Clymer Windshield Spotlight. It was a very popular accessory in the early twenties. Almost half a million Clymer Spotlights were sold during the period of their popularity. The history of the Clymer Spotlight is an interesting story and will be told in some future number of the MOTOR SCRAPBOOK.—*Clymer.*

The Delling Steam Car

1925

SIX PASSENGER SEDAN

Weight of Phaeton Model: Approximately 3100 lbs.

Price of 6 pass. Phaeton: Approximately $2500 t. o. b. factory

"   "   "   Sedan :   " $3200   "   "

ENGINE: Delling three-cylinder double-acting, delivering the same amount of power impulses as a twelve-cylinder gasoline motor. Very long life assured on account of its slow speed (1200 R.P.M. at 60 miles p.h.). Maximum power output 62 horse power. Total space required for engine under the hood only $13\frac{1}{2}$ inches.

BURNER: Our own design throughout. Built on the principle of a miner's lamp and conforming with all rules of the Board of Fire Underwriters. Single ejector nozzle with vertical venturi and mixing chamber. Individual circular grates. Kerosene pilot with electric starter, protecting the car against freezing in winter.

BOILER: Our own design throughout. Straight vertical copper water tubes expanded into steam drum and mud chamber. Non-explosive; no welded seams exposed to boiler fire. Boiler level indicator on instrument board. Automatically regulated water supply.

WATER AND FUEL SYSTEM: Driven from engine. Readily accessible.

CONDENSER: Our own design. Multi stage with separator action, insuring complete condensation under average conditions.

FUEL TANK: 22 gallons, mounted in rear of chassis.

THE DELLING CHASSIS — Note the extreme simplicity

THE 1925 DOBLE STEAM CAR

Doble

LIMOUSINE
Seven Passengers

Doble

DE LUXE PHAETON
Five Passengers

THE DOBLE ENGINE

THE engine is a four-cylinder, double-acting, balanced compound with two high pressure pistons (2⅝ inch diameter by 5 inch stroke), operating the outside cranks, and two low pressure pistons (4½ inch diameter by 5 inch stroke), operating the two center cranks.

The cylinders are cast in pairs, one high pressure, one low pressure, and one valve chest in each block. To insure maintenance of shape and maximum strength, the low pressure pistons are forged integral with the piston rods and are heat-treated before grinding. The cylinders are entirely separated from the crank case so that no deterioration of crank case oil can take place. The cross heads, which take the thrust from the change of longitudinal motion into rotary motion of the crank, are cool at all times and properly lubricated. These cross heads are lined with best babbitt, properly peened and finished in accordance with the best practice.

The connecting rod small end bearings and wrist-pins, on which they turn, are hardened and ground steel, insuring continuance of operation without wear. The crank shaft is a drop forging, all bearing surfaces being hardened and ground. Hoffman hardened roller bearings are used for the four main crank shaft bearings and the eccentric rod and connecting rod bearings on the crank shaft. All valve motion bearings are hardened steel against hardened steel, so that during the lifetime of the automobile no engine bearings should require attention.

The engine is integral with the rear axle, the crank shaft driving the rear axle differential through Maag-tooth, hardened and ground gears. The crank case of the engine forms also the rear axle center housing. Nickel steel tapered tubes, bolted on to each side of this crank case, form the rear axle.

The front end of this engine is supported from a three and one-half inch chrome nickel steel tubular cross-member by a ball-and-socket torque hanger. This cross-member, which forms the engine support, is strongly braced by diagonal tubular struts to the rear spring front hangers, thus tremendously increasing the rigidity of this portion of frame.

THE VALVES—The steam supply to the engine is controlled by two piston valves of exclusive Doble design, one valve functioning for one high and one low pressure cylinder. The valve motion and the ports are so designed that the steam inlet and cut-off and the exhaust opening and closure are precisely the same for each end of each cylinder. This valve combines in its function the steam inlet for both ends of the high-pressure cylinder, transfer of the steam from the high-pressure exhaust to both ends of the low-pressure cylinder, and finally exhaust from the low-pressure cylinder to the condenser. By this arrangement two valves are made to do the work of sixteen. The valves are driven by the Stephenson link valve motion which provides for reversing and also three cut-off points.

out of operation. At no time during the operation of the car is there an exposed flame, as ignition is caused by electric spark plugs located in the Venturi atomizer.

The steam generator is fed with the required amount of water from the water pumps under control by the temperature and pressure of the steam in the generator, this being accomplished electrically, so that instantaneous, accurate and reliable control is assured at all times.

Sufficient steam at a pressure of 750 pounds and a temperature of 750° F. can be developed in this steam generator to maintain a continuous driving speed of 75 miles per hour. The rapidity of steam generation is such that from cold the automobile can be started in from 30 to 45 seconds.

AUXILIARY UNIT

The auxiliary unit, into which is designed all of the auxiliary apparatus of the automobile, is suspended from three points under the front toe boards on the right side of the chassis. Into it are incorporated the water pumps, the vacuum pumps, the electric generator, the oil pump for lubricating the engine cylinders at the rate of one pint of oil to 500 miles, the air pump for fuel pressure, and the speedometer drive.

The water pumps, which feed the steam generator, are four crank driven plunger pumps. Under normal conditions only two of these pumps are working, but under conditions of extreme draft on the steam generator, all four pumps come into operation. The pumps are electrically controlled and their

action is regulated by the temperature and pressure of the steam in the generator.

The vacuum pumps, which are two plunger pumps, are driven from the same crank shaft as the water pumps. They are capable of maintaining a vacuum on the exhaust of the engine under practically all conditions.

The electric generator is so designed that it may be operated as a motor to drive the auxiliary unit independent of the main engine, in case it is required when the car is standing still. This generator is of the constant voltage type, which increases its delivery charge as the battery voltage drops.

Every bearing in the auxiliary unit is automatically oiled by a forced feed circulating system operaced by a pump located in the sump at the bottom of the auxiliary unit crank case. This unit is driven by a short propeller shaft direct from the engine crank shaft.

CONDENSER

The exhaust steam is condensed in a standard type radiator through which a sufficient air circulation is maintained by a fan 24 inches in diameter. This fan, which is driven from the auxiliary unit, turns at the rate of 3,200 revolutions per minute at 60 miles per hour. The exhaust steam from the engine is completely condensed in this radiator under practically all conditions. This highly efficient condensing system assures the driver of a Doble of ample touring radius on one tank of water, 17 gallons, a touring radius far in excess of that assured by the 26-gallon fuel tank.

DOBLE CHASSIS DETAILS

CHASSIS FRAME is made of chrome nickel steel, heat-treated. It is braced by seven tubular cross-members, riveted to the side rails. These are further reinforced and braced by diagonal tubular members, making a very rigid frame construction. The rigidity of the frame forces the springs to take care of the inequalities of the road instead of allowing these twisting forces to react upon the body.

FRONT SPRINGS are 44 inches long, made of chrome vanadium steel according to the highest standards of spring manufacture, with all the leaves polished to avoid friction and give full spring action. Each spring is enclosed in an oil-tight leather boot to keep from it encrustation of mud, and to provide for lubrication.

REAR SPRINGS are constructed and enclosed in the same way and are 58 inches long, being bolted to the under side of the rear axle. The spring bolts are extremely large, being one inch on both ends of the front spring and on the rear end of the rear spring, and one and one-quarter inches on the front end of the rear spring. All spring bolts are bushed with phosphor bronze bushings. Spring action is controlled by Houdaille shock absorbers, which are standard equipment.

FRONT AXLE is an I-beam section drop forging of chrome nickel steel, heat-treated, and is of the reversed Elliot type. The king pins are equipped with two double row annular ball bearings and one thrust ball bearing. The cross steering link is equipped with SKF self-aligning ball bearings.

REAR AXLE driving shafts are of chrome vanadium steel, drilled throughout for lightness, and are of large diameter and heat-treated to insure torsional rigidity so that no vibrations due to road conditions will be amplified and transmitted. The outer end of the drive shafts run in self-aligning SKF ball-bearings.

DIFFERENTIAL is a special Doble design, being so arranged that there is considerable friction developed in the differential in case one wheel rotates faster than the other. This same friction device takes up any wear which may develop, and eliminates any possible noise from backlash in the rear axle. The differential carrier runs on Hess-Bright double row ball-bearings.

STEERING GEAR is the worm-and-wheel type, being equipped with ball-bearings at all points, and so designed that no reaction is felt from the road. It has a sufficient lock

to enable the car to turn in a 42-foot circle. The steering wheel spider is polished cast German silver, insuring continuous good appearance. The rim is selected African ebony, so that no amount of wear will diminish its good appearance and "feel."

THROTTLE WHEEL, which is also of selected African ebony with a polished cast German silver spider, is set within and slightly above the steering wheel. It can be operated with either hand. When the throttle is closed, the throttle wheel may be locked.

BRAKES: The brake drums are made of 50 point carbon steel, heat-treated and ground. Both brakes are expanding, located on the interior of the drum, side by side. The drum is 16 inches in diameter by 5 inches wide. The outer surface of the drum is reinforced by 11 ribs arranged circumferentially, which increase the rigidity of the drum and greatly aid in radiating the heat due to the operation of the brakes.

The brake shoes are made of aluminum for lightness and for heat conduction. They are faced with ferrodo, the best lining procurable for this purpose, which is ground to an exact fit with the drum after the shoes have been completely assembled. In addition to the grinding operation to insure accuracy of bearing, each brake shoe is spotted in to a perfect fit on the brake drum.

These brakes are capable of continuous action under any condition of service without overheating, and show an unusually high resistance to wear.

FUEL TANK, which has a capacity of 26 gallons, is hung at the rear of the chassis. It is made of aluminum plate, all seams being welded to eliminate trouble from riveted or soldered joints, and is suspended in the frame by three points in such manner that no twisting of the frame or unusual shock of the chassis can cause any strain to the tank. The filler neck is also of aluminum, welded into the tank. The filler cap has a hardened steel ring which cannot be damaged by the hose nozzle when filling. No gasket is required.

WATER TANK is constructed, like the fuel tank, of aluminum plate, with all joints welded. A self-cleaning trap is built into the bottom of the water tank to prevent any sediment entering the steam generator. As under practically all conditions all steam is condensed, its 17-gallon capacity gives ample touring radius.

Doble

CHASSIS
Rear and Overhead Views

Herbert Photo

ROAD TEST OF STEAM-POWERED CHASSIS

With a load of 11 tons, this bus chassis, equipped with Frank Curran's newly invented steam power plant, showed great economy in fuel consumption and negotiated with ease and speed all normal street grades. The inventor made these tests in New York City.

Will the Steam Automobile Return?

Success of Recent Tests Renews Interest in Steam as Motive Power for Automobiles

MANY times are the following questions propounded by those who cannot forego the admitted advantages of the steam automobile. Will steam ever come back? Will it ever be a real competitor of the internal-combustion gasoline engine in automotive vehicles?

About 1901 Stanley developed a successful steam automobile which was produced until a few years ago; this was one of the first practical automobiles. It was early proved that steam propulsion was flexible, smooth running, powerful, had a practically continuous torque and at that time produced a horsepower for a low weight of installation.

DOES it not, therefore, seem a curious fact that the steam automobile never attained wide production and that the few manufacturers since Stanley showed the way, have practically all disappeared from the market? It is not because it lacks advantages that steam has been left so far behind in the race. Rather it is a matter of certain disadvantages which heretofore have not been overcome.

Unquestionably the multiplicity of parts, the failures of flash boilers, the large amount of space occupied by the power plant, and the necessity of more than the average mechanical ability in its use and upkeep, together with the remarkable advance in the design and operation of gasoline engines, have been the reasons that have caused the steam automobile to be smothered.

There has recently been tested in New York City traffic, a steam bus which has been so successful that the old questions of the relative value of steam and gasoline propulsion have been revived with considerable pertinency. Our illustrations show the general appearance of the bus chassis and the diagram shows the location of the several units.

Steam of 600 pounds per square inch pressure is generated in a seamless, welded boiler of entirely new construction, the upper part being of the fire-tube type, while the lower part is of water-tube design, the roll of the tubes being welded to the boiler head. Between the above two parts is placed the first superheater. Steam is drawn through this to the throttle, which is operated by foot, from whence it passes to the second superheater which forms the lining of the burner, and is then delivered to the engine.

TWELVE independent water coils all feed a common reservoir and they are arranged so that should one coil prove defective it can be cut out by merely turning a valve. The boiler weighs 400 pounds and delivers 185 horsepower. It is the invention of Frank J. Curran.

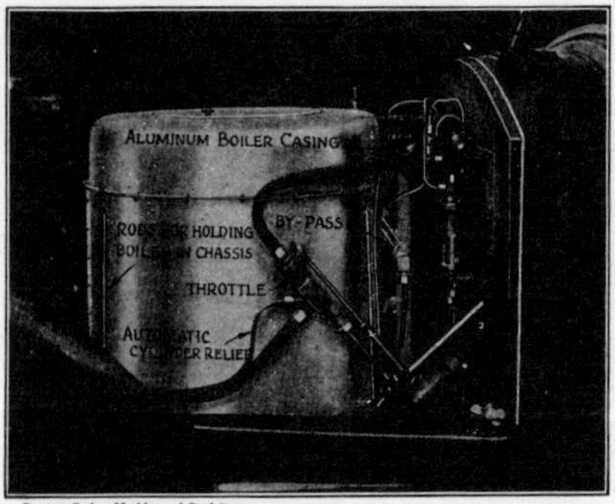

Courtesy Cruban Machine and Steel Corp.

UNDER THE HOOD

Accessibility of equipment may be seen from this photo. Sturdiness and simplicity appear to have been considered in this design

Courtesy Cruban Machine and Steel Corp.
MAIN BURNER, VAPORIZER

This burner and specially designed pilot light burn fuel oil, kerosene, or gasoline

A vaporizing type of burner is used with a specially designed pilot light, both of which burn any grade of fuel oil, kerosene or gasoline, between 23 and 65 gravity without change of adjustments. A steam bus, with 11 tons load was driven over various grades in the outskirts of the city, averaging better than eight miles per gallon.

THE engine is of the three-cylinder reciprocating, simple, uniflow type with improved valve action which regulates cutoffs from full stroke to five percent. Tests show that one horsepower is developed for every 22 pounds of steam consumed. The arrangement of the auxiliary controls is such that by closing all valves, the throttle, automatic by-pass, steam gage, thermo-couple water level indicator and safety valve can be removed for repairs.

Reference to the diagram will show how neatly this engine takes the place of the usual clutch and gear housing

in the gas automobile, and how compact and clean is the design. The exhaust steam enters a radiator or condensing system from which the water returns to a reserve tank. From this tank a small positive-feed pump supplies the boiler again as needed, the water level being controlled by an automatic regulator.

An ingenious hand pump makes it possible to operate the contributory devices to the boiler and burner by hand instantly at any time the auto-

Courtesy Cruban Machine and Steel Corp.
SIDE OF BURNER

Through the open main burner door may be seen the single nozzle and air intake tube

matic devices should fail. The throttle has an automatic by-pass or cylinder relief; when the throttle is closed the pressure in the steam chest and cylinder is immediately by-passed to the condenser.

The engine becomes dead as soon as the foot-pedal throttle is released and itself acts as a brake when desired, thus relieving the wheel brakes when stopping. Many of these features described are the invention of Charles R. Nebelmesser.

The main drawbacks in the past to the adaptation of steam to vehicles, have been the limits of space available, and the weight allowable for horsepower output for large installations.

Courtesy Cruban Machine and Steel Corp.
BURNER AND SUPERHEATER

Superheated steam passes to throttle, thence through the second superheater to the engine

These, it would seem, have been overcome to a large extent in the steam engine which we have described. Whether or not this portends a new development or revival, or whether it is in the end only a particularly good demonstration of an individual machine, time and future experiment alone will tell. But in the search for economical and flexible operation the automotive industry may well pause to give a more than passing inquiry along this line.

TO the average person who must frequent streets which are crowded with traffic, the elimination, at least in part, of some of the obnoxious gases which are the products of combustion in the gasoline engine, will be welcomed as a wholesome boon, for clean air to breathe is rapidly becoming at a premium and no one realizes it more than he who must inhale, almost without cessation, the atmosphere which now is a part of his daily experience.

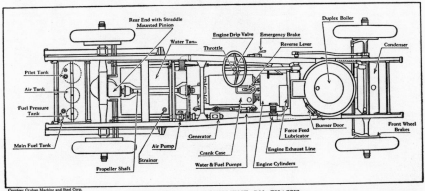

Courtesy Cruban Machine and Steel Corp.
DISTRIBUTION OF EQUIPMENT ON CHASSIS

This view gives an idea of the compactness of Mr. Curran's design in which the parts are not crowded as is usually the case on gasoline cars. Ease of operation, efficient functioning of parts, and cost of upkeep were considerations in the design and location of parts.

AN UNUSUAL STEAM CAR

In 1930 Jeffery Carqueville, the grandson of Thomas B. Jeffery, who once manufactured the Rambler and Jeffery cars, and his partner, Duncan MacDonald, did considerable development work on a steam car.

The body and chassis used were those of a big Nash sport touring car. Mr. Carqueville kindly sent photographs of the car and the steam power plant and gave the following data regarding the car and its construction and operation:

The engine was four-cylinder, the high-pressure cylinders being 2¾ x 5, the low-pressure cylinders 3½ x 5. It was both single and compound, forward and reverse. The engine was a prime mover, operating directly on the rear axle so the rear axle was the crankshaft and the rear wheels were the flywheels. No gears were used. The car was operated on 800 to 1,000 lbs. of steam pressure, the safety valve set to blow at 1000 or 1200 on the flash-type boiler.

Practically no time was required to get up steam, and it was but a matter of seconds before the car was ready to run. The job was fully automatic. A pilot light was used, which kept a section of the coils hot at all times. Then, by pressing a button on the dash, a small amount of water was dropped into the heated section of the coils, and instantly flashed into steam. The moment the throttle was opened and the car started to move, all the automatics came on—the burner was turned on—and the car was in full operation. The boiler was of their own design, employing ¾″ heat-resisting special tubing, coiled around in a rectangle to conform to the shape of the case. The burner was of their own design which he stated might be called multiple Bunsen burner. It was designed to use a low grade of fuel oil or low-grade gasoline.

The water capacity was 30 gallons; and a condenser was used. The speed seemed to be unlimited so long as steam was generated.

THE CARQUEVILLE AND MACDONALD STEAM CAR, USING THEIR OWN STEAM POWER PLANT ON A NASH CHASSIS AND BODY.

(Continued on next page)

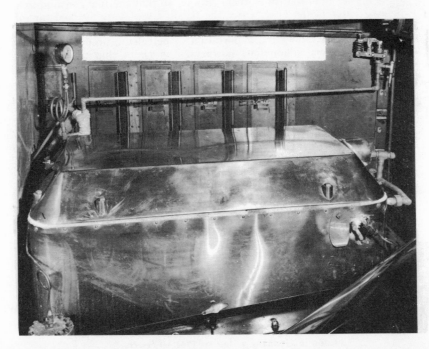

Printed by Horne & Son, Ltd., Whitby.

Published by R. H. & H. W. Bolsover
Nestling House, Sleights, Nr. Whitby, Yorks.

Monthly Ninepence

Steam Car Developments and Steam Aviation

Vol. V	NOVEMBER, 1936	No. 57

New Steam Vehicles

K. Imfeld and R. Roosen describe German-built high-pressure steam equipment developed under the Doble patents and characterised by remarkable flexibility and economy in operation.

Steam-driven vehicles were the pioneers of mechanical road transport and, notwithstanding the remarkable progress of the internal combustion engine, the latest steam equipment offers very attractive features, particularly as regards automatic control of pressure and temperature, and power characteristics inherently suitable for traction service. The elimination of gear-changing alone is an important consideration when it is realised that the drivers of internal combustion engine motor-buses may have to change gears about 4,000 times a day in city service. Even if, in general, the thermal efficiency of the internal combustion engine is higher than that of a steam engine, so that the fuel consumption is greater in the latter case, the feasibility of burning coal tar oil in the steam generator is important both as regards reducing costs and avoiding the importation of petroleum products. From the transport standpoint, however, the claim that 30 per cent. higher journey speeds can be maintained by steam vehicles compared with internal combustion engine vehicles is probably by far the most important consideration. The superiority of the steam vehicle in this respect is due to its smoother and more rapid acceleration and excellent hill climbing qualities.

All these points are illustrated by K. Imfeld and R. Roosen in *Zeitschrift des Vereines deutscher Ingenieure,* in connection with some of the latest steam vehicles built by Henschel & Sohn A.G., Kassel, this firm and A. Borsig, Berlin, having acquired licences under the Doble patents.

STEAM BUSSES AND TRUCKS OF GERMANY

The above article and the one appearing at the top of the next page appeared in an English magazine—"Steam Car Developments and Steam Aviation," in 1936. Firms in Germany were then starting to build steam trucks and busses under Doble patents. Mr. Doble spent almost two years in Germany prior to their entry into the war. On the following pages illustrations are shown of cars, trucks, and busses that were manufactured in Germany and powered by the Doble Flash-Steam Power Unit. It is understood that these units were still in production in Germany as late as 1941.—*Clymer.*

FLASH STEAM GENERATORS

I have been re-reading my collection of Steam Car Developments and Steam Aviation," and, after reading the interesting article on the Doble steam automobile, have come to the conclusion that the flash boiler is the only thing that will enable the steam automobile to displace the internal combustion vehicle. A flash boiler furnishes more steam with less weight than the old fire tube boiler. What we want nowadays is high power with slight weight. When a flash boiler will get up high pressure steam in 15 to 30 seconds, it certainly indicates that the thermal efficiency is very good—that is, a high percentage of the heat of the fire is being transferred into steam or energy to drive the wheels. On the other hand, it requires ten to fifteen minutes to get up steam with a big fire tube boiler. This certainly indicates that much of the heat is being lost through the stack and in heating up the steel tubes of the boiler. What is the advantage of having a big shell boiler with great storage of energy if it lasts for only one fast spurt and then you have to come down to 40 m.p.h. for continuous running? Have a boiler that can maintain 90 m.p.h. continuously, and you won't need any stored power.

STEAM MOTOR FOR AUTOS IS FOUND FASTER

Nov 5- 1936:

German Tests Indicate Lack of Fuel Oil Soon Will Not Be Transportation Problem

KASSEL, Germany, Nov. 4.— Steam-engined automobiles, constructed by a world-famous locomotive works here, have proved so successful after exhaustive practical road tests that the inventors hail them as the beginning of a new era in motoring.

The new car is very easy to handle. With all the engine power always available, regardless of engine revolutions, no gear-box is necessary and the controls consist of merely one pedal in addition to the ordinary brake pedal.

What makes the new car especially important to Germany is the fact that the motor can be driven on pure gas oil or coal tar, always available in Germany, making Germany independent of oil imports.

OIL LONG BIG PROBLEM.

The gigantic progress recently made in the production of artificial gasoline from soft coal, the incessant exploitation of the few German oilfields discovered in recent years in the Hanover district and finally Germany's energetic efforts to perfect the Diesel engine, which runs on crude oil with a smaller fuel consumption than the petrol engine, are all going to the same end; to cut out as much as possible the need for foreign oil.

Strategists in the German Reichswehr Ministry especially have not forgotten how badly the desperate shortage of fuels crippled the German forces' fighting power towards the end of the war.

The steam engine develops 120 horse power and consists of a small boiler heated by coal tar or gas oil and a steam engine of the greatest efficiency. The boiler is heated within two minutes, and the car is then ready for work. Steam pressure or water level in the boiler are regulated automatically.

STARTS QUICKLY, SMOOTHLY.

All the driver need do is to open the gas regulator through the foot pedal, and the car will drive away smoothly. Acceleration is said to be far superior to that of gasoline engined cars of the same size, and higher cruising speeds are therefore attainable.

A series of the new power units has already been ordered by prominent German omnibus companies and even the federal railroads are making experiments now with the intention of using them for small trains on unimportant lines.

184

APRIL 1933.   Filling the Steamer Up with Fuel Oil

Steam Engine Flies Travelair Plane

George and William Besler, sons of the Chairman of the Board of the Central Railroad of New Jersey, gave a demonstration of the use of steam motive power for passenger aircraft propulsion at San Francisco Bay Airdrome on April 20.

The new plane, in its test before officials of the National Aeronautic Association, demonstrated three novel features of great interest to the aeronautical fraternity. First, the operation of the plane is practically noiseless, the only sound being that of the whirling propeller. Second, in landing, the pilot uses the well-known characteristic of the steam engine—he reverses his motor and propellor while in the air and thus is en-

abled to bring his ship to a full stop within a few feet after the landing wheels touch the ground. Third, the plane operating with fuel oil has the advantage of economy, especially because the motor requires practically no servicing.

The engine is a two-cylinder oil burner, developing about 90 h.p. and is said to supply sufficient power to cruise the plane in which it was installed at about 100 m.p.h. It was test flown for only a few minutes, and is said to have performed satisfactorily. Operation was remarkable for its silence.

After the flight the motor was taken from the Travelair plane and will be transported to Davenport, Iowa, where it will be installed as a power plant for a new type railroad locomotive capable of pulling three Pullman cars.

NAZI HERMAN GOERING IN DOBLE-POWERED GERMAN STEAM CAR

This Doble F-35 shows the once powerful head of the German air force giving the Nazi greeting. Alongside of Goering, in the rear seat is the Prince of Hesse-Nassau. The Prince's wife is a daughter of the King of Italy. Hitler made the Prince Ober-Praesidente of the Province Hesse-Nassau, for political reasons. The photo was taken at the railway station at Kassel, Germany in 1933. (Photo, courtesy of Warren Doble.)

These photos show Warren Doble, co-inventor of the Doble Steam Car, and C. T. Briar, long-time Doble enthusiast and Doble owner, at Oakland Airport in 1933. Abner Doble had just left for England, and arrangements were then being made with Lt. Bonnalie, in charge of Boeing School, for use of a Travel-Air training plane to be used in the Besler steam tests. Boeing students were intensely interested in the Doble Steam Car F-30. Warren Doble at wheel of car. — (Briar photos.)

DOBLE STEAM-UNIT-POWERED RAIL-CAR

The first rail car built by the Henschel Locomotive Works at Kassel, Germany, was powered by a Doble steam unit. This photo, taken in 1933, shows the car at Treysa, a few miles South of Kassel, Germany, and was taken on one of the test runs. The arrow shows Warren Doble with some of the officials and mechanics of the Henschel Locomotive Works who were passengers on the first test run.
—Clymer.

A STEAM-PROPELLED SPEED BOAT: This boat was propelled by a Model F Doble, high-pressure steam power plant of 100 HP, which was manufactured in Emeryville, California. Warren Doble, who was a consulting engineer for the Henschel Locomotive Works at Kassel, Germany, is shown at the wheel. Alongside Mr. Doble, is Karl Imfeldt, Chief Engineer of Henschel. In the rear seat are Oscar Henschel and a Nazi officer. The installation of the Doble power plant was made by Warren Doble at a boat works near Berlin, with the help of a half dozen German workers, none of whom spoke English. The power plant was originally designed for automobile propulsion, but was installed in the boat for a demonstration and sales promotion purposes. The body of water is Die Lange See near Koepenick, Germany, 1933. — Clymer. (Photos, courtesy Warren Doble.)

188

Inside view of a Henschel Bus built in Germany just before their entry into the war. . . . Doble Flash-Steam Power Unit is used. . . . Mr. Abner Doble was a Consulting Engineer to the Henschel Locomotive Works of Kassel, Germany. . . . Prior to the war Mr. Doble granted this firm a license to manufacture his Steam units for busses, trucks and other uses. This company was in production of these units for the above uses and they were widely sold throughout Germany.—*Clymer*.

Henschel Trucks using the Doble Flash Steam Power Units in the service of the German State Railway. . . . Doble powered steam trucks and busses were past the experimental stage and were in actual production and use just prior to the start of the war. . . . Mr. Doble is now Chief Engineer of the Stanley Steam Motors Corporation.

A MODERN STEAM BUS

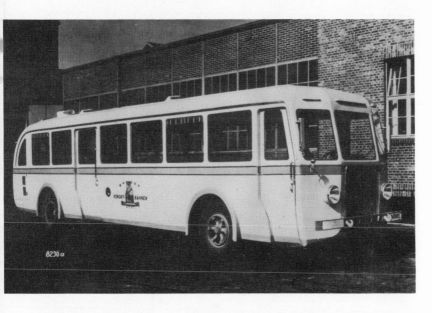

One of the Henschel busses used by several transportation companies in Germany prior to their entry in the war. The bus is powered by a Doble Steam-power Unit.

A close-up view of one of the many Henschel Trucks used before the war by. the German State Railway. The Doble Flash-Steam Power-Unit is used.

Mr. D. A. Warriner of New Orleans is converting a 1939 Dodge into a steam car. The home-made boiler was used in a Model 735 Stanley for 8 years. Lower photo shows the same boiler mounted in the 1939 Dodge. — Clymer.

This steam car owned by Dr. F. P. Luckey, Paterson, New Jersey, uses a Stanley chassis, and is equipped with a Derr boiler and a Marmon body. Howard C. Marks is shown alongside. — Clymer.

(American Steam Automobile Company)

Mr. T. Clarence Marshall of Yorklyn Delaware, owns the unusual Steam Cars illustrated here.

This 1913 Model 76 Stanley is now in operation and in first-class condition . . . It is one of the finest Stanley cars still on the road. . . . Note the Klaxon hand horn mounted on top of right door. . . . Prest-O-Lite tank and tool box on running board. . . . The long hose is used for syphoning water from ditch or creek to fill the water tank every 100 miles or so.—*Clymer.*

This 30 H.P. 1913 Stanley Mountain Wagon was used by Mr. Marshall in 1913 at Gettysburg, Penn., during the encampment of Civil War veterans. For ten weeks it carried thousands of persons over the battlefield. In the winter of 1913-14 it was used as a bus from Yorktown, Dela., to Wilmington, Dela., said to have been the first established bus line in Delaware.—*Clymer.*

A CONVERTED PACKARD!

This 1940 Packard 180 chassis...138″ wheelbase, was converted by Mr. Marshall into a Steam Car.... The inside of the car is shown with the steam instruments attached below the cowl.. the former Packard gear-shift lever is the steam throttle.... Quite classy, I'd say!—*Clymer*.

(Continued on next page)

POWER PLANT OF MR. MARSHALL'S CONVERTED PACKARD

This photo, taken from the underside of the car, shows the 4 x 5 Stanley engine mounted to the Packard rear axle, which is a regular Packard heavy-duty rear end, using a spur gear of 54 teeth. The burner was made by Mr. Marshall and is of the vaporizing type. Either kerosene or gasoline can be used as fuel and approximately 8 gallons per hour is used. The boiler has 152 1¼″ tubes, 22″ long, furnishing 122 sq. ft. of heating surface, which includes the superheater and economizer. The water capacity of the boiler is 16 gallons, which is approximately 80% larger than the standard boiler used in steam automobiles.

The superheater is of nickel-plated steel — ¾″ — and yields 5¼ square feet of heating surface. The steam pressure is 700-750.

The Stanley type water pumps are insulated, making them practically noiseless, and are driven from the engine countershaft at ¼ the rear wheel speed.

The "V" belt drives the generator which is located in the front compartment. Capacity is 35 amperes.

The fan is located behind the radiator and has an automatic cutout.

A fin and tube type radiator with raised heads is used.

Fuel tank capacity is 21 gallons; water tank capacity is 24 gallons. Cochran make oil separator, weighing 13 lbs. is used.

The throttle, hand operated, was formerly the gear shift lever of the Packard before it was converted. The throttle is balanced.

The wheel-base is 138″.

The weight of the car is approximately 4600 lbs.

The tires are 16″ x 7.00″, 6 ply.

The brakes are hydraulic.

Upper photo shows the boiler mounted under the hood of Mr. Marshall's Packard. Lower photo shows front view of Mr. Marshall's Packard with the hood raised.

(Continued from preceding page)

A STEAM-PROPELLED HOUSE-CAR

Through the courtesy of J. Roy Hunt of Los Angeles, we are including in this book some illustrations of the unusual and luxurious steam car that Mr. Hunt built for his personal use. We must remember that much of his work was of an experimental nature — and he sold the car before he had fully completed tests that were satisfactory to him.

The car was constructed before the war and the framework was of chrome-molybdenum tubing covered with aluminum. It was powered by a two-cylinder, 4½ x 5, steam engine, using two high-pressure cylinders. Mr. Hunt also tried compound, but stated that high-pressure cylinders worked best.

A flash boiler of his own design was used — and the superheating tubes were of inconel tubing. The burner was of the atomizing type. The car used Diesel oil costing 6 to 8 cents a gallon. Mileage was approximately 10 miles per gallon. The water capacity was 17 gallons, sufficient for approximately 150 miles. The car would cruise nicely at 50 miles per hour.

The generator and centrifugal pump to return condensed steam to the tank were driven by dual V-belt. The wheel base was 121 inches and the overall length of the body was 18 feet 6 inches. The car weighed 5045 lbs. loaded with fuel and water.

The inside of the car was luxuriously furnished and seated five persons with sleeping accommodations for two. The equipment included electric refrigeration, hot water, shower and toilet, desk, bar, and complete ventilation system.

To avoid fumes, the engine was mounted in the rear — the boiler and engine were included in a unit. The entire power plant could be removed in twenty minutes by the releasing of four bolts. A standard Zephyr differential and splined shaft were used to transmit power from the engine to the rear wheels. A two-stage exhaust turbine was used to turn the fan and condense the steam exhausted from the engine into water for use again.

Mr. Hunt has owned and operated steam cars since 1908. At the present time he scoots around Los Angeles with a very unusual light steam car with a Stanley engine mounted on the rear axle of a model "A" Ford, with the boiler and the burner in the rear. Gasoline rationing does not worry Mr. Hunt. The luxury steam-powered house-car he built indicates he does know his steam engines thoroughly. — Clymer.

(Continued on next page)

THIS VIEW SHOWS DRIVER'S COMPARTMENT, STOVE,
REFRIGERATOR, AND KITCHENETTE.

INTERIOR OF THE HUNT STEAM HOUSE-CAR, SHOWING
DESK AND BAR IN THE BACKGROUND.

(Continued on next page)

(Continued from preceding page)

FRONT END VIEW OF THE HUNT STEAM CAR DURING ITS CONSTRUCTION.

SIDE VIEW OF THE POWER PLANT USED IN THE HUNT STEAMER

DUAL BELT DRIVE GENERATOR AND CENTRIFUGAL PUMP TO RETURN CONDENSED STEAM TO THE TANK. ENGINE AND BOILER ARE CARRIED AS ONE UNIT.

(Continued on next page)

A VIEW OF THE HUNT TWO-CYLINDER HIGH-PRESSURE STEAM ENGINE

(Continued from preceding page)

THE EXHAUST TURBINE USED IN THE HUNT STEAMER.
THE TURBINE IS TWO-STAGE.

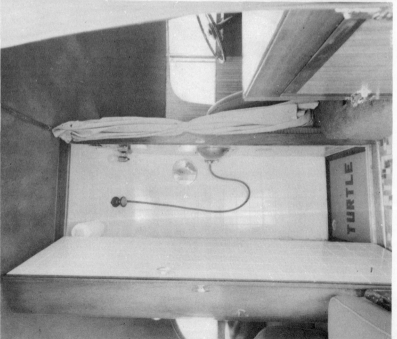

THE SHOWER STALL IS SHOWN HERE IN MR. HUNT'S
UNIQUE HOUSE-CAR.

DOBLE E-19 owned by C. T. Briar, San Diego ,California. Chassis is shown at top.
Center—Photos show chassis and the car with 1929 Stearns-Knight body. Bottom—Mr.
Blair in Doble F-30. Foot throttle and turbo-booster on blower made this car a
"veritable mountain goat." — (Briar photos.)

WHO SAID "GET A HORSE?"

By W. J. RARIDAN

Reprinted from San Diego Union, January 7, 1945

Fifty miles to the gallon — of hydrant water! That's what the age of miracles brought about long ago, but few seemed to appreciate it 'way back when the automobile was in its infancy and nobody knew whether it would live on steam or gasoline when it grew up.

It took rationing to give the steam automobile a chance to snort at its more popular competitors. But it's too genteel to snort — though it does hiss at rivals now and then. Usually it hums as contentedly as if most of its family hadn't been crowded into oblivion by legions of ubiquitous citizens.

Although the original automobiles were all powered by steam, steam-powered automobiles were never numerous. Not many Stanleys or Whites are now to be found. But there's a Doble here in San Diego, owned by C. T. Briar, retired naval aviation pilot, of 1211 Maryland Place.

Many an envious eye follows Briar as he speeds about town in his 20-year-old car using unrationed aqua pura, fuel oil and air. He is, in respect to personal transportation, as much a potentate as one other Doble owner, an Indian Rajah who uses the car in hunting elephants.

Most gas cars need overhauls after they've gone 20,000 miles. That distance only means a rear end lube oil change to the Doble. A set of tires averages 65,000 miles. The car will travel about as far on a gallon of fuel oil as other machines move on a gallon of gas, and fuel oil is much less expensive.

Briar gave other statistics: The Doble engine contains only 35 moving parts, while gasoline motors have hundreds. It will do 60 at an RPM of 900. At 1250 RPM it hits its top speed of 90. The San Diego car, E-19, has covered 183,000 miles. A machine like it in New York has gone 360,000 miles. The steamers have 15-gallon tanks for water, allowing long non-stop trips. They operate slightly more cheaply in hot weather than in cold. Almost anything combustible will serve as fuel in a pinch, including coal dust.

The motor resulted from pioneer experimentation on three now common household conveniences — automatic hot water systems, refrigeration equipment and automatic oil-burning furnaces.

Because of many automatic release valves and special boiler construction, there is no possibility of blow-ups. The boiler is made up of seamless steel tubing coils that expand and contract like the hair-spring of a watch under steam pressure and temperature variance. They are welded in series.

Briar declared that steam cars could be mass-produced more cheaply than gasoline cars. Improvement of metals since the day when steam challenged gas would make possible a steam car that would literally last a lifetime, said Briar.

One factor in which Briar showed pride was the silence of the motor and its completely automatic electric control. When the machine is cold, he turns a switch that lights a fire over the boiler and starts a fan to create draft. Within two minutes he's ready to go. After that, all day long, the boiler stays hot, fire coming on and off under thermostatic control as long as the switch is left on, but the boiler will retain plenty of steam without fire for hours, and a few seconds of fire will build up full 100 H.P.

Some steamers in Europe use coal and others use solid fuels, Briar pointed out. Seven members of the Russian general staff are now using refurbished old Dobles. Japan might be able to send out powerful planes without gasoline supplies, he said, and told how in 1931 he and Warren Doble, co-inventor of the motor, now engineer with an aircraft company in California, made preliminary arrangements with the Boeing aircraft school for the use of a plane, and the successful flight of a steam-powered plane resulted later at Oakland. It was flown by William Besler and financed by Besler Systems. The plane power-unit weighed only 240 lbs., and would have been much lighter if metals since brought into big production had then been available. When no offer for the plane was received from any other direction, it was finally sold to Japan.

Briar predicted steam would "come back" in post-war trucks and busses.

San Diego Union

DIEGO 12, CALIF., SUNDAY MORNING, JANUARY 7, 1945

Doble Steamer Gets 50 Miles a Gallon—of Water

Mr. and Mrs. Charles T. Brier, of 1211 Maryland pl., and their Doble steam auto. They can travel 50 miles on a gallon of hydrant water. With all its manifold advantages over gasoline cars in this era of rationing, Brier said, it has one drawback. He can't leave it parked without guarding it. At every opportunity, curious crowds swarm over it to examine the cheesebox-like boiler and other features. Its originally big, comfortable body has been removed by Brier for streamlined replacement.

Model 740, 1923.
Stanley Steam Roadster.
Owned by Mr. J. B. Van Sciver,
Jr., of Germantown, Penna.

He's hissing all over place in jet-rocket car (Stanley)

Newton A. Brown isn't worried about the gasoline shortage. As long as there are water holes and spigots in Southern California, he'll get along.

The Riverside Western Union employe can't even get steamed up over tire rationing; he'll do his pleasure driving whenever and wherever he pleases and to heck with the OPA.

Newt Brown, a former mechanic, is hissing around these days in a bright red Stanley Steamer, modern version, if you please.

From odds and ends acquired in river bottom or junk yard, Brown built onto the chassis and motor of an old Stanley Steamer—the car that thrilled the world and heckled horses when bustles were seen and not stored.

He's developed a self starter to do away with the required blow torch; he's fashioned a stovepipe exhaust to replace a blower, and he's added electric lights, two-tone horn and a paint job to his "SS" roadburner.

Newt Brown doesn't mind the occasional references to his "rocket" car. He pulls away from the curb in a cloud of steam and a roar of hissing that clears the highway from fright alone.

And the guy who dares to sneak up too close behind Brown's boiler buggy will probably find that his front tires have been scorched to the rim.

The old Stanley Steamer burns kerosene, at 6½ cents a gallon, to generate water steam for propulsion. Actually, it is a "rocket type" vehicle, with its steam jet propulsion driving the motor that pushes it along.

On each gallon of kerosene fuel Brown can travel about 16 miles. And the fuel is unrationed.

Also, Brown can obtain tires for his SS, because it uses an outmoded variety not subject to rationing.

Brown says there's another ration beater like himself in Southern California. His name is Raymond Thompson of Fullerton, and he operates another Stanley Steamer with more or less the same improvements Brown has made.

Neither of them is concerned about service stations closing up. But comes a serious drouth . . .

"HOLD HER, NEWT, SHE'S A-ROARIN'"
Newton Brown pulls away from the curb in his hissing Stanley Steamer ration evader

—Daily News photos by Harry Gill.

THE FUTURE OF STEAM

By BYRON SPENCE, President, The Steam Motor Association

"Will the Steam Car come back?", is a question one very often hears. Perhaps the answer lies in (first) a brief historical look at the past, and (second) a summary of the advantages and disadvantages of Steam as they appear to exist today.

Although it is not generally known, at the beginning of 1908 there were more steam cars on the highways than gas cars. This was the beginning of the period when Ford really started production in volume with the Model T and once he got into volume production of gas cars, quickly became very much in the ascendency, at least as far as numbers were concerned. At that point development and research effort in the automotive field went almost entirely into the gas car field. This became a "trend" or "style", in much the same manner as efforts of our aircraft engineers are now directed so strongly toward jet and turbine propulsion, almost to the exclusion of development work on reciprocating engines. The last White Steamer was built in about 1912, the last Stanley in about 1925, and the last Doble about 1927.

Much of the development of gas cars has been in the direction of approximating in performance the inherent advantages of STEAM. Thus came self starters, 8, 12 and 16 cylinders, Ethyl Gas, overdrives, fluid flywheels and lastly automatic shift devices. The one great advantage of Steam-stored power and flexibility has yet to be equalled by the gas car, which still depends chiefly on speed of rotation of the non-reversible engine to develop its maximum power, and which in turn makes the gas car less flexible than the steam car.

On the other hand, the simplicity and dependability of the present day gas car, in the hands of the average driver, as we steam fans well know, has yet to be equalled by the steam car. And despite much loose talk to the contrary I have yet to see a steam car as quiet as a modern gas car, nor has the freezing problem in the steam car been solved.

While the public has known little of the behind-the-scenes work in the field, the intervening years have produced a certain amount of development work of experienced and competent engineers. The work of Doble, Leslie, Crosby Knox, Snyder, Williams and others has gone more or less unheralded, but their work has been none the less fruitful.

Meanwhile, advances in related fields have been spectacular. To give but one or two examples: Perhaps the most troublesome units of the earlier steam cars were the burners and boilers. The original atomizing burner is believed to have been used by Doble on a steam car. It later became the basic development and patent of the "NoKol" house heating burner. Since that time literally thousands of inventive minds have brought the atomizing burner to absolute dependability and perfection. The developments in metallurgy almost stagger the imagination and now it is entirely feasible to build comparatively light weight, durable, trouble free and compact boilers of high output. Superheaters no longer burn out. Thin-walled tubing can save weight and increase efficiency.

But offsetting almost all advantages of the steam car is the vast network of trained service organizations, spare parts supply depots, repair equipment and tools found in even the most distant and isolated hamlet of North America. As far as cars are concerned it limits the field to the few of us who are dyed-in-the-wool fans, to whom a car is much more than a means of getting from here to there—fans who love their cars enough to understand them thoroughly and do their own service work. This is a limited, but none-the-less real market.

A field of vastly greater possibilities is the city type bus. The bus, more than any other passenger vehicle, requires from a straight dollars-and-cents standpoint alone, smooth, quick acceleration, the least possible wear and tear, freedom from gearshifting, freedom from clutching and declutching and reserve controlled power in abundance. Here in this field, in the hands of each operator, is his own trained service organization. Here indeed is the real field, ready made for an alert manufacturer with a bit of vision and a bit of the good old pioneering spirit which built this country.

As an offshoot of this market, there could easily come a market in the pleasure and fishing boat field, as well as a limited market in the pleasure car field. As a further development of this opportunity can come the heavy duty truck field, especially coal burning units for the coal producing regions.

So steam is indeed not dead, but ready and waiting for a bit of the good old American enterprise, which so successfully built this great country of ours.

Interest in Steam Autos Goes Up in Motor Circles

Opinion Divided Among Engineers Regarding Feasibility of Popularizing Steamer Models

A reported rebirth of interest in the steam automobile as a means of public transportation after the war has Southland motor car men guessing.

Why, it is asked, should a sizeable portion of car driving citizens became intrigued with the idea as well as the ideal of steam propulsion for autos in view of the history of family car development?

For—some auto men say—it is obvious that internal combustion engines of the ordinary type now in use by the millions, long ago outdistanced steam-engined cars. None of the latter have been made for many years.

Interest Aroused

That such interest is manifest, however, is attested by Floyd Clymer of Los Angeles, publisher of a "motor scrapbook" which traces the history of the motor car from its beginnings around 1900. Clymer said yesterday that inquiries on steamers are "flooding my office daily."

According to Clymer, questioners want to know what, if any, plans have been made for manufacturing steam cars after the war and whether modern designs and newly discovered alloys have reached the point where their use in steam automobiles will improve the mechanism.

"My replies to these questions are along historical rather than technical lines," Clymer said. "I'm not an engineer. But of one fact I am sure: There are two schools of thought on steam cars.

"One school holds that the automobile steam engine has reached its limit of development, that it has been proven impracticable by the very fact that internal combustion motors have utterly displaced it on the commercial market.

Improvement Possible

"Opposite opinion is just as positive. Its proponents say that 'nothing ever reaches perfection' and that the steam auto engine can and will be vastly improved.

"I believe it is a fact that scores of inventors and designers are at work today to make the steam car better. Who can say what the final outcome of their efforts will be? Americans have a record of licking mechanical problems."

Lloyd Lanterman of La Canada, mechanical engineer and veteran steam car experimenter, believes that present data on engineering points definitely to a successful steam automobile in the postwar picture.

"Right now, said Lanterman, "it is possible to engineer a steam car with a lightweight, 200-h o r s e p o w e r engine that could be built in quantity to compete with any passenger car on the roads."

Lost Markets

Lanterman declared t h a t a "stodgy self-complacency" on the part of early makers of steam cars was partly responsible for their l o s s of markets which eventually brought their business to an end.

He said that year after year steam motor designs were virtually f r o z e n and that only slight changes in body configuration marked yearly models.

He put no credence in the oft-repeated assertion that machinations of the "big interests" were instrumental in p a v i n g the downhill road which steam cars followed to oblivion.

"Competition between internal combustion and steam was completely fair," he asserted. "Once the gasoline engine got the jump on steam, however, most of the good engineers devoted all their time and efforts to gasoline car development, for the public was sold on gasoline."

There never has been any question, Lanterman averred, about the smooth-running qualities of a steam car in operation. Power is fed by one hand throttle direct to the rear wheels without transmission or drive shaft. There is no involved ignition system, no clutch or transmission, no drive shaft and no right-angle turn in power delivery at the differential.

He believes that water-tube boilers—in which t h e water is turned to steam inside a tube—will be used in the successful steamer of the future. These boilers, he emphasized, must be of the "water level" type rather than the "flash" boiler.

Art Austria, Los Angeles garage o w n e r and collector of early American automobiles, doubts that steamers will again compete, even for a short period, with gasoline motor vehicles.

Needs Attention

He declared that "it will always take an expert to operate a steam car. So long as it's in good running order the steamer, admittedly, is easy and smooth to drive. But in order to keep it in tiptop shape it must be regularly i n s p e c t e d and cleaned. This applies to burners, water and fuel supply valves and pumps and to the boiler itself.

"With a gasoline engine, you are always ready to go at the touch of a button."

"Steamers are simple, direct, quiet and smooth operating," steamerites reiterate. "T h e y have none of the many complications of the gasoline car such as clutch, transmission, ignition system, drive shaft and a right-angle turn to the rear wheels."

STEAM DRIVEN MOTORBUS MAY SOLVE PROBLEM

Investment Banker Sees in This Development Chance For Railroads in Field

New York, Feb. 3.—Steam will replace gasoline in providing the motive power of a nation-wide chain of passenger buses, which will be co-ordinated with the railroads in the development of an interlocking transportation system, in the opinion of F. J. Lisman, who points out that in plans conceived by the railroads steam may eventually be used because it provides lower initial cost for buses, lower operating costs and in the final analysis gives longer life to equipment.

Mr. Lisman, whose experience in railroad financing dates back more than 40 years, said that while the gasoline-driven private automobile had proven practical, the large operating cost of the internal combustion motor used in motorbuses had prevented many of the steam carriers from going into the bus operation on a large scale. scale.

"The continuous shifting of gears in the large buses," said Mr. Lisman, "and the high operating cost of running in low and second speed are factors that weigh against the gasoline bus. Many bus companies sprung into being without taking into account these high operating costs and the result has been that they are not making money. Operation by steam, I believe, provides the answer to their problem, and certainly no one is better equipped to know the advantages of steam than the railroads.

CHICAGO TRIBUNE—1939

THE STEAM AUTOMOBILE

Chicago, March 2. — I have often wondered why the steam driven automobile has not had more success in the American car market. Although I possess a gas car myself, I believe the steamer has every advantage over the gas car except quick getaway from a cold start, and even there a steamer gets under way in less than two minutes from a cold condition.

Once in motion, the steamer has it all over the gas car; more speed, more acceleration, no gears, quieter machine, no stink, more rugged engine, and burns any kind of liquid fuel.

Evidently the gas car manufacturers have reached their ultimate in engine improvement and are now tinkering with body designs in the effort to be progressive. Now is the time for the steam car manufacturer to start something; borrow the excellent body design of the gas car and turn out a steamer of as good appearance and better engine than the present boulevard fumigator.   J. S. Pollack.

WHY DID THE STEAM CAR FAIL IN POPULARITY?

By FLOYD CLYMER

Since I started publishing my Motor Scrapbooks I have received hundreds of letters asking my opinion as to why steam-powered automobiles failed to maintain the popularity they once enjoyed in the United States.

First of all, let me say that I am not a steam engineer and I most certainly do not know all of the answers. I do know, however, that there is a tremendous interest in steam automobiles—and in this article I will state only some of the reasons why I believe steam cars disappeared from the market.

In the earlier days and up until such time as automobiles would cruise at 50 to 60 miles per hour, the steamer gave a fairly good account of itself. However, in recent years, when speeds of 70 or 80 miles per hour were not unusual, the steam car had difficulty in generating steam as fast as was necessary to sustain high speed. Most of the early manufacturers of steam cars were quite conservative—and in most instances were not as progressive as were the manufacturers of gasoline cars. It seems to me that steam developments did not keep pace with the development of the gasoline propelled car; and that while many of the faults of the steam car might have been overcome, no one seemed to be progressive enough in the steam field to improve and profitably merchandise a successful steam car.

The magic of steam power holds a fascination for millions of motorists. Many recall their early experiences either in driving or in riding in a steam car, and they are inclined to remember the most favorable features of the steamer. These were: the tremendous acceleration; constant power; the smoothness and lack of vibration; the elimination of clutches, transmissions, carburetors, ignition systems, and other units necessary on a gas-propelled car. Many of these same steam car enthusiasts have overlooked the difficulties of the earlier steam cars, such as scorched boilers, delay in starting, lack of proper service facilities, and the problem of maintaining a steam generating unit so that it would operate at its highest efficiency under all conditions.

As I have stated in other publications, I sincerely believe that steam power will again be used in propelling road vehicles in the United States. I believe that steam propelled units will first appear in large busses and trucks and it is quite likely that some light, steam-powered passenger car may appear. Needless to say, the first steam car that does appear will find an immediate market, with a large number of purchasers ready to lay "cash on the line." However, it remains to be seen whether or not the user will be content to give attention to the many small details necessary to operate the steam car.

As automobiles were improved throughout the years, many of the troublesome gas car features of years ago have been eliminated. It may therefore be that if steam cars are again produced for sale in this country it will require many months and perhaps years of testing in the hands of the private owners before some of the troublesome features of the steam car are eliminated.

I do believe, however, that the great strides which have been made in the development of metals, oils, fuels, boilers, burners, etc., will enable manufacturers to produce steam cars that will be fairly satisfactory in operation. Most certainly the steam car does have some highly desirable features; and perhaps the objectionable features can and will be overcome.

Doubtless thousands of my readers have heard the story, as I have, many, many times, that the steam car was eliminated from competition due to the efforts of the large oil companies. I have never believed this statement to be true—and as stated herein, the steam car was eliminated through the complacency of some of the early steam car manufacturers and the lack of advanced engineering which did not keep pace with the progress made by the gasoline car manufacturers.

It would have been interesting to have watched the development of the steam car in America had such men as Ford, Chrysler, Kettering, and others—with their inventive minds and manufacturing genius—turned toward the development of the steam automobile instead of the gasoline car. Had these men been steam engineers and devoted their efforts to the steam car, it is quite possible that the motorists of America would today be enjoying the many acknowledged advantages of the steam car, plus the elimination of the troublesome things so common in the steam cars of the early days. It would be interesting to know what the results would have been had the steam car been given preference over the gasoline car. Had this been so, it is possible that many of our large service stations would now be featuring "boilers cleaned while you wait," "Let us check your burner and water; no charge"—and "Steam engines serviced overnight." On the other hand, the service station as we know it today would long ago have passed out of existence had steam cars maintained the early-day sales percentage that they once enjoyed.

THE TIMES-PICAYUNE NEW ORLEANS STATES, SUNDAY, JULY 16, 1944

Steam for Cars of China May Bring New Auto Era

(The Associated Press)

Washington.—One of these days you may step on the steam instead of the gas. Automotive engineers are thinking about steam-powered autos, trucks, busses and tractors for postwar transportation—although not as an immediate prospect.

The return of steam is considered possible because of modern automatic fueling devices and thermostatic controls, and because of the light stainless metals which have been developed in recent years.

Steam power lost out years ago because, for one thing, if the fire died out in the boiler it took around half an hour to get up steam again. This defect largely was overcome, but in the meantime the automotive industry was putting the quick-starting gasoline motor into so many cars that steam became almost forgotten.

Yet steam is efficient. One of the last steamers developed 150 horsepower with a motor weighing 150 pounds. Compare that with the horsepower-weight ratio of your own car.

The other day the writer rode in a steam car built in 1925. It took less than two minutes to get up steam. This car has traveled 340,000 miles and today runs as smoothly as a 1940 gasoline coupe which has less than 40,000 miles on its speedometer.

Like all steamers, this one had no gearshift, no clutch. There was an accelerator, a steering wheel and a brake. To back, you simply reversed the motor—not a gear.

The new thinking about steam is primarily a Chinese idea. The Chinese asked American engineers: "How about designing us a steam-powered vehicle—one that will be simple to build and take care of, that can be adapted to burn anything from coal dust to tung oil or alcohol, that dust and corrosion won't harm, and will be just as powerful high in the mountains as at sea level."

So the engineers looked up designs of the last steamers made a decade ago and tackled the problems involved in applying new devices and materials discovered since then.

The basic job is to develop the essential units of a steam vehicle to the point where they can be produced cheaply and efficiently enough to interest capital for mass production.

The engine, a simple unit of around 30-horsepower, is no great problem; it's the boiler they're concentrating on. One engineer envisions a small, compact unit of stainless metal. He has an idea that instead of using conventional boiler tubing there must be some way of using the corrugation principle you see in heavy paper boxes. Such a method would, he hopes, permit cheap mass production.

The engineers found there still are several hundred steamers operating in this country, carefully kept by owners who like the smooth, steady power, along with freedom from stalling and gear shifting.

The American Steam Car, Sedan Model

The Possibilities in Steam

By
" SLIDE-RULE "

The Pros and Cons of an Alternative Propellant to Petrol

" CARBON " can be relied upon to produce some unusual statistics every so often, but probably many more besides myself were surprised by his statement that during 1943 no fewer than 101 steam motorcycles were actually taxed for use on the roads. Readers may remember descriptions in this journal of one or two such vehicles constructed by steam fans for their own use, and as there are no manufacturers producing this class of machine obviously the whole lot have been built privately.

As a prime mover for road vehicles the internal-combustion engine can be criticized on many scores, the chief being that it must be started by some external means, and even when started cannot develop any respectable torque unless it is turning over fairly fast. To overcome these fundamental short-comings one has to resort to all the paraphernalia of starting mechanism, clutch and gearbox. Of recent years, in the car world far more ingenuity has been applied to the latter two items than to the power unit itself. Self-changing gearboxes, " electric hands," push-button changing and similar devices have been developed and marketed, and, in some cases, makers have produced most extraordinarily complicated automatic gear-shifts and simultaneously provided overriding controls to put the automatic feature out of action !

Complications

Motorcycles have not progressed (?) as far as this—although one well-known engineer is advocating synchromesh gears, which, to my mind, would be an unnecessary complication—but, nevertheless, t h e i r transmission systems, including clutches, are fairly intricate and expensive pieces of mechanism which everyone would be glad to throw away if they could get equal results without them.

Because the working medium is admitted to the cylinder under pressure and has not first of all to be compressed and fired therein, a reciprocating steam engine is self-starting, even under load. The converse is also true; if the load becomes greater than the engine can overcome, it will come to a stop without any sign of distress, instead of labouring, knocking and finally stalling as would a petrol engine. Also, it can exert the same, or almost the same, torque through the whole of its speed range, from zero up to maximum revs. All these properties combined do away with the need for any form of starting mechanism, clutch or gearbox, and, of course, the controls necessary to operate these items. The engine can be driven entirely by means of a throttle control, although to obtain maximum economy in running another control is required to vary the " cut-off," i.e. to alter the proportion of the stroke during

which live steam is admitted to the cylinder. The action of the two controls is roughly as follows :—The throttle controls the *rate* at which live steam can pass from the boiler to the valve chest, and after that the steam is admitted to the cylinder by the valve for a portion of the piston stroke. The valve then closes and during the remainder of the stroke the steam is expanding and thus dropping in pressure. By varying the valve timing, and so making the cut-off point at which steam admission ceases come earlier in the stroke, a smaller amount of steam is admitted, but it expands more and thus gives up more of its energy with a proportionate gain in steam economy.

Conversely, when maximum power is required, as when accelerating or hill-climbing, the cut-off is made later and full steam pressure is allowed to act on the piston for a larger proportion of its stroke. The mechanism which so varies the valve timing can also alter it in such a way that the engine can run backwards. It can even reverse (or rather exercise a torque in the reverse direction) while still running forward, thus acting as a sort of mechanical " back-pedalling " device—a feature which gives very good manœuvrability in congested areas, although not perhaps of much value on a solo motorcycle. This simplification of control is, of course, a very good thing, but there are other matters needing the driver's attention which, to a large extent, offset this advantage.

Mechanically, steam engines are very quiet; they do not need high revs. to develop their power ; the pistons run reasonably cool and at so nearly a constant temperature that clearances can be accurately controlled, and side-thrust—the cause of piston-slap—can be eliminated by using piston rods passing through glands in the cylinder covers and guided externally by cross-heads. This construction permits steam to be admitted to both sides of the piston, thus making every stroke a power stroke, so that " four-cylinder " torque can be obtained from a single-cylinder engine, and two such cylinders operating on cranks set at 90 degrees provide an almost continuous turning effort.

As a steam engine needs no cooling—in fact, the cylinders are usually lagged with asbestos to keep them hot—it does not have to be placed where a draught can play upon it and can be mounted horizontally, vertically or at any intermediate angle without detriment. Neither does it need to run at colossal revs. in order to develop its power; the Stanley steam car—a sample of which I had quite a lot of fun with many years ago—pulled a gear of 1½ to 1, or something equally fantastic, and could restart with ease on a grade of 1 in 5 without juggling with foot brake and clutch.

However nice all this may appear, there is another side to the picture. What the steam engine gains in simplicity of construction and control it loses in the complexity of the boiler feed-water and fuel-supply arrangements. The Stanley just mentioned had more instruments on it than any car I have seen before or since ; not only was the whole dashboard full of them, but there were even three set into the side of the front seat and visible only when the door was open. Admittedly these merely showed the quantity of oil, water and kerosene fuel in the respective tanks, but as running out of water in a country district in summer-time might be disastrous, and running out of fuel in any case meant a lot of snaky work relighting the Primus-type burners underneath the boiler, one had to bear these indicators in mind.

Limitations

On the whole the steamer is in the end more complicated than the petrol vehicle, and, unlike the latter, which is only limited in power by its own characteristics, the performance of the former is settled not so much by engine size as by its boiler, for the power which can be developed continuously is entirely dependent upon the rate at which steam can be evaporated therein. Very high pressures (600 lb. per sq. in. in the case of the Stanley) are necessary in order to get anything like a respectable continuous horse-power figure from a boiler in the restricted space available on a passenger vehicle, and it does not seem likely that there would ever be enough room available on a motorcycle.

Of course, even with a small boiler high power is available for a limited time following a period of running light, but that does not help the motorist desirous of covering a long, easy stretch at the highest possible velocity. Roughly speaking a large express locomotive turns out the same power as a modern combat aeroplane engine, and although the comparison is scarcely fair the enormous difference in their respective bulk is largely accounted for by the huge dimensions of the boiler required for sustained high speed in the steam device.

It is possible to make boilers occupying less volume per horse-power, but it seems unlikely that it would be possible to make one small enough to fit into the confines of a normal motorcycle frame and yet able to develop a horse-power equivalent to that turned out by the modern sports engine. I am inclined to think that most of the 101 registered steamers have their boilers mounted on sidecar chassis. Perhaps some enthusiast who really knows something about steam will give us an outline of his " ideal " machine, because I am certain many of us will be interested in what he has to say.

This article regarding the possibilities of Steam Power for use in motorcycles appeared in the English publication "Motorcycling," March 30, 1944. One hundred and three steam motorcycles were licensed for road use in England in 1943.—*Clymer.*

STEAM...
A POSTWAR POWER POSSIBILITY

BY WILLIAM B. McGORUM

OF ALL THE COMBINATIONS of rubber-tired power thus far put into urban transit use, the trolley coach is outstanding. It is not any automotive vehicle, any more than is the trolley car; its pure performance and the overall transit selling job it does stands unmatched by any automotive vehicle in service today. The public likes it primarily for characteristics which are the antithesis of those inherent in the internal combustion powered vehicle.

In the trolley coach we already have the formula for the successful postwar bus.

Among the outstanding reasons for its popularity are these: that it moves silently and has a high, sustained and smooth acceleration. The trolley coach is warm in winter and the absence of fumes and engine noise and vibration is pleasing both to its riders and the public at large. Drivers like the ease with which it can be operated. The maintenance forces have found in the trolley coach the simplicity and dependability in hard service for which the trolley car has long been noted.

The over-all postwar transit job for which the trolley coach would be so admirably adapted except for certain physical characteristics which limit its scope, could be served admirably by steam power.

The magic that lies in the vapor of water has never ceased to occupy the serious thought and consideration of forward looking men in our industry since the hybrid buses appeared. To many, the increasingly complex-mechanical arrangements employed as means for adapting internal combustion power to transit needs represent a sort of Rube Goldberg approach to the problem when viewed in the light of the innate fitness of steam power for such service. As one of the leaders in the industry recently remarked, "It is like building rubber gloves for leaky fountain pens."

Consider what steam power has to offer in transit service.

Maximum torque, to the point of slipping a tire on dry pavement is available from this form of power without any mechanical movement occurring. This torque, converted to motion is capable of producing in a heavy vehicle a rate of acceleration greatly exceeding

LOOKING TO THE FUTURE

the limit useable in passenger service. Such acceleration, governed to practical limits as in the operation of trolley coaches and P.C.C. cars can be merchandised in the form of higher scheduled speeds and resultant passenger satisfaction. From corner to corner the private automobile driver will hardly care to compete with the performance at the disposal of an operator upon the mere pressure on his throttle pedal. Our customers will experience a real sense of superiority over all other street traffic in riding in such a vehicle.

Steam Is Silent

Steam is the only power medium other than electricity which can deliver silent motion. For others than those of our patrons accustomed to the silent movement of the trolley coach this will be a new and ever welcome sensation. Comparison with even the relative quietness of the modern passenger automobile will be impressive. Favorably associated in the passenger's impressions with silence of movement will be the smooth and purposeful response of this form of power to the wishes of the operator.

During even extreme cold weather the steam powered bus will offer heating and ventilating comfort unmatched except by the trolley coach and the modern trolley car. As a practical matter exhaust fumes will be non-existent. Both

(Continued on next page)

(Continued from preceding page)

gasoline and Diesel engines are offenders in this respect. The burning of Diesel or even low-grade furnace oil in a steam powered vehicle is quite a different problem than that posed by the practically instantaneous combustion of so relatively heavy a fuel inside an internal combustion engine.

Drivers will like the steam powered bus, and such work will be considered attractive in any community. Clutching and gear shifting will disappear as a part of driving. This of course is the goal in current attempts to design practical and long-lived torque converters and automatic transmissions for application to the internal combustion engine.

Provides Power Breaking

The driver will have power braking at his disposal. Except for air brake application means to be used at times when four-wheel braking is desirable, as on icy streets, his entire operating control will consist of two pedals, one for power forward and another beside it in the customary brake pedal position for power braking and reverse operation.

Service braking will be by vehicle application of power controlled by this pedal through reversed engine valves with the same smoothness as forward acceleration. Operation at hilly stops will simply consist of holding the bus stationary against the grade of whatever amount of forward foot throttle is required. Resumption of movement will only require stepping down further on the throttle.

The driver will have no water, pressure or fuel controls to be concerned about as was required by steam vehicles of some twenty years ago and which in that respect were not too greatly different in the technique required of the driver of gasoline vehicles of the same vintage. The generation of pressure will be quite simple and entirely automatic, relieving the operator entirely of any concern for the development of power.

And, for those older operating men whose trolley cars in other than modern form it may be expected to render obsolete, the steam powered coach will be a blessing. Traditionally and not without good reason these men have dreaded the transition from trolley to bus operation. In the steam vehicle they will discover standards of ease and comfort of operation they not only did not experience in their rail service, but which in harking back to the days of the open platform they could not be expected to believe would happen in the transit industry.

The postwar advent of automotive steam propulsion will result in new concepts of bus maintenance. Shop

W. B. (Bill) McGorum

Twenty-two years ago the writer of this article poked thoughtful and inquisitive finger into transportation, found it entirely to his liking and, as a consequence, has had an unflagging interest in transportation ever since. Graduated from M.I.T. in 1921 he began his transportation apprenticeship in the statistical department of Stone & Webster, Inc. in Boston in Feb. 1922. Next he was a student engineer with Key West Electric Co. until 1924 when he became assistant to the chief electrical engineer of the Columbus (Ga.) Electric & Power Co. Between 1924 and 1927 Mr. McGorum successively became junior secretary to the division manager of Stone & Webster, bus master mechanic, Tampa Electric Co. and assistant office manager of the Stone & Webster New York office.

In September 1927, he was appointed assistant superintendent of equipment, Virginia Electric & Power Co. at Norfolk and became manager of transportation for that company, a position he held until Feb. 1936, when he resigned to become vice-president and general manager of the Charleston (W. Va.) Transit Co. Mr. McGorum resigned from the latter organization in May 1938 to accept a position with similar title and responsibilities with the Lehigh Valley Transit Co., Allentown, Pa.

For nearly two decades, Mr. McGorum has been interested in the mechanics as well as the economics of transportation. In 1926 he recognized the advantages of steam power for bus and truck application generally and meanwhile has encouraged and participated in the development of heavy duty steam power as it embodies modern concepts of performance, safety, low cost maintenance and trouble-free, automatic operation. In this article he presents in a clear and concise style some of the reasons why he believes that steam has a real future in highway transportation.

production lines established for the rebuilding of engines, transmissions and clutches may be expected to virtually disappear, so drastic will be the shrinkage of this class of work for a given fleet. Inspections will be lengthened to periods unbelievable as measured in terms of requirements of the internal combustion vehicle. A smaller force will be seen around the garages. Men now of less than top mechanic grade who have been struggling upward through the classifications, engaged in the dirty and laborious work of manhandling driving units into and out of buses can be expected to gradually forsake that kind of work for the jaunty cap and well paid job of coach pilot.

For as this vehicle begins to replace fleet units of internal combustion powered buses, whether in kind or as the result of replacement of power plants in existing vehicles, the amount of brute maintenance work required will begin to decrease sharply. The maintenance pattern will eventually require only a few classes of garage employees, such as top-grade mechanics, servicing men and cleaners. The steam generator is a static device designed to absorb heat and handle pressure. The moving parts associated with it consist mainly of its controls, the understanding and maintenance of the proper adjustment of which will compose the principal duties of the mechanics of steam propelled buses.

Pint-size Engine

The driving engine, a relatively pint sized affair developing one bhp per cu. in. of displacement, and located under the bus, runs in roller or ball bearings on both crankshaft and connecting rods. No flame is produced within this powerplant and it is free of carbon, sludge and fuel dilution. Being directly connected to the rear axle it is never operated at a speed greater than called for by the road speed of the bus, which at some high figure such as 65–70 mph. might amount to a maximum of 3000 rpm. It is not considered that such an engine will need to be opened oftener than each 200,000 miles. The friction braking system will be used so seldom that the dirty, laborious work of relining brakes will for practical purposes disappear.

It has been unthinkingly said in the past that steam propulsion could not expect to return to the American scene, because the men who were familiar with these vehicles have largely disappeared. It was pointed out that at almost every crossroads garage there have long been men who know how to make a gasoline engine run, but to whom the appearance of a steam vehicle would mean nothing in terms of past experience, knowledge or ability.

These considerations do realistically apply to any thought that steam may reappear in the passenger automobile. However, neither the urban transit industry nor the long distance bus lines have in the past depended on cross roads garages to keep their vehicles running. In fact fairly few mechanics outside of the garages of bus and trucking companies could do much with a Diesel engine in trouble except to make it worse.

Changes Taken In Stride

We are operating fleets, and as fleet operators we have taken radical changes in the forms and accessories of the internal combustion engine in our stride. We organize ourselves in the ways necessary to do this, and we train our men to handle and service the products in widely varying physical form and design of many different vehicle manufacturers.

The mechanics who maintain the steam powered bus will have had special training. They will understand cutoff, release and compression for the steam cycle as intimately as they now do the two- or four-cycle gasoline or Diesel engine. Experience with war training gas demonstrated how quickly and satisfactorily the fundamentals of entirely new techniques can be taught. These postwar mechanics who deal with steam—rather than internal combustion power will have predominantly as their stock in trade skill of mind rather than primarily of the hand. The mechanisms they tend will be long-lived, requiring only tuning rather than constant rebuilding.

Here, then, is the formula, reduced to the tangible picture of the postwar bus. All the progress of past years in body construction, axle, steering, lighting, seating and other similar development is not only retained bue enhanced. But the old, too familiar power plant with its supporting and modifying mechanisms is missing. Something new will be added to the bus, and that something new is in reality very old, automotively speaking. It is the same power but in how different a physical form that White, Locomobile and many other early auto builders made history with over 40 years ago.

It is the same basic power that brought most of our forebears from the old country as immigrants; the power that opened the west and which has played and is today playing such a part in making and keeping our country what it is.

Ever since gasoline overtook steam, put 27,000,000 cars in the hands of the American people and incidentally nearly wrecked our business—public transportation—there have been men who knew

implicitly that steam power would return as the salvation of the burden vehicle. There has been little serious thought that this form of power could or should have risen to the popularity of the internal combustion engine for passenger automobile application. The modern automobile in its present excellent and future improved form is here to stay. Who could really want a more satisfactory or more practical mechanism for the purpose!

But commercial truck and bus fleet operators long ago have had enough of the type of power plant which in contrast to its unsuitability in the burden field is so successful and satisfactory in the private automobile. Its limitations and weaknesses in heavy duty applications have cost the business which use and depend upon vehicles so equipped millions of dollars in wasted resources of materials, labor and manufacturing facilities.

Research Continues

It is to this field that able men of engineering talen and with vision have been quietly and implacably pointing their research and development of embodiments of steam power generation and conversion suitable for heavy duty automotive application. They have been biding their time and saying little of what they have been doing, the while a steady tide of need for the realization of their far-sightedness has been rising.

The results of this work are now flowing into the hands of manufacturers. Some designs are on the drafting boards, while others are already taking physical shape in pre-production experimental form, all jealously guarded. All concerned have listened closely and carefully enough to realize that the best postwar bus with internal combustion power and super-converter drive will actually be as prewar as a 1930 model as soon as the first steam powered bus of respectable parentage makes its debut in the transportation field.

Revenue Potentialities

Considering its potentialities in respect of revenue building and operating economy the advent of steam bus power may well mean the difference between continued existence and failure of many a company in the marginal days that are almost certain to result from postwar resumption of private automobile purchase and operation in the grand manner. For other companies, less critically affected, the timely appearance of this vehicle on the transit scene may enable the desirable retention of relatively high wage levels while at the same time making possible the realization of satisfactory operating profit.

LIST OF 125 MAKES OF STEAM CARS ONCE MANUFACTURED IN THE UNITED STATES

1. American, 1900
2. American, 1922
3. Artzberger
4. Aultman
5. Austin
6. Auto-Loco
7. Baker
8. Baldwin
9. Ball
10. Best
11. Binney-Burnham
12. Boss
13. Brecht
14. Bristol
15. Cameron
16. Cannon
17. Capitol
18. Century
19. Cincinnati
20. Clark
21. Clermont
22. Coats
23. Conrad
24. Cotta
25. Crompton
26. Crouch
27. Delling
28. Detroit
29. Doble
30. Dudgeon
31. Eastman
32. Eclipse
33. Elberon
34. Elite
35. Empire
36. Endurance
37. Essex
38. Federal
39. Field
40. Foster
41. Gaeth
42. Gearless
43. Geneva
44. Grout
45. Hartley
46. Hess
47. Hoffman
48. Holland
49. Holyoke
50. House
51. Howard
52. Hudson
53. International
54. Jaxon
55. Johnson
56. Keene
57. Kellogg
58. Kensington
59. Keystone
60. Kidder
61. Kraft
62. Lane
63. Leach
64. Locke
65. Locomobile
66. Loomis
67. Lutz
68. Lyons
69. Malden
70. Mason
71. McKay
72. Mercury
73. Meteor
74. Mills
75. Milwaukee
76. Mobile
77. Morse
78. New England
79. Ormond
80. Overholt
81. Overman
82. Oxford
83. Pawtucket
84. Peerless
85. Porter
86. Prescott
87. Puritan
88. Randolph
89. Reading
90. Remel-Vincent
91. Rogers
92. Ross
93. Scott-Newcomb
94. Simons
95. Skene
96. Spencer
97. Springer
98. Springfield
99. Squier
100. Standard
101. Stanley
102. Stanton
103. Steamobile
104. Stearns
105. Sterling
106. Stewart-Coats
107. Storck
108. Strathmore
109. Stringer
110. Strouse
111. Super-Steamer
112. Taunton
113. Terwilliger
114. Thompson
115. Toledo
116. Tractmobile
117. Trask-Detroit
118. Trinity
119. Victor
120. Waltham
121. Watt
122. Webb-Jay
123. Westfield
124. White
125. Whitney

—————

125 Total